W9-AGU-137

PUBLIC POLICY AND PRIVATE EDUCATION IN JAPAN

Also by Estelle James

THE NONPROFIT SECTOR IN INTERNATIONAL PERSPECTIVE: Studies in Comparative Culture and Policy

THE NONPROFIT ENTERPRISE IN MARKET ECONOMIES (*with Susan Rose-Ackerman*)

HOFFA AND THE TEAMSTERS: A Study of Union Power (*with Ralph James*)

Public Policy and Private Education in Japan

Estelle James
and
Gail Benjamin

St. Martin's Press   New York

LIBRARY

© Estelle James and Gail Benjamin, 1988

All rights reserved. For information, write:
Scholarly and Reference Division,
St. Martin's Press, Inc., 175 Fifth Avenue, New York, NY 10010

First published in the United States of America in 1988

Printed in Hong Kong

ISBN 0–312–01337–X

Library of Congress Cataloging-in-Publication Data
James, Estelle.
Public policy and private education in Japan/Estelle James and
Gail R. Benjamin.
p.   cm.
Bibliography: p.
Includes index.
ISBN 0–312–01337–X: $39.95 (est.)
1. Education and state—Japan.   2. Private schools—Japan.
3. Public schools—Japan.   I. Benjamin, Gail R.   II. Title.
LC94.J3J36   1988
379.52—dc19   87–35606 CIP

C
4
13
J36 1988
Contents

List of Tables

List of Figures

Preface

This monograph on the Japanese educational system grew out of a research project analysing the role of the non-profit sector and the public–private division of responsibility for education in a variety of modern and developing countries. Several other papers that have emerged from that project are listed in the Bibliography and a comparative volume is now in process. However, we felt that the case of Japan was sufficiently intriguing to merit a book of its own.

Data for this work was gathered during a research visit to Japan by both authors in 1983. We wish to thank the numerous people in Japan who helped us to gather material for this monograph, including Shogo Ichikawa and Hirumitsu Muta of the National Institute for Educational Research, Toru Yoshimura and Yoshinobu Yamamoto of Saitama University, Ken Ogata of Hosei University, Takao Maruyama of the Association of Private Universities, Yasuo Kai and Tetsu Beppu of the Foundation for the Promotion of Private Schools, Akio Nakajima and Akimasa Mitsuta of the Ministry of Education and Noboru Ukawa, headmaster of Toin Gakuen. We appreciate the capable data analysis carried out by R. S. Huang and H. K. Lee of the State University of New York (SUNY) at Stony Brook and Amy Salzbury of the Brookings Institution, as well as the translations provided by Shigeru Kishikawa of SUNY, Stony Brook, Chika Murakami of Sophia University, Tsuneo Shiobara of Saitama University and Isamu Maruyama of International House of Japan. Most of the typing was done with great efficiency and intelligence by Linda Josephs.

Parts of Chapters 8 and 9 were previously published in 'Educational Distribution and Income Redistribution Through Education', *Journal of Human Resources*, vol. 22, no. 4, ©1987, reprinted by permission of the University of Wisconsin Press. An earlier version of Chapter 10 was published in 'The Private Nonprofit Provision of Education: a Theoretical Model and Application to Japan', *Journal of Comparative Economics*, vol. 10, ©1986, Academic Press; reprinted by permission.

We are grateful for the financial support for this and related projects received from the Exxon Education Foundation, the National Endowment for the Humanities, the Social Science Research Council, the Agency for International Development, the AAUW

Education Foundation and the Spencer Foundation. The over-all study began in 1981 while Estelle James was a Fellow at the Woodrow Wilson International Center for Scholars, the bulk of the writing was done while she was in residence at the State University of New York, Stony Brook, and finishing touches were put on this book in 1987 while she was a Fellow at the Netherlands Institute for Advanced Study. All the assistance received from these institutions is appreciated. Especially important were the moral and material support received from the Program on Nonprofit Organizations at Yale University (and its Chairman, John Simon), which has encouraged research and the exchange of ideas on the role of 'third sector' institutions. Without this support the work on Japan as well as the continuing work on other countries would not have been possible.

ESTELLE JAMES
GAIL BENJAMIN

Introduction

This book is about the public and private school systems in Japan and how they interact to provide some of the highest educational achievement indices in the world. In sharp contrast to those of the USA and UK, Japan's educational system features a large private sector and an élite public sector at the secondary and higher levels, an impressive level of mathematical and scientific literacy for all, and very few 'second chances' for students. We suggest that we can judiciously use Japan as a laboratory from which we may learn valuable lessons about the educational options available to us.

But first, a word about definitions:

In this book the term 'public schools' means those schools which are largely financed by public funds and managed by governmental authorities, while 'private schools' have a large private funding and management component. In the UK the term 'public schools' commonly refers to a group of high standard private schools, but this is not the meaning we shall adopt. To avoid confusion, references will often be made to 'state' and 'independent' schools in the UK. The 'state' schools largely correspond to the American and Japanese public schools and the 'independent' schools are private.

A major debate on the American and British educational scene over the past few years has concerned the quality of our public school systems and the advantages and disadvantages of a heavier reliance on private schools. Public policies such as tuition tax credits and voucher schemes have been proposed, which would encourage the growth of the private sector. Would this have the effect of reducing government expenditures and quality in the public schools? Conversely, if real public spending on education declines, because of budgetary stringency and/or removal of tax advantages (e.g. if state and local taxes, which are used to finance education in the USA, became non-deductible on federal returns) would this lead to a larger private sector? If so, what would be the impact on stratification within the educational system? Would it imply class or racial segregation, with better education for the economically and socially more advantaged groups? One must beware of facile generalisations from a very homogeneous country such as Japan to countries characterised by cultural and socioeconomic diversity, such as the UK and the USA. Nevertheless, the experience of Japan suggests that the private sector is not necessarily preferred to the public, and private sector growth does not inevitably have dire consequences for the well-being of the public schools and the educational system as a whole.

What then determines the nature of this interaction? One key to the puzzle is the kind of access we choose for our public school system. In Japan the public sector is deliberately kept small, selective, differentiated, high quality and therefore élite, while the private sector is large, with more open access and (therefore) less preferred. The nature of the public sector determines the nature of the private sector that will develop as its mirror image, and the availability of a private sector sets constraints for the kind of public sector that can be sustained.

Another key to the puzzle is found in the link between the labour market and the educational system. Employers' recruitment practices determine the ranking (or non-ranking) of universities, and university admissions policies in turn determine the hierarchy among high schools, as well as the placing of public and private institutions within the hierarchy. Thus, stratification within the educational system and the labour market are closely related. In this book we try to delineate some of these interrelationships, both for Japan and for other countries as well.

The private education sector in Japan is unique among modern industrial societies. In most Western countries the provision of private education is a response to cultural heterogeneity. From the demand side, linguistic, religious and income differences create differentiated choices about the preferred type or quality of education. Since the government is often constrained to offer a relatively uniform product, some people opt out to the private sector, even if it costs more. From the supply side, most private schools differ from ordinary businesses in that they are run by non-profit organisations, where monetary dividends and capital gains are ruled out as motivating forces. Non-profit organisations, sometimes called charities, trusts, foundations or associations, are organisations that can earn a profit but cannot legally distribute these profits in monetary form nor can shares be sold by 'owners'. Instead all earnings must be reinvested in the activities of the organisation. Around the world religious organisations constitute a major source of entrepreneurship and venture capital in the non-profit sector, motivated by their desire to increase faith and adherents rather than their desire for monetary profits. Therefore, private education is stronger in countries with greater cultural heterogeneity and with strong independent organised religious groups.[1] While the provision of privatised education in some countries, such as Holland and Belgium, is clearly consistent with this description, the case of Japan is a clear contradiction.

Indices of income equality show Japan to be relatively egalitarian. For example, in the 1960s, the period of great expansion in the Japanese educational system, after-tax Gini coefficients in Japan were lower, and the income share of the bottom 20 per cent higher, than in other OECD countries. Unemployment has been low, severe poverty absent.[2]

Culturally, Japan is one of the most homogeneous countries in the world. Japanese is the uniform universal language. Koreans, the only major ethnic minority, are less than 0.5 per cent of the total population. Japan has refused entry to refugees, foreign workers and other immigrants in order to maintain its cultural homogeneity. Moreover, the predominant religions, Shintoism and Buddhism, are neither proselytising nor institutionally organised to provide secular services.

Yet, at the secondary and even more so, the higher educational levels, the Japanese system is heavily private. In 1982, 28 per cent of the high school students and 76 per cent of those in higher education, were attending private (usually non-profit) institutions.[3] How then do we explain this phenomenon? Why have people demanded private education and what is the source of entrepreneurship, where the profit motive is ostensibly absent?

The Japanese experience suggests an alternative reason for a large private sector: it is a response to an excess demand for education in the face of a deliberately limited government supply. We would expect to find this phenomenon in developing countries, where the scarcity of public resources and entrepreneurial talent often make it difficult for the supply of public schools to increase as fast as demand. Japan can no longer be characterised as a developing country, but it has made the transition to modern industrial state more rapidly and more recently than most Western countries and the large private education sector may be a legacy of earlier periods.

In addition, since the end of the Second World War, Japan has been controlled by the conservative Liberal Democratic Party (LDP), which has maintained the lowest rate of government expenditure and taxation among modern developed countries. This policy of limited government production, as applied to education, meant that only the minimum quantity deemed necessary for national purposes was provided publicly, while everything else was considered a consumer good and left to private enterprise. Since demand far exceeded the available public supply, the private sector flourished. The case of Japan suggests that whereas cultural heterogeneity may lead people to prefer variegated privatised services over the uniform government product, the lack of any government product for many prospective students is an even more compelling reason for private sector growth. It also suggests that, contrary to popular belief, a high level of educational enrolments and achievement is possible on the basis of private funding and initiative, when governmental production is absent. It should come as no surprise that the supporters of the LDP were the chief beneficiaries of this policy of restricted public provision of education. Indeed, one focus of this monograph is the political economy of public spending and production of education: who benefits and who loses from the current policy toward public and private schools and what light this throws on the operations of the political process.

The private educational sector in Japan is beset by paradoxes. Legally, all private schools must be non-profit yet people speak of them as being highly profitable. The growth of private schools is evidence of a well-functioning product market yet it has depended, in large part, on imperfections in the factor market. The private sector serves the upper classes disproportionately and in that sense is 'élite', yet quality and selectivity indices point to the public schools as being élite. The social rate of return appears to be higher in the private sector, the private rate of return higher in the public sector. One of the main reasons for this irony is the lower expenditure per student in privatised education. Yet the government is now undertaking measures designed to equalise expenditures and thereby lower the social rate of return to private schools and universities. Each of these paradoxes will be explored.

In Part I (Chapters 1, 2 and 3) of this monograph we describe the historical, social and cultural setting in which the educational sector as a whole is embedded in Japan, and we also survey major issues and non-issues on the contemporary education scene. In Part II, which is the heart of our study and its original contribution, we focus on the role of the private sector, contrasting it with the public sector in Japanese education. While earlier works have focused on one level of Japanese education, this study considers all levels, since the division between public and private operates throughout.[4] However, high schools and universities, where the private sector is largest, receive most attention.

Chapter 4 sets forth basic data on the relative size of the private sector in education, both past and present, placing these data within the general Japanese context in which limited government spending, production and taxation are considered best. Chapter 5 deals with a fundamental question: where does the entrepreneurship and venture capital come from; what are the motives of the founders and funders, in an enterprise which is supposedly non-profit? Institutional and market forces that make the founding and funding tasks easier will also be examined. In addition to describing the Japanese situation, this section aims to illuminate the theory of non-profit production more generally. Chapters 6, 7, 8 and 9 deal with important differences between the public and private sectors: differences in clientele, benefits, prestige, quality, costs, efficiency and redistributive effects. The object is to discover systematic reasons for these differences, reasons that might help us to predict what would happen in other countries if privatised education were encouraged. With a similar purpose, differences across Japanese prefectures in the size and nature of the private sector are examined in Chapter 10 and the political reasons for these differences are explored. Chapter 11 continues with a discussion of two important policy reforms: the Tokyo attempt in the 1960s to make public education more uniform, and the institution of government subsidies to private schools in the 1970s. As is often the case in such reforms, their effects may be quite different from their intent.

Finally, the Conclusion draws out implications of the Japanese experience for the USA and UK. In many ways, the Japanese public and private school systems are different from ours. Nevertheless, we believe that we can learn much about the interrelationship between these two sectors, and the effects of policy alternatives, by studying the Japanese case.

Part I

Education in Japanese Culture

1 Historical Background of Education in Japan

Schooling in formal institutional settings has been an important feature of Japanese society since the early nineteenth century, and a large part of the success of modern Japan has been attributed to the effectiveness and adaptiveness of its educational system. The institutional settings of education in Japan have been very different from those in other industrial countries and the character of the education offered has also had a distinctive Japanese cast. In this book we are primarily concerned with the allocation of educational functions among different sorts of institutions, and in order to understand how and why and to what effect this pattern has developed, we will look at schooling in its broader social setting as well. Some of the most striking characteristics of modern Japanese education – a clear distinction between élite education and mass education, a division of responsibility between the state and private institutions which roughly parallels that distinction, a widespread 'taste for education' among the populace and a notion of students as learners of what is known rather than as potential innovators – can be seen as long-standing cultural patterns which can be discerned from the seventeenth century on.[1]

PUBLIC EDUCATION UNDER THE TOKUGAWA SHOGUNATE

Japan's modernisation is traditionally dated from the Meiji Restoration in 1868, and the modernisation of the school system from the education reforms promulgated in 1872. But the 200 years before the Meiji Restoration were years of social, educational and economic vitality which left Japan in a position to cope with an apparently sudden cleavage from traditional patterns and enabled it to move rapidly to industrialisation and modernisation.

The Meiji period was preceded by the Tokugawa Shogunate, which lasted from 1604 to 1867. While across the world the American colonies were being established and eventually cohered into a single federal system and the nation-state was gradually developing in

Europe, internal warfare in Japan was creating a semi-feudal political
regime known as the Tokugawa Shogunate. The importance of the
warrior class was assured by the long wars preceding Ieyasu Tokugawa's final victory, and the relative precariousness of the regime
during its early years. This warrior class – samurai, daimio and the
Shogun's family – constituted about 5 per cent of the total population
and had complete control over the administration of the rest of Japan,
maintaining peace, administering justice, collecting taxes, etc. As the
Tokugawa regime continued in power and the potential for civil war
receded, this class, commonly referred to as the samurai class (though
it also contained people of higher status) changed in function from
being primarily a warrior class to being primarily an administrative
class. And the education and training needed by the regime for these
people also changed.

In response to these needs a system of schools for males of the
samurai class was developed. One set, the leader, was established
under the auspices of the Shogunate central government in the areas it
directly controlled, roughly 15 per cent of Japan. These were known
as *bakufu* schools. Other parts of Japan were administered by feudal
lords pledging loyalty to the Shogunate, and these individual fiefs also
established schools for their samurai-class males. There was wider
variation among these fief schools, since they were dependent on the
interest and patronage of individual feudal lords.

The overt function of these schools was to prepare young men to
move into their proper roles as rulers of the society, and the
curriculum changed over time as the job of ruling changed. A covert
function of the schools was also undoubtedly to control and occupy
the energies of young men of the warrior class in the absence of
warfare. In general, males spent much of their time between the ages
of 10 and 25 or 30 primarily occupied in attending these schools. It is
difficult to tell just how many hours a day, or how many days a year
were spent in 'educational' activities, but this was construed as the
major occupation of these young men.

The curriculum which was considered appropriate for training
future leaders of Japan was basically twofold. First was military
training, which decreased in importance as stability continued, and
finally became an athletic pursuit with Zen flavourings incorporating
physical training and Zen philosophy. The modern Japanese approach to fencing, archery and other traditional sports still emphasises these aesthetic aspects.

The second part of the curriculum was a study of the classical

Chinese writings on political philosphy and history. In spite of the fact that the Japanese have borrowed Chinese ideographs as an integral part of their writing system, Chinese and Japanese are unrelated languages, no more closely connected than English and Japanese or English and Chinese. Studying the Chinese classics therefore entailed, first, learning to read Chinese. The Chinese writing system is one which is not based on any correspondence between sound and symbol, but rather on an arbitrary relationship between a word and a symbol. The number of symbols, called ideographs or characters, which must be learned to read the classics studied in the Japanese *bakufu* and fief schools ranged from about 1000 to 3000 or more, depending on how far one progressed. The standard pedagogical approach called for an initial memorisation by rote of the texts (in Chinese), followed by memorising a way of reading these off in a sort of pidgin Japanese, followed, if students persevered, by interpretation and study of the meaning of the texts.

The texts which students were given first were moral and exhortatory in character, and Confucian in content. (Indeed, by the middle of the Tokugawa period, only Confucian works, and only orthodox interpretations of those works, were allowed in the schools.) These were followed by works of political philosphy which outlined a Confucian approach to the proper ordering of social life and the role of the rulers and ruled, and the most advanced works were historical studies of China.

It is easy to understand that, given this curriculum, many students never got past the tedium of the first works. For those students who did reach the stage of being able to understand the later works in the sequence, however, those works presented a sophisticated approach to governance, and even – since Japanese conditions never matched either the ideal states of the philosophical works or the descriptions presented in the Chinese historical works – a sense of comparative studies and multiple possibilities for arranging political systems.

Mathematics as needed by administrators, that is, fiscal accounting, percentages, money exchanges, some surveying, was also taught in these schools for future administrators, though reluctantly. Such pursuits seemed too petty and practical for samurai, and smacked of the practices of merchants. By the end of the Tokugawa period, however, such practical pursuits, combined with the excitement of 'Western learning' in astronomy, medicine, engineering and military strategy, were drawing more and more students away from the sterile pursuit of orthodox Confucianism, and even garnering extra rewards from rulers.

It is important to recognise that although literacy in Japanese and a knowledge of basic arithmetic played no part at all in the curriculum of the *bakufu* and fief schools, all the students at these schools had learned these at home or on their own during their school years.

These *bakufu* and fief schools were instituted as training grounds for the ruling élite of Japan, and as such they had important social functions. It was in this context that each generation of élite men learned to know each other, to deal with both the established rankings of the traditional hierarchy, into which each was born, and with the natural hierarchy of ability, application and interest among individuals within the class. It was also a place for a current ruling group to evaluate and select men for jobs as they came of age. In this context it is instructive to compare a description of the periodic examinations held in the *bakufu* and fief schools with a much later description of a job interview in modern Japan:

Each student was summoned before the examiners and given a passage from the books he had studied either simply to read, or to expound, according to the state he had reached. Examination etiquette was precise. Students of the two upper ranks of samurai were allowed to remove their short sword after they had moved to their place before the examiners in the centre of the room. Those of the next two ranks had to remove it at the entrance before they moved to the centre of the room. The next rank, as well as removing their sword at the entrance, had to kneel not more than one mat's length within the room, and the next rank half a mat, while such luckless foot-soldiers as were emboldened to enter such exalted company had to leave their sword in the waiting-room and proceed no further than the threshold of the room itself. Students (of the upper four ranks only) who proved the most able in these trial runs were selected to appear at the more formal examinations, held, either at the school or at the castle, in the presence of the daimyo or his chief minister and a retinue of other officials. These followed the same pattern. It seems that all who were selected to appear on these grand occasions received a first prize of approximately a gallon of *sake*.[2]

Upon entering the room you are to stop at attention at the

entrance, bow once and wait for an examiner's 'please' and some
gesture leading you toward the chair. Your standing posture must
be straight; both arms are to stay down naturally at the sides, your
palms touching lightly the outer sides of your legs. Your head must
be straight, chin slightly pulled in ... You ought to examine
yourself in a mirror. Proceeding toward the examiners and stop-
ping by the chair, you are to bow to them again. You are to face
them, straighten your posture, and then bend your upper body
about twenty degrees. Bend your head slightly further. It would be
unslightly if your arms did not stay at your sides.[3]

The importance of training in etiquette, in ritual behaviour, in ability
to present oneself acceptably in a highly circumscribed framework of
ascribed statuses, is evident in both eras.

It was also in its role as a training school for the ruling élite that the
fief and *bakufu* schools had to deal with some basic contradictions in
Japanese society. On the one hand, these schools – and also the
commoner schools – were intended to train men to take their
appointed places in a rigid and unchanging hereditary ranking
system. There was no opportunity or occasion for individual movement between commoner and samurai status, and very limited movement between ranks of the samurai class. The occupational slots were
established, and the young men to be prepared for those slots were
selected by birth, not by any other criterion. This matched well with a
long-standing disposition on the part of the Japanese to see children
as relatively undistinguished by special abilities or handicaps at birth,
and to see differences between people as the result of different training
and different degrees of effort that the child puts into his training.
American observers at the present time are universally struck by this
aspect of Japanese educational philosophy, and it is well attested for
Tokugawa times, too. If innate ability is considered to be relatively
uniform, then people can be arbitrarily assigned to occupation
according to their family background, with no loss of talent or
efficiency. Schools need not be used as a screening mechanism,
matching people with jobs for which they are suited, but rather as an
institution preparing them for pre-ordained jobs.

It was understood that some people might reach an educational – or
moral – goal more quickly than others, but this difference was not
considered very important, and the appropriate goals were felt to be
within reach of all, with proper application and effort by the student.
One of the features of fief and *bakufu* schools which made this attitude

plausible was their emphasis on education as primarily moral education:

> There is no need to become a scholar widely read and with encyclopaedic knowledge. It is enough to get a thorough grasp of the principles of loyalty, respect, filial piety and trust. Wide learning and literary accomplishments are not necesary. Anyone can manage to get hold of the general principles of the Four Books and the Five Classics by the time he is thirty or forty. It all depends on diligence. Even the dullest of wits can manage it if he applies himself earnestly enough.[4]

Still, individual differences in ability tend to surface in academic settings, and the *bakufu* and fief schools sought an alternative to potentially embarrassing conflicts between ranking by heredity and displayed ability by concentrating on age differences, or seniority differences in the school, as principles for regulating social interactions. (Social interactions not based in a clearly understood hierarchical relationship were even less comfortable to Japanese in Tokugawa times than today.) Since students were instructed individually much of the time (though they all remained in the same room for study and practice), direct comparisons and competition were not forced to the forefront.

Though the tensions between ascribed status and achieved knowledge are inherent in the school situation, they could be effectively played down as long as society remained stable and unchanging, and as long as the occupational skills of administrators remained relatively simple. The increasing rate of economic change and the challenge from the West that became apparent by about 1800, however, caused increasing strains in the educational and governmental systems. More direct competition was gradually introduced into the schools, more administrative jobs carried direct salaries, more ranks became eligible to hold them, and more samurai (and commoners) deserted the fief and *bakufu* schools to enrol in private schools which emphasised intellectual liveliness and the exciting new Western learning. (At about the same time, the burgeoning entrepreneurial class in England was becoming dissatisfied with classical education as taught in traditional grammar schools, and was beginning to demand more 'modern' subjects such as mathematics and science.)

It was perhaps fortunate for Japanese society that an increase in the openly competitive nature of society could be associated with an external threat from the West. For outside observers, the particular Japanese way of reconciling intense competition, a belief that everyone is substantially equal in ability, a strong cultural commitment to harmony in social relationships and a high level of achievement is Japan's most intriguing and distinguishing characteristic.

PRIVATE EDUCATION UNDER THE TOKUGAWA SHOGUNATE

As a result of the educational system sketched here for the samurai class, Japan at the time of the Meiji Restoration and the embarkation on self-conscious modernisation found herself with a ruling class that was well educated in traditional learning and well on the way to becoming educated in Western learning. The habit of education was established, the content was not trivial, education had already become a primary qualification for holding office and an established means of social mobility. At the time of the Meiji Restoration, Japan also possessed a population of commoners who were quite well educated.

Unlike samurai education, which was supported by the government, education for commoners developed totally out of private initiative, and private desires for education, both practical and elegant. These schools for commoners are usually referred to as *terakoya*, a word which etymologically means 'an establishment for temple children', since at an early point in Japan (as elsewhere in the world) temples were the locus of most commoner education. However, they soon lost any significant connection with temples and with Buddhist clergy.

Increasing stability and prosperity throughout the Tokugawa period brought a widespread demand for education, primarily in Japanese literacy and numeracy, from merchants, tradesmen, village headmen and finally farmers. These schools were locally organised and supported, by a combination of direct fees paid by students' families and community support. The ratio of these two forms of support varied, but in the cities there was less reliance on community support and more on direct fees to users. This was only to be expected given the different kinds of support required for teachers to make a living in the two environments: rural communities could provide housing and produce out of local community resources, while city-dwellers themselves were involved in a more heavily cash-dependent economy, and so paid for schooling for their children in cash also.

How many children attended these privately supported, fully voluntary schools? Though it is extremely difficult to arrive at hard figures, because the records available are scattered and unrepresentative, Dore makes an effective argument that by 1868, the end of the Tokugawa era, about 45 per cent of commoner boys and 10 per cent of commoner girls were attending school for long enough periods to become effectively literate.[5] These numbers are much higher than education or literacy rates for most underdeveloped countries at a comparable stage of pre-industrialisation. They may be compared with estimates for England for this period before public schools were started, when education was conducted mainly by voluntary religion-based schools and private proprietary schools. These estimates vary widely depending on whether the source was demonstrating that public schools were necessary or unnecessary. For example, Cruickshank and Simon argue that as late as the 1860s only one-third of English children aged 6–12 were in satisfactory schools, that attendance was irregular and usually ceased at age 12, while West maintains that a school place existed for almost everyone and 90 per cent could read and write.[6]

In any event, the Japanese figures imply that there were professional teachers and schools available to form the basis for the expansion of education following the Meiji Restoration, and that commoners were ready and willing to pay for education, on a voluntary basis, from a very early period in Japan. Therefore, resistance to a governmentally sponsored and tax-supported education system was minimal after the Meiji Restoration and supplementing the government system with private schools was consistent with tradition.

What did children learn in these private commoner schools? They learned to read and write Japanese, using both the syllabaries and Chinese characters. (That is, Japanese was and is commonly written with Chinese characters standing for Japanese words, with the inflections added to the stems using the Japanese syllabary. The syllabary is phonetic, but the Chinese characters are totally arbitrary in relationship to the sounds of Japanese words, and largely to the meanings of the words.) There were different textbooks for children destined for different occupations – farmers, shopkeepers, traders. These texts were often ostensibly in the form of letters on different subjects, written in such a way as to hang a large vocabulary on a slender storyline. Some model letters for different occasions in life were also commonly presented, along with much useful or esoteric information in list form: for example, charms for combating illness or snake-bite, lists of alternative Chinese and Japanese names of the months, ways to wrap presents for ceremonial occasions, lists of characters used in personal names, affinities between male and female names for arranging marriages, and how to tell time by the position of the Big Dipper, etc.[7] There was also usually a large dose of Buddhist moralising involved in the *terakoya* curriculum, and in some parts of Japan important folk music or dramatic traditions were handed down in the *terakoya*.

Besides learning of this encyclopaedic sort which was considered mundane, practical and 'Japanese', there were eventually a significant number of commoners who wanted to participate in the Chinese studies which were the basis of the samurai education. Thus there arose private schools catering to the desire for a classical education among the commoner class. The teachers were usually samurai who had been educated in the *bakufu* or fief schools, and used this as a way to make a living. Basically they followed the curriculum and traditions of the fief schools, but sometimes they were more inclined to literary studies, such as Chinese poetry and prose literature, and sometimes they were havens for teachers who were not satisfied with the orthodox interpretations of Confucianism that were the only ones countenanced in the official *bakufu* and fief schools. As Western learning insinuated its way into Japan, some advanced private schools for teaching this new learning were also established, and commoners as well as samurai found their way to these schools as students.

In numerical terms, which give some indication of the breadth and reach of education at the end of the Tokugawa Shogunate, it has been estimated that there were 177 *bakufu*–fief schools, about 1500 *shijuku*, or private academies organised by individual teachers, usually teaching a few disciplines in advanced subjects, often those outside the more official curriculum of the first two types of schools, and as many as 11 000 *terakoya*, providing instruction to commoners.[8]

THE MEIJI RESTORATION

The Meiji Restoration in Japan, dating from 1868, is called this because it was the result of a political movement ostensibly to restore the emperor of Japan to a position of primacy that was obscured during the Tokugawa and earlier shogunates. In practice, however,

the emperor ended up with little more power than before, and real
power passed to a different group of samurai (largely drawn from
those families which had reluctantly and belatedly supported Ieyasu
Tokugawa in 1600) who instituted a constitutional monarchy. This
form of government was chosen in conscious imitation of what the
Japanese modernising élite saw as the most effective forms of government in Europe and the Americas, and as they were willing to borrow
wholesale a form of government, they were willing and eager to
borrow other institutions including an educational system. If the
prime model for government was the UK, the prime models for
education were the USA and France. The USA impressed the
Japanese with the way it managed to get a great number of children
into schools, and France impressed the Japanese with its high level of
advanced training for a political and technological élite. So the ruling
groups in Japan made the decision to establish a system of universal,
compulsory elementary schooling and very high quality selective
post-compulsory training. While this was based on a foreign model, it
is hardly surprising that the foreign model chosen was very compatible with the traditional élite and hierarchical nature of Japanese
culture.

When studying education in Japan between 1868 and the Second
World War it is necessary to consider simultaneously two streams of
education, the mass compulsory level and the élite training level.
Largely because of the educational legacy of two such systems already
in place during Tokugawa times, Japan was able to move quickly and
effectively to enlarge its educational reach. Education was compulsory and roughly uniform for all at the primary level, i.e. for the first
six years. Beyond that, however, education was differentiated, vocational and highly selective. In its widespread compulsory primary
stage the Japanese system was similar to the American; in its limited
differentiated post-primary stage it was similar to systems prevailing
in England, France and other European countries, which featured
highly selective education.

One immediate measure of the government's success at the compulsory level lies in the school attendance figures within a few years of the
initiation of the central schooling system. Table 1.1 shows how the
number of students and schools had grown rapidly by the turn of the
century. By 1902, 90 per cent of the children were attending school.[9]

The most dramatic change was surely in the proportion of females
in school. This expansion of education for women was confined to
compulsory schooling as far as the government was concerned,

Table 1.1   Public and private primary schools and students, 1883–1980

	Number of schools			Number of students (in 000s)			
	Total	Public	Private	% Private	Total	Public	Private	% Private
1883	30 156	29 589	567	1.9	3 238	3 193	45	1.4
1893	23 960	23 418	542	2.3	3 338	3 281	56	1.7
1903	23 648	23 354	294	1.2	5 084	5 037	47	0.9
1913	21 149	21 001	148	0.7	7 096	7 069	27	0.4
1923	20 732	20 618	114	0.6	9 137	9 109	28	0.3
1933	20 724	20 627	97	0.5	11 035	11 009	27	0.2
1943	21 309	21 227	82	0.4	12 848	12 816	32	0.3
1953	21 735	21 611	124	0.6	11 225	11 193	32	0.3
1960	22 701	22 540	161	0.7	12 591	12 544	49	0.4
1970	22 444	22 283	161	0.7	9 493	9 439	55	0.6
1980	24 945	24 779	166	0.7	11 827	11 767	60	0.5

Sources: 1883–1970 data from Ministry of Education, *Education in 1968–70*, Part II on 'Historical Statistics', pp. 102–7; 1980 Data from *Mombusho*, 1981, pp. 3, 15, 18.

however; post-compulsory education for girls was left to missionaries for quite a number of years and even now females are greatly underrepresented in public universities.

As we noted above, the mass compulsory education was not oriented to narrow vocational ends, but was aimed at producing a work-force that at the end of formal schooling was undifferentiated – the curriculum was no different for children intended for different occupations. The content of education at this level remained, as it had been in the *terakoya* and as it is in most countries, concentrated on teaching literacy and basic mathematics. Literacy was made some-what easier by standardisation of the syllabaries used and by a significant reduction in the number of Chinese characters that were needed. This movement culminated in 1946 in a list of 'Characters of Standard Usage' containing only 1850 characters, plus some extras for personal and place names. (This helped, but not as much as might be supposed. Each character has several different readings, depending on context, so must in effect be learned several times.)

Western learning and eventually science were also parts of the curriculum. It is significant that moral education always played an important role. A distinction between moral education, as the respon-sibility of institutions other than the state, and secular education, as the responsibility of the state, simply never developed in Japan as it did in the USA and most European countries.

This is partly because in Japan moral education means something different from its Western meaning. It did not – and does not now – concern itself with such issues as the proper relationship betwen man and God, nor with private relationships between people, nor with sex as a particular arena for moral conflict. Instead, moral education in Meiji Japan referred to the proper ordering of relations between individuals as role-players in a social structure and its object was to integrate what had been a fragmented feudal society. Regional differences were still salient at this time in Japan, and the aim of the Meiji Restoration was to minimise the continuation and disintegrating impact of these differences. When the new Meiji government took the first step to institutionalise a modern educational structure in Japan in 1872, one of its major goals was to use that system to create a united citizenry which would enable Japan to compete on an equal basis with other nations in the modern world. Just as the USA used education as a means to indoctrinate immigrants from diverse countries into US citizenry, so Japan set out to do the same, for different regions within the country, and this was accomplished through the moral education curriculum.

As developed during the early Meiji period, moral education had two philosophical bases. First was Confucian political doctrine, and second was a movement called *kokugaku*, national learning. In contrast to Western political philosophy, which emphasises individual rights *vis-à-vis* the state, Confucian political philosophy is primarily concerned with outlining the duties owed by an individual to others and to the state (usually in the form of a person, such as the emperor or other high official). This philosophy emphasised the importance of each individual carrying out his status and role responsibilities, so as to contribute to a rightly ordered society.

Confucianism is a universalistic philosophy. A second source of moral education, however, was *kokugaku*, 'national learning', which stressed the uniqueness of the Japanese experience and identity. *Kokugaku* had developed during the late Tokugawa period as a revolt against the non-Japanese, Chinese emphasis of Confucian studies, and it involved a study of Japanese language, Japanese history, and Japanese religion. *Kokugaku* combined with Confucianism to place the emperor of Japan at the head of the Japanese state as a god, to whom all Japanese were bound by both mystical and moral ties. These two strains of thought were combined to provide a workable political and moral philosophy that would, it was hoped, enable Japan to enter into a modern, competitive relationship with the outside world as a nationally unified and distinctive people, with a stable political and social order.

During the time that an effective national compulsory educational system was being developed, the field of secondary and higher education was also developing rapidly. New schools and new kinds of schools were started, both by the government and even more so by private initiative from Japanese educational entrepreneurs and missionaries. There were a number of changes in the organisation and legal status of both government and private schools. Many of these were granted governmental recognition, and were either absorbed by the governmental educational system or came to be an institutionalised supplement to it. These developments, especially those in the private sector, will be discussed in much greater detail in Chapters 4 and 5.

The chief characteristic of these high schools and universities was that they were were selective, career-oriented in conception and highly differentiated into different trades and different curricula. Both vertical movement into these schools and horizontal movement from one trade to another were extremely difficult.

Though hereditary rank was no longer the official basis for assignment to post-compulsory education, it is true that former samurai continued to dominate the élite track for some time to come. Several factors worked to mitigate continued samurai dominance, however. First, the mass compulsory educational system had as one of its functions the selection of promising material for élite education. Innate ability and effort were now seen to matter, as education and occupations became increasingly complex. Second, because another function of the educational system was national integration, the content and quality of mass education were centrally controlled and so tended to erase any barriers to élite education that arose from regional differences. Third, because this was a time of massive economic and political change in Japan, there were many more and different kinds of élites to which people could be recruited, so that the samurai class could not provide all the candidates needed, and the kinds of new jobs were not always those that seemed naturally suited to samurai in any case. And perhaps most importantly, because of the base laid in Tokugawa times, the population's appetite for education was enormous, and well informed. It could not be bought off with ineffective schooling. If the government wanted to control education –

16

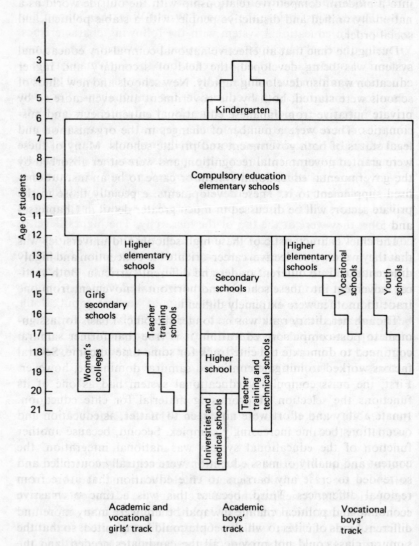

Adapted from Anderson, *Education in Japan*, p. 41.

Figure 1.1   Structure of the Japanese educational system, 1939

and it did – it had to offer a superior education, and this opened the door to upward movement for all classes.

By the years just before the Second World War, then, Japan had developed an educational system with the following characteristics. Virtually universal education was provided for six years, with a small portion of students in an élite stream but the vast majority in a nationally uniform curriculum. This was oriented toward general education, including moral education for nationalism. Very few private schools existed at this compulsory education level. Post-compulsory education tracked females separately from males and tracked males into different vocationally oriented schools, some technical, and some leading to the professions and government service. Those schools were both public and private. But since the public institutions were very limited in size, selective by ability and trained their students for the prestigious civil service examinations and jobs, they were at the top of the hierarchy. The highest level of education was found in the government Imperial Universities, and the greatest prestige as well as the most desirable jobs accrued to graduates of these universities. One is hardly surprised by the prevailing belief that the most meritorious students found their way to these institutions. Thus, both the high quality of student input at the beginning and the high status of jobs at the end enhanced the prestige of these public institutions. A small but significant number of students were sent to Europe or the USA for graduate training. Figure 1.1 outlines this schooling system.[10]

EDUCATIONAL REFORM UNDER THE AMERICAN OCCUPATION

The next major watershed for Japanese education came with Japan's defeat at the end of the Second World War and the American Occupation. The Americans hoped to change the education system in such a way that the population would be immune from any future militaristic adventures, and the Occupation authorities instituted both organisational and content changes hoping to achieve this goal. As is the case with most seemingly dramatic changes in society, an evaluation of the American changes leaves one feeling that it is difficult to sort out the permanent and ephemeral changes, the important and trivial ones. Continuities seem as significant as changes.

The immediate post-war years found the education system in total disarray – for several months before the formal end of the war the schools had ceased even to be convened. The physical plants were in disrepair or destroyed, and the institution shared in the general discrediting of old social arrangements that had led to the débâcle of the war, especially since the school system had been so heavily ideologically instrumental from the 1930s until the end of the war. It was in the name of the emperor, and the duties owed by all to him, that the state apparatus had justified the cooperation, sacrifices and obedience that enabled Japan to industrialise, militarise and move swiftly along the course that led to their entry into the Second World War. The Ministry of Education had played a leading role in the political–moral indoctrination during this period. It follows that, in the general discrediting of wartime institutions that followed Japan's defeat (including the psychologically devastating disavowal of divinity by the emperor), the prestige of the Ministry and the credibility of its doctrine of morality fell precipitously. Thus, the system at first seemed receptive to American-induced ideas of change, both with respect to ideology and institutions.

The organisational changes that the Occupation authorities put in place were designed to achieve several results. First, they hoped to decentralise control of education and make education a local responsibility as it is in the USA. It was felt that this would prevent political exploitation of the education system and abuses such as had taken place between 1930 and the end of the war. Second, the school structure and curriculum were simplified in such a way as to eliminate the relatively early vocational tracking that had characterised pre-war education in Japan. Thus the 6–3–3 grade structure, six years of elementary school, three of junior high school and three of senior high school, with no overt differentiation of curriculum before high school, was put into place. The separate tracking of males and females was ended, at this level. Post-high school education was made less specialised, and a number of steps were taken to reduce the prestige differentiation of universities, particularly the differentiation between the Imperial Universities (especially those at Tokyo and Kyoto) and all other schools. The most lasting part of this effort was the upgrading of selected institutions, so that each prefecture would have at least one national university, all of which were supposed to be equal in quality.

The American authorities also took several steps designed to modify the political content of education. First, they did away with the role of the central Ministry of Education as the selector of textbooks and the originator of curriculum. These were both to be under local control and it was hoped that a free market-place of ideas and textbooks would prevent the kind of uniform propaganda which the Americans thought characterised pre-war education. Second, they eliminated moral education as a subject for the school curriculum at any level and oversaw the development of social studies, history and civics curricula which were supposed to foster democratic ideals among students.

How long-lasting were these reforms? We consider this question at greater length in Chapter 3 on 'Current Issues and Non-issues in Japanese Education'. Here we simply note that while some local responsibility for education has developed, by 1985 the Ministry of Education had regained substantial control, including control over curriculum and textbooks. Moral education had been reinstated by the Ministry as an important course in the national curriculum, albeit with less militaristic overtones.

In keeping with American desires, and the wishes of the Japanese population, undifferentiated compulsory schooling has been extended from six to nine years, through the junior high schools. Junior high schools became non-selective and comprehensive, as in the American model. On the other hand, senior high schools remained highly selective and differentiated, as in most European countries at the end of the Second World War. Despite this selectivity and differentiation, the growth in schools, students and teachers at non-compulsory levels was dramatic, as indicated in Tables 1.2, 1.3, 1.4, 1.5, and 1.6, which give this data for different types of institutions.

Secondary education has become available at the world's highest rate – 90 per cent of the age group now finishes high school – but many of these graduate from private high schools. Higher education has also exploded, enrolling 38 per cent of the relevant age cohort, but most of these are in new privately funded and privately managed universities. Thus, movement from one level of the system to another is much more universal, much less selective than it used to be. However, in light of this vast expansion of educational opportunity, the differentiation within each (post-compulsory) level has become even greater, the status hierarchy even more pronounced – contrary to the initial intent or expectation of the American Occupation. In this sense, the greater the change, the more everything has remained the same. An outline of the present educational structure is given in Figure 1.2.[11]

Table 1.2 Public and private secondary schools and students, 1883–1980*

	Number of schools			Number of students (in 000s)			
	Total	Public	Private	% Private	Total	Public	Private	% Private
1883	202	185	17	8.4	16	15	1	6.3
1893	124	96	38	30.7	25	19	7	25.7
1903	1 925	1 798	127	6.6	216	191	24	11.3
1913	9 188	8 701	487	5.3	681	614	67	9.8
1923	16 873	16 457	416	2.5	1691	1546	144	8.6
1933	17 710	16 998	712	4.0	2287	2013	248	10.8
1943	20 284	16 575	3709	18.3	5222	3706	1516	29.0
1953	15 678	14 112	1566	10.0	7715	7046	670	8.7
1960	15 759	14 146	1613	10.2	9126	7994	1132	12.4
1970	14 950	13 150	1800	12.0	8948	7522	1427	15.9
1980	16 001	14 208	1793	11.2	9716	8226	1450	14.9

*Includes both lower and upper secondary schools. The former is almost all public; the latter has a large private sector. In 1980 the percentage private at the lower secondary (junior high) level was 2.9, at the upper secondary (high school) level it was 28.1.
Sources: As Table 1.1.

Table 1.3 Public and private higher educational institutions and students, 1883–1980*

	Number of schools			Number of students (in 000s)			
	Total	Public	Private	% Private	Total	Public	Private	% Private
1883	147	118	29	19.7	15	12	3	22.4
1893	98	66	32	32.7	21	14	7	32.3
1903	129	101	28	21.7	53	39	14	26.7
1913	195	139	56	28.7	84	59	25	29.9
1923	327	234	93	28.4	145	86	59	40.9
1933	403	264	139	34.5	218	111	107	48.9
1943	438	272	166	37.9	398	202	196	49.2
1953	461	150	311	67.5	536	219	317	59.2
1960	525	171	354	67.4	712	242	470	66.0
1970	930	235	695	74.7	1714	423	1291	75.3
1980	1025	270	755	73.7	2253	536	1717	76.2

*Includes technical colleges, junior colleges and universities.
Sources: As Table 1.1.

Table 1.4 Students and teachers in public and private high schools (upper secondary schools), 1960–82

	Enrolments (in 000s)				Teachers				Enrolments/Teacher			
	Total	Public	Private	% Private	Total	Public	Private	% Private	Total	Public	Private	Private/Public
1960	3239	2310	929	28.7	131 224	100 891	30 333	23.1	24.69	22.90	30.64	1.3
1965	5074	3409	1665	32.8	193 524	144 539	48 985	25.3	26.22	23.58	33.99	1.4
1970	4232	2947	1285	30.4	202 440	154 478	47 962	23.7	20.90	19.08	26.78	1.4
1975	4333	3025	1038	30.2	222 733	171 311	50 847	22.8	19.45	17.60	25.73	1.5
1980	4622	3322	1300	28.1	243 627	189 227	54 400	22.3	18.97	17.55	23.90	1.4
1982	4601	3322	1278	27.8	248 495	193 167	55 328	22.3	18.51	17.20	23.10	1.3

Sources: 1960–75: Educational Standards in Japan (Ministry of Education, 1975) pp. 256–9, 314–15; 1980: Mombusho (Ministry of Education, 1981) pp. 1, 15, 18; 1982: Calculated from information provided by Japan Foundation for the Promotion of Private Schools.

Table 1.5 Students and teachers in public and private junior colleges, 1960–82

	Enrolments (in 000s)					Teachers (in 000s)					Enrolments/Teacher			
	Total	National	Local	Private	% Private	Total	National	Local	Private	% Private	Total	National Local	National Private	Private/Public
1960	83	7	11	66	78.8	6	1	1	5	82.2	13.05	15.59	12.90	0.8
1965	148	8	14	126	85.3	9	1	1	8	86.8	15.83	17.56	15.57	0.9
1970	263	10	16	237	90.1	15	2	2	14	89.5	17.18	16.15	17.30	1.1
1975	354	13	18	323	91.2	16	2	2	13	85.4	22.74	13.70	24.29	1.8
1980	371	34 {		337	90.9	16	3	3	14	84.3	22.67	13.12	24.44	1.9
1982	373	16	20	337	90.4	18	3	3	14	81.0	21.22	10.70	23.70	2.2

Sources: 1960–75: *Educational Standards in Japan* (Ministry of Education, 1975) pp. 270–7, 314–15; 1980: *Mombusho* (Ministry of Education, 1981) pp. 1, 15, 18; 1982: Information provided by Japan Foundation for the Promotion of Private Schools.

Table 1.6 Students and teachers in public and private universities, 1960–82

	Enrolments (in 000s)					Teachers					Enrolments/Teacher				
	Total	National	Local	Private	% Private	Total	National	Local	Private	% Private	Total	National	Local	Private	Private/ Public
1960	628	195	30	404	64.3	44 434	24 410	4725	15 299	34.3	14.14	7.98	6.27	26.35	3.3
1965	938	238	38	661	70.5	57 445	29 828	5089	22 528	39.2	16.32	7.99	7.52	29.34	3.7
1970	1407	310	50	1047	74.4	76 275	36 840	5342	34 093	44.7	18.44	8.40	9.38	30.70	3.7
1975	1734	358	51	1325	76.4	89 648	42 020	5602	42 026	46.9	19.34	8.51	9.08	31.54	3.7
1980	1835	407	52	1377	75.0	102 985	47 843	5794	49 348	47.8	17.82	8.50	8.99	27.90	3.3
1982	1780	405	50	1325	74.5	107 486	49 944	5766	51 766	48.2	16.56	8.10	8.60	25.60	3.2

Sources: As Table 1.5.

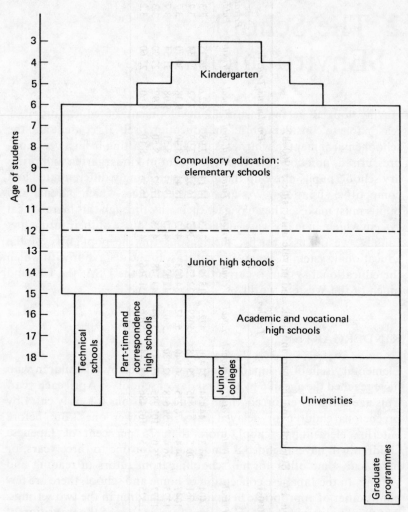

Age of students

Kindergarten

Compulsory education: elementary schools

Junior high schools

Technical schools

Part-time and correspondence high schools

Academic and vocational high schools

Junior colleges

Universities

Graduate programmes

Adapted from Anderson, *Education in Japan*, p. 106.

Figure 1.2   Structure of the Japanese educational system, 1972

2 The School Environment

Having looked at the historical development of education, it is reasonable to consider in brief the education itself, its content and the school environment in which it is imparted. Starting from a very non-pressurised, non-competitive environment in kindergarten and primary school, pupils move up the line to increasingly differentiated and competitive situations. We consider the choices which parents and pupils must make as they navigate their way through this hierarchical system which, in many ways, determines the course of their future life. Finally, we discuss, briefly, the reasons for the popularity of the educational system in Japan – in contrast to the disfavour with which the educational system is currently viewed in the USA, the UK and much of the Western world.

KINDERGARTEN

Elementary school in Japan requires attendance by all children who have reached the age of 6 by the first day of school – 1 April each year. This age is rigidly enforced; there are no provisions for early entry by precocious children or delayed entry for slower ones. But before entering elementary school, more than 75 per cent of Japenese children will have attended a kindergarten for one to three years, or have had some other formal schooling from tutors in reading and writing. In the Japanese conception of home and school, there are few continuities of appropriate behaviour for children in the two settings. The chief value of kindergarten, therefore, is to ease the transition of children into the very different set of demands which they will face in elementary school.

In the Japanese view, the major difference between home and school is that children must adjust to and participate in group life at school. That is, a child must move from home, where the ordinary child-rearing patterns have led him to believe that there is no distinction between his own desires and what is desired for him by his parents (read: mother). In psychological terms, Japanese child-rearing practices, which are quite uniform throughout the society, are not intended to foster independence and a sense of separate self in children, but rather to gain necessary compliance by minimising overt demands on children, and by encouraging them to want what their mothers want, because of an emotional bond between mother and child. Japanese mothers not only reason less with their children, but also are less authoritarian than American mothers. In addition, they are willing to absorb more verbal and physical abuse than is common in American homes, with no overt signs of anger or anything other than patient long-suffering. Since there are few children in a family, and competition for the mother's attention is limited, children come to feel that it is normal for the world in general to be organised as they would prefer it.

This is not to say that pre-school Japanese children are not well-behaved. They seem remarkably well-behaved, in situations that Americans regard as trying for children, such as relatively long rides on public transportation, or accompanying their mothers on the many errands that are part of the housewife's job in modern Japan. They also absorb very early a concern for decorum that requires a great deal of discipline. At one kindergarten sports day which we observed, for instance, not only were the 3-, 4- and 5-year-old students in attendance, but there were many younger siblings. We ate lunch seated on plastic groundsheets, with shoes placed neatly off the cloths. The young children were not required to stay still all during the meal, but jumped up and down, ran off to play and returned for a few more bites. By the age of 2 children in this group could be trusted to remember to take off their shoes each time they returned to the cloths, and to put them on again to play.

But pre-schools in Japan emphasise to children and parents that in school the demands of group life take precedence over individual impulses, and they teach this concept through highly ritualised group activities. Snacks or meals, for instance, are conducted differently. At home, families rarely sit down for a joint meal, and children typically eat as they play, or eat a bit, play, then return for more food. At kindergartens, however, a lunch requires that all children sit at once at assigned seats, that they arrange their lunch-boxes in a prescribed way, wait to be served drinks by other pupils, listen to announcements by teachers, eat together, eat all their meal, and remain sitting together until everyone is finished. Other group activities, such as listening to stories, also encourage long spans of attention and respect for the group. In the groups that we observed, potentially disruptive behaviours were given minimal attention. A teacher would not interrupt reading a story to tell a talking child to be quiet, but would reach over to touch his head or shoulder while continuing the story. A child being rowdy at lunch-time would attract the presence of the teacher to his side, but no comment on the inappropriate behaviour, nor would he be allowed to become the focus of group attention. Without the reward of attention, such non-conformist behaviour seems to wither very quickly.

Other situations which call for long periods of quiet behaviour in a group are the frequent ceremonies of opening school, or marking new terms of school, or visitors' days, or religious holidays. Many of these ceremonies not only involve group activities such as marching onto the stage together as a class, performing together, sitting quietly as other parts of the ceremony proceed, but also performing individual parts smoothly, such as going, in turn, to bow to the principal and receive a certificate. At the school we observed, a teacher was waiting at the gate to receive each child's greeting and bow each morning, and each child waited in line at the end of school to say good-bye and bow to the teacher before leaving.

On the other hand, a majority of the time in kindergartens is spent in free play, and during this time the children are given a good deal more freedom than in American pre-schools. There seems to be almost no activity the children could do in the school grounds that is forbidden, whether it is digging holes in the playground or using sharp knives and scissors for craft activities. Nor do the teachers feel a need to engage in very much direct supervision. Children are allowed to play in rooms with no teacher present, to play individually or in groups of their own choosing, at activities of their own choosing. Again, disruption and arguments are handled in the quietest way possible, without becoming noticeable to any but those immediately involved. *Genki*, liveliness, is a desired characteristic of Japanese children, and during this free playtime is much in evidence, enough to be unnerving to American observers. Neither parents nor teachers of children this age seem to worry at all about their getting physically hurt, and getting dirty is fully expected.

Though children at kindergarten are encouraged to be independent in feeding and dressing themselves, this behaviour is much less expected at home, where children are still allowed or encouraged to avail themselves of the mother's help for many small activities. A common theme of the mothers' club meetings we attended was the teachers' suggestion that mothers should expect more independent behaviour from their children to reinforce the lessons of school, but it was clear from discussions after the meeting that both mothers and children would be reluctant to dispense with these intimate shared activities.

PRIMARY SCHOOL

Even for those children who have attended kindergarten, however, the entry to first grade marks the beginning of proper education, of a new status, of a serious competition. The change of status is marked at home with the purchase of new clothes and especially of a new book bag, of heavy red or black leather, expensive, and expected to last for six long years of elementary school. At school there is a formal greeting ceremony, with a welcome from the principal, all the children already separated from their watching parents and gathered together to face a new teacher and a new life.

Japanese elementary-school classes are large, about forty pupils, with one teacher for all subjects and no aides, in spartan buildings.[1] Because first grade is considered a crucial foundation for the rest of school, especially in terms of discipline, experienced teachers are assigned to these classes, and a great deal of effort is put into making the class a working, organised group during the first part of the school year. There is also a demanding curriculum prescribed by the Ministry of Education. Observers in Japanese elementary schools are almost always struck by the enthusiasm and high level of activity that is apparent, and are amazed at how much of this activity is actually directed at the curricular material. Japanese elementary-school pupils are not expected to be quiet in order to learn, but they are expected to focus on the material being presented. Teachers work hard at making this material interesting and lively, and seem generally to succeed. It is during these years at elementary school that the egalitarian, child-centred, whole-child approach to education is dominant. Though children must work hard to keep pace with the curriculum, teachers are able to develop techniques for pulling the slower students up to an acceptable level of performance, somewhat at the expense of faster pupils. But during these years, teachers can feel that they are not hurting faster pupils by this, because they will have chances to pull ahead later on in the more competitive years. (And differences among pupils at that stage are not very great by American standards, because of the relative similarity in home environments, the high degree of socioeconomic and cultural homogeneity in Japan.)

Among the most important of the tactics for encouraging high achievement from all pupils while at the same time minimising direct competition is the elaborate group-structuring that Japanese elementary teachers use. A class of forty children will be broken up into different sets of four to eight children to work out problems in class, discuss issues before presenting a group report to the class, do classroom chores, and work on assignments. The groups are changed regularly. The principles used by teachers to form these groups are such as to discourage social cliques and to avoid homogeneous groupings, instead resulting in groups that are all about equal in performance. At the same time, grades do not mask differences in performance between individual pupils. Cummings reports that elementary schools with strong union sentiments toward equality nevertheless give grades that approximate very closely to a normal curve, and that this is a matter of school policy.[2]

Children spend 240 days a year in school (33 per cent more than in the USA and 20 per cent more than in the UK), 36 hours per week, with only short vacation periods, during which there are daily assignments. School is almost the only place where they can meet with other children to play, the activities and materials covered in school are interesting, and, in short, as the work-place tends to become a total environment for men at work, so school comes to be the major focus of a child's life. And children like school. Most of them are able to achieve at acceptable levels, none are excluded or shamed by classroom practices, and all adults regard school as a serious, important and difficult occupation. If children are doing as well as they can in school, they are successful children.

Nor is there any parental opposition to the practices, demands or standards of the schools. Parents are not cut off from what goes on in elementary classrooms and schools, since there is frequent communication between home and school. Some adult from nearly every family participates in the PTA meetings, attends special functions such as sports day or opening and New Year's ceremonies, and attendance at the monthly observation days usually runs at about 75 per cent of the mothers of a class. Parents put no other demands on children in terms of chores, family activities are structured to conform to the demands of school and parents help children to achieve to the limits of their schooling or financial resources to do so.

The elementary school curriculum concentrates most heavily on literacy, mathematics and social studies, but there is also a serious curriculum in art, music and physical education. The attitude that

innate abilities have relatively little to do with differences in performance extends not only to academic subjects but also to the arts, and it
is simply and accurately assumed that every child can learn to play
several instruments, read music, paint, draw and sculpt satisfactorily.

The years at elementary school then, are ones which children enjoy,
which are designed by the teachers to be rigorous and enjoyable, and
to emphasise development of capacities in a number of different areas
of life. They are relatively immune from the competitive pressures of
the later school years.

JUNIOR HIGH SCHOOL

It is in junior high school, still part of the compulsory school system,
that the beginnings of competition and pressure appear, and become
part of the mood and approach of parents, teachers and students.
Most children are still in public schools, even where private junior
high schools are available, and there is still little differentiation
between the student bodies of different schools in terms of achievements or family background. But it is at the end of junior high school
that pupils will be divided into different categories for high school,
and thus have some part of their destiny set. Therefore the curriculum
at junior high school becomes more demanding, and is geared to the
preparation for high school entrance examinations. The emphasis
moves toward material to be covered, facts to be learned, quick recall
of information and direct competition. There are still some features
which are intended to foster group cohesiveness – for example, home-
room groups stay together for all subjects and it is teachers who are
transient between rooms while students stay put, there are sports and
entertainment competitions between home-rooms and trips for home-
room groups. However, actual study or classroom performances that
are mediated through a group structure are much less common, and
differences between the achievements of children become very
obvious. Teachers may use techniques intended to shame low per-
formers – making a child who cannot answer a question remain
standing beside the desk until he is asked a question he can answer,
for instance, or calling a child to the teachers' room for a scolding in
the presence of other teachers.

One of the most important functions of teachers in junior high
school is 'guidance', that is, helping parents to judge which of the high
school examinations their child should enter. Accurate information
about each child's performance is necessary for this, as well as

accurate information about the possible schools. Singleton describes how the teachers in different junior high schools traded information with each other about the range of their pupils' scores on practice examinations at that time given in the schools, and with high schools on the scores of accepted pupils in order to advise parents accordingly.[3] (Misinformation becomes ultimately dysfunctional for all teachers and schools involved, so a self-policing system was in operation.) At the time Singleton was writing, students could apply to only one public high school, and there were few private schools, and fewer desirable ones, in the area, so the decision about which examinations to take, and to which schools to apply, were indeed consequential. Recently, the schools themselves have stopped giving practice examinations, and this has become part of the profit-making publishing industry surrounding education in Japan. The publishers provide practice tests, grading, advice, cram materials and information about schools and their requirements.

Classes in junior high school are almost exclusively conducted on a lecture basis, depart very little from the outlined curriculum and the textbooks, and are presented to well-behaved but often bored pupils. The ten-minute breaks between classes, when pupils are left in their room unsupervised, see explosions of liveliness that, for all their noise, are not regarded as anything to worry about by teachers.

THE HIGH SCHOOL ENVIRONMENT

The high school entrance examinations divide the undifferentiated populations of the junior high schools into hierarchically distinguished, permanent categories. From this point (age 15) on, competition becomes regional and even national in scope, not local. Each school is distinguished from those above and below it by the examination score needed for entry and therefore serves a very narrow range, in terms of ability and prior academic achievement. Students are not guaranteed a place in their local high school nor, indeed, in the academic track of any public high school. Those who are left out must attend a vocational school, perhaps at night, or a private school. As a result, high school student bodies are distinguishable in terms of the examination skills of their students, and also in terms of family characteristics, such as family size, proportion of working mothers, father's education and occupation, and number of broken families.[4]

However, the curriculum does not become different for the great majority who pursue the academic track. This is still standardised by the Ministry of Education, and high schools that have students at lower levels of achievement are given very little leeway to address the needs of these students. The curriculum and the prospect of university entrance examinations that are perforce based on that nationally standardised curriculum are challenging enough for even the brightest of Japan's hard-working high school students.

School remains the major occupation of children at high school age. They are indeed described as 'children' by parents and teachers, and scant attention is given culturally to differentiating their status from that of younger children. They still do very little to help at home; spend little time with their peers outside school, whether with friends of the same sex, in mixed groups or dating; do not hold part-time jobs; have little spending money, cannot drive, and have little time to spend outside the two contexts of school and family.

The high school curriculum is much less diversified than that of most American high schools or even most British comprehensives, and does not offer electives or choices within prescribed fields, such as a choice between studying short stories or plays to fulfil requirements for Japanese literature. Neither in high school nor at other levels do students do much writing. They are not assigned research projects or asked to do any original work. They do study intensively a core of basic subjects with teachers whose major qualification is knowledge of the subject matter. They learn a great deal that can be tested on objective examinations given to large numbers of students.

During these years, they face the most intense competition of their lives. (Competition is not absent from later life, but it is more diffuse.) For it is at the end of high school that they must face either immediate employment or the competition for university entrance, which will largely determine their later occupation and economic and social levels. Attaining a good grade on the university entrance examination is the overriding goal of the high school years. The few months immediately preceding the examinations are popularly known as 'Examination Hell'. By comparison, for those who get in, college is a vacation.

UNIVERSITY LIFE

For most students who are accepted into a university, their four years there are the most relaxed and pressure-free years of their lives between the ages of 6 and 55.[5] Since it is admittance into a particular university which is of the greatest importance in determining job prospects, and since few have ever dropped out of university (or any other level of Japanese education) because of failing grades, students do not study much. Instead college life is characterised by a rich and warm social life, organised around clubs which reflect an interest in some leisure-time activity – skiing, folk music, jazz, archery and so on. These clubs become groups which provide for all their members' social needs. Some courtship takes place in these groups, but students do not marry while in college, and most college students will still enter into marriages arranged for them after the end of their formal education.

The better the university into which a student has been accepted, the more relaxed and enjoyable his college years are apt to be. This will be true of nearly all students at national universities and at the most prestigious private colleges. For students at lesser private institutions, however, the placement officers who control access to job openings do use grades as a sorting device, and students will have to work harder and show more concern for grades. At the major private universities, some employers use the seminar courses of certain professors as their main source of job-candidates, and there is thus competition to be accepted into those seminars. Those students who during their college years decide they want to do graduate work will also be harder-working undergraduates, but this number is minuscule in Japan.

The first two years of undergraduate education are primarily general education and introductory courses. At national universities the classes might be as large as 100–150 students, and the format is, of course, lectures. In private universities the classes are generally much larger. At national universities, the classes of the last two years, when students are specialising, generally have about twenty students each. At the private universities they will again be much larger.

Japanese who are discussing their country's education system often conjecture that the major purpose of college for all but a few very motivated students is to act as a long decompression period after the rigours of the entrance examination preparation. But the demands of the employment which students enter after university are after all very different from taking exams. And it may be that the style of teaching, the kind of work that is required of students during the four years at university and the camaraderie that develops there, is a preparation, in a useful way, for the more realistic tasks students will face after college.

EGALITARIANISM, HIERARCHY AND COMPETITION IN JAPANESE EDUCATION

Japanese culture is characterised by what is perhaps a unique blend of egalitarianism and hierarchical organisation. The egalitarianism lies partly in the conviction that people are innately all about the same, and that in the equation:

$$\text{Hard work} + \text{Ability} = \text{Educational attainment} = \text{Status}$$

the more important variable is the hard work, not the ability. The standard ways of judging school quality (space, expenditure per pupil, teacher qualifications, etc.) indicate that compulsory schools are very standardised throughout the Japanese school system, and the results, as measured on achievement tests (at the end of primary school especially) are very standard, too – less variation in achievement than in other countries.[6] Very few private schools exist at the primary and junior high levels, which comprise the compulsory years of education.

The famous Japanese propensity for hierarchy, however, is expressed in almost every human interaction, in a predilection for ranked lists of this and that, and a belief that there really is a difference between the no. 1 *tempura* restaurant in Tokyo and the no. 2 *tempura* restaurant in Tokyo, with the ranking criteria being self-evident, or wholly agreed upon. No one questions rankings – of companies, of restaurants, of stores, of high schools or universities. It is also believed in Japan that it is not innate qualities that are reflected in hierarchies, but developed qualities: that one's final place in the hierarchy depends on the effort one is willing to make, not on innate differential endowment or starting-place in the social order. For the Japanese, the ranking criterion for universities is the jobs their graduates get. And for high schools, the criteria are the number of students who go on to university, and the ranking of the universities which accept them. In general in this hierarchy, 'public' ranks above 'private'.

Now for the parents and students trying to navigate their way through the educational system to a desirable adult life and status, what are the choice points and the options, given this hierarchical system?

At the pre-school level, about 75 per cent of the 4- and 5-year olds choose to go to kindergarten, although this is not compulsory. These are mostly privately run, by non-profit organisations, many of them affiliated to a religious organisation, either Buddhist or Christian. Some children are also enrolled in government or private day-care centres, but apparently a decision has been made, *de facto*, not to increase the number of places in these facilities, but to increase the number of places in kindergartens, which do not act as day-care facilities.

As we have seen, except for a few ambitious families in Tokyo, the pre-school years are optional and low-pressure. These one or two years of pre-schooling probably make adjustment to primary school easier, so that while there is no great advantage one way or the other, most families think kindergarten is a good idea. Reading is not taught in kindergartens but many families begin some tutoring at this age, either at home or paid for, so that probably 80 per cent of the children in the first grade can read in the syllabaries before starting school.

The next choice point is not perceived as such by most Japanese families; that is, almost everyone sends their children to the local government primary school. There is little segregation by income in Japanese neighbourhoods, so most primary schools have a similar mix of pupils in terms of family backgrounds. The inputs to primary schools are uniform, both from students and schools, and the outputs are undifferentiated. Beginning in primary school, however, half or more of the students are paying for additional private education. For some students this is remedial, for a few it is to push them ahead of their classmates, for most it seems necessary to keep up with the demanding curriculum, and some of it is enrichment – piano lessons, judo, calligraphy and so on.

Similarly, for most Japanese parents and students, junior high school is a matter of attending the district, local government school. Some élite private high schools have an attached junior high school and families hoping to send their children to those schools will have begun serious tutoring for the junior high school's entrance examinations, in the fourth grade.

For most families in most parts of Japan, however, high school is the first big decision-point and the first point at which hopes may be frustrated. It is also the first point at which background differences among students are reflected in classroom compositions.[7] High school is not compulsory in Japan, and the government, while it has expanded the number of high school places over the years, has not been required to meet all the demand for high school education. In most areas of Japan the status hierarchy of high schools looks about like this (figures give rough proportions of the age cohort in each type of school; these are subject to regional variation):[8]

1. élite private high school (1 per cent) (not found in all areas)
2. public academic school (37 per cent)
3. private day school (25 per cent)
4. public vocational high school (23 per cent)
5. public night, correspondence or special school (7 per cent)
6. no post-compulsory-schooling (7 per cent)

The government academic high schools enrol just over a third of the age cohort, and some of these students are in academic but terminal courses, not university preparatory courses. Entrance to these schools is competitive, by examination. Everyone who wants to apply to a given high school may do so, multiple applications are common, and each school makes its selection, primarily on the basis of examination scores. Therefore, both the student and the school exercise choice; this is not an open-access, neighbourhood school system, nor is it a system of centralised assignment of pupils to schools. Those students who have attended cram schools or had tutoring are at a distinct advantage, so family financial resources become a factor at this point. Spending on cram schools during the junior high school period is common because it may help a family to avoid the expenses of private high school. Except for a few élite schools, moreover, the quality of education in the government schools is considered superior: spending per capita is higher, teachers are paid more, facilities are better, students get higher scores on university entrance exams.

Ethnographic evidence presented in Rohlen's study of five high schools, public and private, in Kobe, Japan, contrasts the attitudes of students, their varying commitment to education, the different support they receive from families and teachers and the clear understanding of everyone concerned as to the career possibilities that remain open to students in different schools.[9] A study of values and attitudes among students in Japanese high schools showed that the academic high schools in both sectors had more in common with each other than with the vocational schools in the same sector. In the academic high schools, both the students and the teachers were likely to have a good relationship with each other, whereas these characteristics are not ordinarily present in the vocational schools. Along the public–private axis, private schools are more likely to emphasise school history and tradition, special school events, etc. An interest in moral and international problems characterises the religious private schools; high costs, in terms of tuition and commuting time, characterise the private high schools with university affiliations.[10] In Part II we present detailed quantitative evidence that high schools of these different categories are really different, in terms of the students they attract, the number of students they place in universities and the lifetime earnings which these students can expect.

The proportion of the age cohort enrolled in university preparatory courses, either in public or private schools, is 45–50 per cent and the proportion of the cohort that enters higher education – junior college, private university or public university – is close to 40 per cent. In this sense there is a place for almost everyone who wants one, but the fierce competitive factor comes from the fact that the quality of the higher education is believed to vary enormously, and the value of a degree from one university is very different from the value of a degree from another university. These differences are closer in magnitude to the American than to the British system – perhaps because Japan and the USA both enrol very large proportions of the age cohort in higher education so that differentiation among students requires differentiation among institutions. This differentiation is only partly related to the 'quality' of the education imparted by the schools in question. It is more importantly a reflection of great differences in the student input, with corresponding differences in the hiring patterns of employers. Almost without exception these employers use 'feeder' colleges, so a student accepted at Waseda University, for instance, knows in advance which of the big companies of Japan hire Waseda graduates, and which never hire them.

The degree of competition to get into a good university is indicated by the fact that overall, about 40 per cent of the freshmen each year are students who have spent one to three years or more in full-time study, probably at a cram school, after completing high school. (These students are called *ronin*, the term used in Tokugawa times for itinerant samurai who did not have a permanent attachment to a lord but were seeking one.) The percentage of *ronin* freshmen varies by 'desirability' of field; it is lowest for education students (about 20 per cent) and highest for medical and dental schools (about 60 per cent). So each year's batch of potential students is really competing with a pool of applicants larger than that year's cohort, some of whom have been busy for up to three years preparing for the entrance exam. This in turn means that many of those in a given cohort who wish to enter university cannot do so immediately but must wait two or three years, while improving their examination scores.[11] The 40 per cent of the cohort who eventually enter higher education include the *ronin*.

It is this intense competitive situation with regard to higher education that determines the character of education in Japan, from the top down. Very public, very detailed records are kept of which high schools succeed in placing their students in which universities, and a school's prestige is determined solely by this criterion. Getting into a high school which places students in the universities which the student hopes to attend becomes a goal for junior high students and their parents, and so on down the line.

Alongside this panoply of public and private non-profit institutions has developed a large for-profit educational industry. First, there are firms which develop and administer examinations for different schools, and practice examinations for cram schools to use. And there are cram schools, and private academies, which specialise in preparing students for specific examinations, or types of exams. A part of the private education industry also prepares information about type and content of exams, later careers of school graduates and examination scores for different schools that are essential guides to parents and children in wending their way through this competitive and complex educational system. While similar data are also published in the UK about secondary schools and in the USA about universities, the flow of publicly available and demanded information is much greater in Japan, corresponding to the wide range of options available to students and the perception that their choice crucially determines their future life.

THE POPULARITY OF THE EDUCATIONAL SYSTEM

Whatever its shortcomings, the Japanese educational system is by and large popular, effective in achieving the goals of its participants – in contrast to the American and British systems which are constantly under critical attack. We can suggest a number of reasons why this may be the case.

First and foremost is a genuine and near-total consensus on the goals and purposes of the educational system, and these goals are limited. Schools in Japan do not have the large variety of social missions expected of inner-city schools in the USA and UK. In Japanese schools the goals are to provide high-quality compulsory education for all, to achieve a common level of competence, citizenship and experience, and beyond that level, to be the instrument by which a legitimate ranking of people and sorting into social slots in a hierarchically organised society can take place. They do not have to deal with students from very diverse backgrounds and therefore have not been assigned the task of equalising opportunities for those from disadvantaged homes.

Beyond the junior-high-school level (i.e. age 15), each school deals with a narrow spectrum of ability and can therefore concentrate on that range. The public schools, being selective, get the best students who achieve the best results. Students at the tail end of the distribution are relegated to private schools or to 'invisible' vocational high schools, which receive little popular attention. The academic curriculum is narrow and geared to the interests of the academic students – the university entrance examinations.

Furthermore, these examinations are regarded as fair at all levels, a good and proper tool for choosing people for scarce goods – school places and jobs – in the society. Since children spend most of their time in school (much more so than in the USA or UK) and since their time in school is oriented toward taking examinations, it is hardly surprising that they achieve more and that those in the public schools achieve most of all.

There seems to be very little feeling in Japan that the schools are being used to reproduce an exploitative class structure or to keep some groups 'in their place'. In this regard, Japan has benefited from a remarkably sustained period of economic growth, which has dampened potential class conflict. One can anticipate more difficulty as economic growth slows down and upward social mobility can take place only if offset by downward mobility – a sure source of social conflict.

Finally, social and family support for education and the educational system is strong. This support is expressed in public and private spending on education, in the wages and respect given to teachers and educators, in the time allocated to it and the seriousness with which children's efforts to learn and succeed in education are taken. Evidence for this degree of support ranges from comical anecdotes (the stereotype of the 'education mama' that appears so often in the popular press, and the study desk equipped with a buzzer to ring for mother to come with academic help, a word of encouragement or a snack that is part of so many Japanese households), to finding that Japanese husbands rate their wives' ability to handle the children's education as the second most important characteristic they can have (following being an interesting person to talk to).[12] It is indeed the case that a Japanese family has been successful if their children do well in school, and on the child's part this is almost the only thing he needs to do to be a successful child. In such circumstances, and where there are few cultural barriers to academic performance, taken in the aggregate, that performance can be very high.

3 Current Issues and Non-issues in Japanese Education

Our account of the development of Japanese education so far has given no hint of discord or disagreement within Japan over education, but in Japan as in most countries, education is important enough to be the focus of political and philosophical controversy. In the case of Japan, the issues that gather public attention are in large part a legacy of the pre-war pattern of political indoctrination carried out in the schools and the post-war reforms which were intended to wrest control of education away from the central Ministry of Education. It is significant that these issues have not yet been totally resolved today. It is also significant that many of the issues which are considered most important and controversial in countries such as the USA and UK – the role of education in achieving racial and socioeconomic integration, the relative roles of public and private schools, the quality and funding of public education – are not salient questions in Japan. In this chapter we assess these issues and non-issues and their interrelationship with broader aspects of Japanese culture and life.

The central issues in Japanese education for the past forty years have revolved about the power of the national Ministry of Education (*Mombusho*) versus the local and prefectural governments on the one hand and the Teachers' Union on the other. These three groups constitute the major actors in most disputes. The major areas where the lines have been drawn concern questions of élitism versus egalitarian access, Ministry 'censorship' of textbooks, and moral education.

As noted earlier, the Occupation forces wanted to decrease the role of the Ministry, which it considered unduly nationalistic and militaristic, and increase the role of the localities, following the American model. Local communities were to choose their own textbooks, curriculum, etc. Occupation forces also aimed to increase the control of the teachers over the schools, and to purge the ranks of teachers of the most militaristic among them. During this period, about 20 per cent of the teachers left the profession, either because of economic hardship or fear of purge. Left in the leadership core of the teachers was a small group who had taken an anti-militaristic position throughout the pre-war and war years, and who now formed an effective bread-and-butter trade union, the Japan Teachers' Union. The JTU supported local control of education rather than Ministry control, opposed moral–political indoctrination in the schools, favoured egalitarian rather than élite education, and opposed 'education by examination'. Thus, it would have seemed to be the natural ally of the Occupation. However, it also had a strong socialist or communist ideological bias, which effectively prevented this alliance, and its policy consequences, from coming to fruition.

Despite its initial anti-Ministry position, the Occupation forces never got around to purging the *Mombusho* after the war. This was in part because such a purge would have been very difficult to accomplish and in part because during the Cold War which quickly ensued, the primary goal of the American forces changed from creating a democracy in the ruins of an empire to promoting Japan as a bastion against Communism in Asia. Since the Teachers' Union was steadfastly leftist, the natural enemy of the Occupation from this perspective, its opponent, the *Mombusho*, gradually became worthy of Occupation support.

At the national level these two groups were and are relentless ideological opponents, maintaining rigid and pure positions over a long period of time. But only a few issues can actually be resolved at the national level, because the Occupation forces did indeed leave considerable power, particularly over bread-and-butter issues, in the local school districts and prefectures. To see how this tripartite struggle plays itself out, we examine a few of the issues that have been most salient for these involved in the Japanese educational system.[1]

MORAL EDUCATION AND CENSORSHIP

Among the first of the changes after the Occupation was the reassertion of Ministry control over textbooks and curriculum. The Japanese were very uncomfortable with the strong degree of local control proposed by the Occupation forces, mostly because they envisaged, accurately, a national market for education beyond the high school level. Local control of educational materials, such as exists in the USA and the UK, seemed too chaotic, and too likely to leave some students at a real disadvantage in the examination competition. Standardisation of curriculum and of curricular material seemed to the Japanese to be the only way to ensure equality of educational opportunity. Under the system that was developed, authors of text-books were informed of the national curriculum 'suggested' by the Ministry, and submitted texts to the Ministry for approval for use with that curriculum.

Then as now, use of the Ministry's curriculum was not mandatory for local or prefectural schools, but in effect it is extremely difficult for school districts to deviate from the national curriculum, since the examination system exerts a strong pressure for all schools to cover the same material in the same way. National or regional examinations serve as an important central control mechanism in all countries (such as the UK) where they exist. Their absence from the USA is one of the major reasons why local control and diversity persist. This diversity in achievement is now becoming a source of controversy, with more people demanding a national exam as a tool of accountability. Most Japanese have long felt that national standardisation is in every child's best interests. Thus, this reassertion of central control by the Ministry of Education met with very little opposition on general principles from rank-and-file teachers or parents and the public at large.

The two areas in which this was politically sensitive, however, are the inclusion of a specific course on 'morals' in the national curriculum, and the preparation of teaching materials under the direction of the Ministry, particularly the 'censorship' of textbooks dealing with the Second World War.

The overt reason for the opposition to a course on morals was the memory of the role such a course had played in the indoctrination of students during the pre-war years. Most teachers and most members of society wanted to avoid such practices and consequences in the new era. At the same time, there were and are powerful cultural reasons for including a morals course in the schools. Though Japanese did and do practise religion, mainly Shinto and Buddhist, these religions in their Japanese context do not emphasise ethics and morality, and there is no institutional way for them to impart such instruction to children as there is in most Western countries. (Shintoism emphasises a relationship between people and supernatural forces associated with places and natural phenomena; Buddhism emphasises the relation-ship between people and personalistic spirits, including most impor-tantly one's family members as they become less human and more divine.)[2]

Nor do Japanese consider the family a proper arena for moral training. Such training, with its inherent focus on rule-governed patterns of behaviour between individuals, is inconsistent with the emotionally based patterns of behaviour within family groups. Japanese parents do not feel they want to impart to their children particular religious, moral or ethical values which they cannot trust a public body, such as the education system, to reflect adequately and accurately. This attitude, which sharply contrasts with that in many Western countries, is one of the most telling of the signs of cultural homogeneity among the Japanese.

Again, since morality and the content of the morals course in Japan deal primarily with the relationship of individuals to a group, it seems only reasonable to Japanese that such instruction should take place in the institution for children which is characterised by group life. Thus, in spite of opposition by the Teachers' Union on the national level, the Ministry of Education's plan to reinstate moral instruction was adopted, because of the pressure from parents and the population in general who felt that this was necessary and proper. It is interesting that the absence of 'moral' or 'religious' education in the public schools is a source of concern to many parents in the Western world, but the existing cultural diversity makes it difficult, if not impossible, to agree on the content of such instruction which would satisfy most people. In Japan such agreement was reached with relative ease.

The morals instruction issue, then, is one which was resolved in favour of the Ministry of Education, but only because the Ministry proposal was resonant with strong cultural convictions of parents and members of the Teachers' Union were willing to implement it in the classroom. The issue of textbook censorship is more complicated and publicly strident, and the main subject area of controversy has been the modern history of Japan.

In general, the Ministry of Education and the members of the national legislature most concerned with education would prefer to present that part of Japan's history in terms that are less harsh than those favoured by the Teachers' Union and the political left. The Ministry gives these texts meticulous scrutiny, often insisting on minute but crucial changes in the text – saying that Japan 'entered' Korea, not that Japan 'invaded' Korea, for instance. The Japan Teachers' Union and the leftist political parties also watch for such censorship, and make it a major public issue. In 1982 and 1983 such a vocabulary choice also became an international issue for Japan, as those countries which had suffered under Japanese occupation lodged formal public protests against softening the description of Japan's activities during this period of history. In this dispute, though the left may win a few skirmishes on vocabulary, the Ministry of Education has generally prevailed in establishing the tone of the textbook material mastered by all Japanese high school students.

Overt practices that foster nationalism are quite absent from Japanese schools, however. Schools do not usually fly the Japanese flag, these are not displayed in classrooms, patriotic songs are rarely sung, there is no ceremony comparable to the daily recitation of the Pledge of Allegiance so common in American schools.

ELITISM VERSUS EGALITARIAN ACCESS

Once its control over curriculum was re-established, the Ministry began to change the course of study to make it more demanding, more oriented to examinations and more suited to acting as a screening device to place students in academically appropriate secondary and post-secondary schools. The Teachers' Union opposed these initiatives because of their élitist consequences, but has not been able to alter fundamentally the Ministry's objectives, especially at the junior high and high school levels. This *Mombusho* policy apparently has strong popular support.

More troublesome to society at large is the problem of children who do not do well in school, particularly those who make some level of violent protest. In Japan, this sort of juvenile delinquency is most manifest in junior high schools and its most troubling form is violence directed at teachers. Since it is in junior high school that education becomes specifically geared to examination performance for high school entrance, and since entrance into a desirable high school is by no means assured for all students, students at junior high school are under a great deal of pressure. Class sizes are large, the curriculum is extremely demanding and teachers do not mask performance differences between children. It becomes apparent to some children during the years at junior high school that they cannot and will not gain access to the education and jobs to which they aspire, and it is during these years that Japanese schools experience the most difficulty with behaviour problems. Teachers, those on the political left and some parents are apt to feel that the age of 15 is too early for decisions about strongly differentiated education to be made. But so far the *Mombusho* has not felt pressure to change its policy on this issue.

A more generalised case of this problem concerns 'Examination Hell' – the intense competitive pressure all students face when they graduate from junior high and high school and take a series of demanding exams which stress detail or memory and which will determine their future. Entry to universities is strictly governed by examination performance and future employment prospects are strictly governed by which university is attended. Thus, students know that a tremendous amount depends on the results of these examinations, leading to the common sobriquet, 'Examination Hell'.

This is perhaps the most widely discussed issue in Japanese education today. As expected, the Teachers' Union vigorously opposes this system in favour of one which is less pressured, more open-access. (But even teachers have acceded to the pressure, take great pains not to send their pupils ill-equipped into the real world of examination competition, and take great pleasure in their students' successes.) The Ministry supports the system as being the best way to allocate scarce student places and jobs. It is perceived as meritocratic; no matter what a student's connections, there is no way to get past the barrier except to succeed on the examinations. There are no admittance quotas of any other sort and places cannot be bought, especially at national universities. The selectivity and differentiation of public schools inherent in the examination system is also viewed as a way to maintain high quality educational institutions. Goals are clearly defined, students are grouped with others of like ability so that instruction can be geared accordingly, and teachers can be held accountable for the results in their classes.

The general populace is torn between these arguments of the Teachers' Union on the one hand and the *Mombusho* on the other. On the one hand, it is generally recognised that some desirable qualities are stifled and the teenage years are made miserable by an education process that focuses exclusively on highly competitive examinations. On the other hand, since the examination system is so honest and since to get through the examinations a student has to develop highly valued personal traits – perseverance, docility, a good memory and a high degree of achievement – the process is thought to select legitimately the most talented students of the best character for the best opportunities. The idea that class origin rather than individual effort may determine examination results is not widely accepted or even discussed. Thus, public opinion vacillates.

During the period of general unrest in the late 1960s, a partial reform was attempted in Tokyo which played down the role of examinations and selectivity among public high schools. Those who passed the examinations for academic high schools were assigned to one on a random basis. As discussed in Chapter 11, the result has been a shift of the prestige hierarchy, with private schools (which remain selective) moving to the top, displacing the non-selective government schools. The Tokyo experience, which is seen as an élite migration from the public sector, has apparently convinced most parents and politicians that competitive examinations and selectivity are, if not an unmixed blessing, at least a necessary evil, and the Ministry of Education continues to have its way.

BREAD AND BUTTER ISSUES: LOCAL CONTROL

Though the Ministry of Education has reasserted itself and in many ways become the most powerful actor in a truly national educational system, it is also true that the post-war reforms left enough traces so that prefectures and municipalities have significant control over education. In this sense, the Japanese situation resembles the English system, with its tension between central and local control, more than the American system, where local control clearly dominates. As in the UK, localities with a different political complexion may be slow to implement and may at times reverse centrally determined policies.

In particular, prefectures and municipalities in Japan handle contract negotiations with local branches of the JTU, and any educational issues that are at the same time contract issues are subject to local rejection of central Ministry directives. This is one of the ways in which local governments can respond to constituency demands and reflect the political leanings, leftist or rightist, of the local population. Thus, the Ministry of Education at one point wanted to establish a new position of head teacher in the hope of gaining more direct control over classroom practices, and this became the focus of a bitter battle between the JTU and *Mombusho* at the national level. Because it had to be implemented at the local level, however, and because many prefectures were more in sympathy with the teachers' position, the Ministry's plan was not implemented.

Another issue in which the Ministry of Education has not been successful in persuading prefectures and localities to follow its recommendations is the field of vocational education. Though the Ministry feels that Japan needs a stronger emphasis on vocational training at the high school level and in post high school technical institutes, consumers of education do not agree, and prefectures have spurned central government funds for vocational high schools while continuing to push for the building of more academic high schools and for more funds for their maintenance.

Vocational education is unpopular in Japan, despite employer outcries for more of it, basically because firms expect very little job preparation from their new employees and do not reward those who have it. This is certainly true of those who go to work after high school and is surprisingly true even for university graduates. Vocational education at the secondary-school level is therefore unpopular, because it does preclude some options later on, without providing any offsetting benefits.

As one consequence, a great deal of job training and technical education is conducted by employers. The very low level of graduate education in universities can probably be explained this way: it is, instead, provided on the job, by employers. If so, this is another example of the privatisation of education in Japan. Firms (and their workers) bear most of their own training cost but they also get the returns, and they avoid the (tax) costs of training workers for other companies. They also avoid overtraining workers whose skills cannot be used. Since inter-employer mobility is very low in Japan, most training can be viewed as specific rather than general, so this private investment in worker training is very safe for both worker and firm.

NON-ISSUES IN JAPANESE EDUCATION

It is also appropriate to mention some educational issues that arise in many other countries, but are not of overt concern in Japan. First among these is the role of education in altering prevailing patterns of economic and political integration. Because of the homogeneous nature of the Japanese population, it is not part of the function of education to better the status of disadvantaged groups nor to integrate cultural minorities or new immigrants. Thus decisions about tracking in the educational system do not come in for criticism because they are perceived as unfair or as instruments to reproduce an unjust social structure. Schools can base their entrance criteria solely on examinations and feel no need to use any other kind of quota. In contrast, even before racial considerations played a major role in American universities, many colleges and universities tried to ensure a geographical representation among students or gave preference to applicants who had alumni connections with the school. These considerations are absent in Japan. Schools are seen as agents for education and job selection and nothing else. In this sense their task is simpler than in many other countries.

If there is a group or category of students who consistently fare less well in the educational system in Japan, it is women. Though their entrance into some sort of post-secondary education is only somewhat lower than that of men, they usually end up in junior colleges which are primarily for females and are popularly known as 'brides' schools'. Their entrance rates to universities, particularly good universities, is very much below that of men. The academic performance of girls matches that of boys throughout elementary school, but is noticeably lower by the middle of high school. A large part of the explanation may lie in the prospective rewards of education for women, since everyone agrees that learning in high school is gruelling and unpleasant. Women are excluded from the labour market for most jobs which require a college education. Teaching is open as an occupation, and women do fairly well as pharmacists, doctors and dentists (which are not top-status professions in Japan as in the USA and UK). But they are almost categorically excluded from the jobs with large corporations, premised on lifetime employment and an overwhelming commitment to the employers' organisation, that are the career goal of most young men who study hard enough to get a university education. In these circumstances it is understandable that families, schools and the girls themselves should make a less serious commitment to study for examinations. For men, their employment is the most important determinant of status and life quality; for women, their marriage is the most important determinant of life-style and success (and education is not always an advantage in the marriage market). While equality for women on the job scene is just beginning to be discussed in Japan, it will take many years before it reaches the forefront as a salient issue on the educational scene.

Significantly for the topic of our book, there is no concern in Japan with the divisive effects of a large private sector in education. The private sector is not viewed as élitist; rather, the public sector is. It does not weaken the government schools, which remain strong and well-funded. It does not divide the population along religious or class or linguistic lines, as in some countries. Instead, the private sector models itself on the public sector to the greatest extent possible, and public examinations drive the education given in all schools. Thus, privatisation of education is not seen as a problem, but rather as a solution to the problem of inadequate supply. Even the recently instituted subsidies to private education have been relatively non-controversial. But that is getting ahead of our story. We move on now to tell it more systematically.

Part II

The Public and Private Sectors in the Japanese Educational System

4 Overview of the Private Sector

As we observed in Chapter 1, Tokugawa Japan was feudal, with each feudal chief running (government) schools to train the sons of samurai families and local leaders in administrative and military skills. Basic literacy and numerical skills were provided to merchant families and some farmers by (non-government) temple schools, locally supported. The modern educational system began in the Meiji Period, when the feudal system was overthrown and a national government instituted, with the major goal of modernising Japan. Education was viewed as an important tool for catching up with the West, both economically and militarily.

The 1872 Education Code embodied the major elements of the modern Japanese education system, elements which have remained to this day. First, the national goals, to be achieved through the government, were seen to require widespread basic schooling for the masses, quality advanced training for the select few. Specifically, a high level of verbal and mathematical literacy was to be imparted to all by public primary schools, during the six years of compulsory education (increased to nine years, including junior high school, after the Second World War). While localities were responsible for running these schools, much of the funding was provided by the central government and national standards were imposed. In terms both of quantity and quality, this system must be judged a success. Currently, 99 per cent of all Japanese students are enrolled in public elementary schools, and their mathematics and science achievement rates are the highest in the world. In an international comparison of mathematical achievement, based on tests given to all 13-year-olds and to the entire grade level in which most 13-year-olds are found, Japan ranked first among ten industrial countries for the former, second (to Israel) among twelve industrial countries, for the latter. In both cases, Japan's mean score was double that of the two lowest-ranking countries, Sweden and the USA.[1] Japan also scored the highest by far among twelve industrial countries in science achievement overall, as well as in separate tests in biology, earth science, chemistry, and physics for 10-year-olds and 13-year-olds.[2]

In addition to the compulsory level of schooling for all, a very

53

limited number of places at high school and unversity levels were needed to educate members of the élite civil service and professions, and this, too, was viewed as a public responsibility from 1872 on. The public secondary and higher educational institutions, therefore, were selective, rationing entry to the most desirable lifetime career paths, and highly sought after. Most of the public high schools are funded and run by local governments (municipalities and prefectures), although a few are national. Most of the public universities are national although a few are run by municipalities or prefectures. The public high schools and universities which were started during the Meiji Period remain the most selective and prestigious even today, with Tokyo and Kyoto Universities at the apex of the hierarchy. Their peak position is reinforced by a highly favourable funding formula.[3]

For those who could not get into these public institutions, a whole range of private secondary schools and colleges developed. Most of the high schools prepared students for the university examinations and most of the colleges specialised in business, law, and literature, low-cost fields which prepared students for jobs in the private sector. At first the private higher educational institutions were called *senmon-gakko* (second-class 'specialised schools') but after 1918 they were allowed to attain university status. Many of the earliest colleges were started by Christian missionaries and had foreign financial support (consistent with the pattern in other developing countries at that time), although two of the most famous, Waseda and Keio, were started by Japanese idealists (influenced by Western ideas). Post-compulsory schools for women, in particular, were nearly all private, Christian and specialised, since the government saw little practical value in educating women, whose place was in the home, not the labour force. Their legacy today is the junior college system, which is 90 per cent female and 90 per cent private.

Thus, while the American Occupation is sometimes credited with the vast expansion of the private educational sector, this system was actually firmly established before the Second World War, as the major mechanism for meeting the growing Japanese demand for secondary and higher education. Also firmly entrenched was its competitive, stratified nature, with older institutions usually more selective and prestigious than new ones, and with élite public institutions at the top of the hierarchy.

The expansion of the private sector, as demand for education exploded during the twentieth century, is documented in Tables 1.1–

1.6. There we see secondary education enrolments more than doubling every decade before the Second World War. By 1980, 90 per cent of all 18-year-olds were graduating from high school, 28 per cent of them from private high schools. (By comparison, only 74 per cent of the relevant age-group graduate from high school in the USA, 90 per cent of these from public schools. And in England less than one-third of the cohort stays in secondary school beyond the compulsory age of 16 but 20–25 per cent of those who stay and pass the pre-university (A-level) examinations are in independent schools, although these schools account for only 7 per cent of total secondary enrolments.)[4]

At the higher educational level, the overall growth rate was almost as rapid, as a college degree was seen as the major avenue to social mobility and economic well-being, and most growth took place in the private sector. Thus, enrolments in colleges and universities rose from 53 000 in 1903 to 712 000 in 1960, the private percentage increasing from 27 to 66.

The period of greatest growth in higher education, however, was yet to come. Demand for university education had increased because of rocketing incomes and high school education which had saturated the relevant age group. Between 1960 and 1980 higher educational enrolments went up threefold, almost all of it in burgeoning private institutions. By 1980, 38 per cent of all 18-year-olds were entering junior colleges and universities, over 80 per cent of them entering the private sector. (Since some private sector students were in two-year junior colleges and most graduate students were in public universities, the private percentage of total enrolments was a bit lower, 76 per cent.)[5] The average years of schooling for the age-group 25–34 was second only to that in the USA, where 23 per cent of enrolments are private, and slightly higher than in the UK, where practically all higher educational enrolments are in publicly funded institutions.[6]

Yet despite this impressive quality at the primary level and quantity at the secondary and higher levels, the costs to the Japanese treasury have been low. In 1973, for example, the Japanese government spent 5.5 per cent of its national income on education, compared with 7.1 per cent in the USA, 7.7 per cent in the UK and 8.8 per cent in the USSR.[7] The Japanese experience shows that education need not be compulsory, nor need it be provided publicly, to be acquired by a large proportion of the population, in the presence of strong labour-market incentives.

The private sector can thus be seen as 'the other side of the coin' from what the government decided it would provide. The government left major gaps, which the private sector promptly filled – a response to excess demand.

The private sector also serves as a shock absorber, responding rapidly to ups and downs in the relevant population, while the public sector gradually adjusts. This is shown, for example, if one examines yearly changes in high school enrolments in the Tokyo metropolitan area, 1950–70: the peaks and valleys of private enrolments closely follow those of the total number of high-school graduates, while the public sector shows a consistent small secular increase.[8] Since the number of private schools remains relatively constant, changes in average school size was the main adjustment mechanism. This is also consistent with our discussions with officials of Saitama prefecture, who indicated that the private sector was expected to bear much of the adjustment to demographic change in the 1980s and 1990s.

Underlying these developments is the fact that, beyond the level of compulsory education (junior high school), the Japanese government is not obliged to provide a space for everyone. In particular, spaces in the academic high school track which prepares students for the university are severely limited: only 40 per cent of those who attend high school can be accommodated in the academic course in public schools, and these are always filled to capacity. The rest must choose between the two less desirable alternatives: private schools, which are predominantly academic, accommodate 28 per cent of the cohort and public vocational or night courses accommodate 32 per cent.[9] The former are a varied group, some highly selective and others struggling to survive. The latter are at the bottom of the pecking order and often have excess capacity.[10]

However, the most vivid evidence of excess demand occurs in the higher education sphere, where we observe high application rates for entry, low succcess rates, and large numbers of *ronin* – students who, having failed the entrance exam to universities and colleges the first time round, try again in future years. As we see from Table 4.1, the application rate (row 1) among high school graduates has been rising steadily (from 26 per cent in 1960 to 46 per cent in 1980), but their success rate in getting into college has always been less than 76 per cent (row 2). If we measure 'excess demand' as (1 – the success rate), this has been in the vicinity of 30 per cent for most of the post-war period. It increased greatly during the 1960s, as the number of high school graduates and their application rate to universities steadily rose (row 7). The 'left-overs' typically became *ronin*, who constitute approximately 30 per cent of next year's applicant pool (see row 3).

Table 4.1   Demand and excess demand for higher education, 1960–80

	1960	1965	1970	1975	1980
(1) Application rate among high-school graduates	0.26	0.33	0.35	0.47	0.46
(2) Success rates among high-school graduates	0.66	0.76	0.70	0.72	0.68
(3) Ronin applicants ÷ high-school applicants	n.a.	0.28	0.39	0.31	0.35
(4) Total success rate	0.57	0.67	0.68	0.73	0.71
(5) Total number of applicants	n.a.	493 408	676 806	820 557	863 000
(6) Total accepted	n.a.	330 583	460 228	599 006	590 652
(7) Excess demand	n.a.	162 825	216 578	221 551	273 000

Sources: Rows 1 and 4: *Mombusho*, p. 36; rows 2, 3 and 5: *Educational Standards in Japan*, pp. 261–7; rows 6 and 7: our calculations from (4) and (5); 1980 data for rows 2, 3 and 5 from *National Education Standards*, 1981.

The proportion of *ronin* peaked dramatically in the late 1960s, because of the rapidly expanding demand and excess demand.[11]

The excess demand in higher education occurred in a national market, in secondary education in a local market where demand and supply varied widely by prefecture. This point will be developed further using regression analysis in Chapter 10. The remarkable alacrity with which the private sector responded at both levels will be discussed at length in the next chapter. Here we simply make a few key points.

First, the Japanese response was in sharp contrast to the situation in the USA and other Western countries, where the large excess demand after the Second World War, particularly in higher education, was met by the government, not the private sector. How do we account for this international difference? In the UK and several other

European countries, higher education is provided free of charge by the government – presumably to assure access to lower income groups, although universities always end up populated by higher socioeconomic classes. In the US, where many private universities have long existed, the expectation was that they would choose increased selectivity over quantity as demand for higher education rose – and this was one of the reasons for strong political pressure to build new public institutions in the 1960s. On the other hand, in Japan the public institutions are the 'élite', 'high quality' ones, and they maintain this status, in part, by restricting enrolments. This meant that most of the post-war expansion had to take place in the private sector. Moreover, the concept of paying privately for higher education was generally accepted by the Japanese ruling group.

As we shall see when we discuss redistributional effects and prefectural differences in Chapters 8, 9 and 10, the pattern of service delivery chosen by Japan was consistent with the interests of the supporters of the Liberal Democratic Party (LDP), which has consistently governed Japan since the 1950s. Only when its power began to wane and new coalitions had to be forged, in the late 1960s and early 1970s, did its policies begin to change. This suggests that, ultimately, the public/private division of responsibility for education (and other quasi-public social services) may be designed to maximise the welfare of those in power and provide necessary pay-offs to allied groups.

Second, the public/private division of responsibility for education is consistent with what we find in other parts of the Japanese economy, possibly with the same underlying forces at work. Direct government production and consumption is limited, as evidenced by its average tax rate of 25 per cent of GNP in 1982, one of the lowest in the industrialised world. In the medical sphere too, services are provided largely by private doctors and hospitals, paid for by compulsory insurance.

However, this does not mean that the government is uninvolved; rather, its influence is pervasive, albeit indirect. In Japan, as in other countries we have studied, a favourable government policy is probably the single most important factor explaining the growth of a large private sector in education.

Beyond the clearly demarcated limits of public educational institutions, the government left the door open for private schools to develop, and facilitated this development. To begin with, the government recognised the legitimacy of private high schools and, after 1918, private universities. In addition, by educating the masses at the lower levels, but only a small group at higher levels, the government was creating a huge potential demand for private schools. The scarcity of those with further education created a high rate of return, hence a demand for private schooling on the part of the 'left-overs'. Had the government built fewer primary and junior high schools, or more high schools and universities, this excess demand for private advanced education would not have been so great.

Moreover, the public universities based their entrance on a strict examination system, thereby creating a demand, in particular, for schools that effectively trained students to pass these exams. Many private high schools gear their teaching specifically to these exams, attracting students who want that preparation. In addition, outside the regular school system, there has developed a whole system of private profit-making cram schools, or *juku*, whose entire purpose is to coach students for high school and university examinations. Over half of all junior high school students in large cities attend *juku* or hire private tutors to help them to get into top high schools; two-thirds of the successful entrants to Tokyo University in 1980 had attended *juku*. *Juku* range from simple enterprises set up by former teachers or housewives and run in their homes to elaborate franchise operations established by movie companies or department stores. They advertise their success rate on examinations and sometimes even select their clientele to maximise this rate.[12]

Finally, while government approval was needed for starting new schools, this was freely granted in the 1960s. Thus, the approval rate rose from 50 per cent in 1960 to 90 per cent in 1966, for new private universities.[13] During the peak years of 1964–7, 122 applications for new university charters were received and 80 per cent were granted. Regulations regarding student–faculty ratios, library size, minimum capital requirements, maximum size, etc., were all overlooked, in the haste to get institutions started to meet the popular demand. For instance, legal standards required that at least 50 per cent of the faculty be full-time. Yet a 1970 survey of thirty-four private universities showed that sixteen violated this condition overall and the remaining ones violated it in some fields. Similarly, standards required that there should be no more than twenty students per library seat, but half the universities surveyed violated this. Virtually all private universities exceeded their authorised enrolment quota, two-thirds by more than 50 per cent and one-third by more than 100 per cent.[14] This choice of quantity over quality, large numbers and low cost per student is, incidentally, characteristic of many developing countries during their periods of rapid educational expansion. It is ironical that Japan, which is today one of the most developed countries in the world, made a similar choice in expanding its higher educational system.

Perhaps most significantly, the government permitted extensive bank loan financing of private educational institutions, during a period of stringent credit-rationing; the private schools were getting an indirect subsidy, in the form of access to loans below equilibrium market rates, without which they could not have grown. More will be said about this in the next chapter.

In effect, the government was saying to the private sector: 'We will not start the educational facilities ourselves, but we expect you to do so, and we will make the process both easy and profitable. This will relieve the pressure on us, and will be consistent with our mutual goals.' And, consistent with other aspects of Japanese society, the private sector responded, doing a job which is now done by government in most other modern industrial countries.

5 The Founding Decision: Who Starts Private Schools and Why?

In Japan, as in many other countries, private schools and universities are legally required to be non-profit organisations (NPOs) – organisations which do not have 'owners' who can sell their stock and receive profits. The earnings of NPOs must be reinvested in the organisation, they cannot be distributed – presumably to reduce the incentive for downgrading an educational product whose quality consumers may not be able to evaluate. The question then arises: who starts these schools and why?

Starting a new enterprise involves three elements of entrepreneurship: organisational labour, risk-taking and venture capital. In economic models of profit-maximising enterprises, these real costs are rewarded by access to profits, in the form of dividends or capital gains. The NPO founder, however, does not get these monetary rewards. What, then, are his incentives to serve as entrepreneur; what objectives guide his behaviour? This is an important issue in the theory of non-profit organisations. Our intent is to approach it inductively, by observing the behaviour of non-profit entrepreneurs in many different settings, and in this paper we explore the insights provided by the Japanese educational experience.

FOUNDING

In other countries we have found that a large proportion of NPOs providing services such as schools or hospitals, are started by other more basic organisations – usually religious groups, sometimes political parties or labour unions. These 'ideological' organisations view schools as important institutions in the formation of taste, hence a mechanism for extending their influence and increasing their adherents. This is particularly true of proselytising religions, and their actions have evoked a similar defensive response from other religions faced with such competition. Religious groups can readily generate an initial demand for their own educational product from among their

61

membership (hence, minimise their risk) and can generate the supply by using their own sources of capital, labour and organising ability. Thus, organised religion turns out to be the main founder and religious motives the *raison d'être* for the non-profit sector in most countries we have studied, including the USA and the UK.[1]

What of Japan? Religious groups did, indeed, found a large number of Japanese private schools and universities. In 1980, 638 out of the 1959 private primary and secondary schools – 33 per cent – were run by religious organisations, 70 per cent of them Christian. Similarly, 30 per cent of the 432 private junior colleges and 319 universities were religious, largely Christian.[2] Among these are the earliest and most prestigious private educational institutions (such as Jochi and Doshisha, which rank among the top five universities in many fields). While these numbers are substantial, they do not constitute a majority. Most private schools in Japan are secular, and this has been particularly true of schools started during the great expansionary period after the Second World War.

Virtually none of these schools have been started by political parties or labour unions. Unions are weak and the LDP, the only strong political party in post-war Japan, is not organised to provide education or social service to its constituents. Who, then, were the founders of these secular non-profit schools and what were their motivations? This question, which we asked of many informed educators, scholars and bureaucrats, usually evoked surprise, followed by a variety of (non-testable) hypotheses. We present here the most plausible explanations.

First, it should be noted that, while most schools are not started by 'ideological' organisations, neither are they started by individuals. Instead, vertical integration is characteristic of the private school system – one school starts another. For example, a university provides the small venture capital needed for a 'feeder' high school, knowing it faces an assured demand – since entry to an affiliated high school typically means preferred entry to the university. That is, the university promises to accept a specified number of students from its feeder schools, on the basis of grades or teacher recommendations, and parents are willing to pay to spare their children the agony of 'examination hell'. Or a high school integrates upward, into a university, out of retained earnings, knowing that it is generating a potential clientele for education. The risk is therefore minimal, particularly in a period of excess demand for education.

How widespread is this phenomenon? Our survey of the 376 private secondary schools in Tokyo showed that only 47 of them were not affiliated with other schools at higher or lower levels. This pervasiveness of vertical integration not only helps us to understand who starts new private schools, it also affects the fundamental nature of the private-school system which, in effect, is made up of many vertically integrated subsystems. Students who enter such a ladder at the primary level are likely to remain within that subsystem through the university level. This segmentation is an even more important characteristic of the private school system in other countries, such as Holland and India, as well.[3]

Vertical integration is consistent with the hypothesis that non-profits have, as a major objective, sales or output maximisation. A small number of individuals or religious groups are the original founders, driven by pecuniary or non-pecuniary motives. They find that starting another school increases gross revenues *per se* and, in addition, may increase revenues from the first school as well. In a statistical regression analysis of the pricing and output behaviour of a random sample of private Tokyo high schools we found that the acceptance rate of its students to universities was a major determinant of tuition and other fees and the acceptance rate was significantly higher for secondary schools with affiliated colleges (see last page of Chapter 6). Sales maximisation has been viewed as a possible supplementary motivation for normal profit-making firms in general, especially for Japanese firms.[4] Surely, it is an even more plausible motive for NPOs, where profits have ostensibly been ruled out.

As a second motivating force, it appears that disguised profit distribution can and does take place in a variety of ways, both legal and illegal, in institutions which are technically non-profit. The illegal ways are only occasional and are well publicised when discovered, as when student places or professional appointments are 'sold' to families who give large gifts to the school or its administrator or 'kickbacks' are given to school managers by equipment companies. During the summer of 1983 such a case was highly publicised. An influential senior professor at Tokyo Medical and Dental University was alleged to have received a large gift from a colleague who wanted a faculty position there. Investigations then showed that the professor's family ran a medical equipment sales company which might have sold equipment to the school at a large profit.[5]

The legal ways to earn disguised profits are more common and more interesting. For example, the school founder is often its principal and on its Board of Directors as well. These are paid positions, so the founder quickly finds himself remunerated for his time; little volunteer labour is involved. In some cases, the founder may be paid beyond the market wage, i.e. beyond what he could earn elsewhere; he is, in effect, receiving monetary profits, albeit in disguised form. This situation may be particularly attractive for risk-averse entrepreneurs and for founders who face mandatory retirement from the government or corporate bureaucracy at age 55, with few alternative uses for their time. The disguised distribution of profits in non-monetary form, as non-taxable perks – expense accounts, free houses and cars – is especially valuable and difficult to trace.

Benefits to founders may take intangible form: perpetuation of a family name on a school; status and prestige from being connected with education, which is highly regarded in Japan; an opportunity to try out a new pedagogical technique. On the whole, Japanese schools do not engage in pedagogical experimentation, but some do. A recent best-selling book by a noted Japanese TV personality described the innovative private school she attended as a child, and the devotion of its founder to his experimental pedagogical techniques. These motivations are more common in the USA. Less familiar in the USA, but found in many other countries, including Japan, is the political motive for founding private schools: a community is more likely to vote for a person who has brought it a highly valued enterprise, a school.[6] A politician who does not have the power to start a public school, then, may start a private school.

We have, thus, identified several plausible motives for non-profit founders: the religious motive being the single most important, albeit far from universal; the objectives of output maximisation, disguised profit distribution, prestige and political power dominating the secular scene.

FUNDING

Once having the motivation to start a school, and the promise of remuneration for their labour, the task of these non-profit-oriented founders is to raise venture capital. How is this accomplished, in a setting where the usual rewards – dividends and capital gains – are ruled out by the non-profit constraint?

As noted above, this problem has been solved partially by vertical integration, with retained earnings from one school constituting the initial investment in another. Data from the early 1960s, for example, shows a steadily growing 'surplus' of revenues over current expenditures for private universities; indeed, the net profitability of higher education was rising faster than in other consumer goods industries (such as department stores) or corporate enterprise generally.[7] During a period of excess demand, when education is a profitable industry, the creation of new schools is a logical response to the question of what to do with net earnings that cannot be distributed to owners.

Another contributing factor is the concentration on labour-intensive activities, with a low capital/output ratio. High schools, for example, are relatively small-scale labour-intensive enterprises, and therefore, well suited to operation by non-profit organisations which cannot raise equity capital. The same is true of junior colleges. Private universities in Japan tend to specialise in teaching rather than research, and concentrate on a small number of low-cost areas, such as law and economics, again minimising the need for capital. For example, two-thirds of the private colleges and universities are single-subject institutions – only 10 per cent teach five or more disciplines.[8] Some capital is required, however, for buildings and modest equipment. Where does it come from?

In the USA buildings and other capital facilities for NPOs are often financed by donations, in lieu of stock ownership. This is also true to a limited extent in the UK, where donations are much less than in the USA. In Holland and Sweden, buildings and other facilities are typically supplied by the government to NPOs – at little or no cost. In Japan, government funded 2 per cent of private-school expenditures during the expansionary 1960s, and 'donations' another 7 per cent.[9] However, fixed assets are generally financed by loans, which can then be repaid, with interest, out of revenues generated in later years. Most of these were bank loans although after 1965 a special government-created foundation played an increasingly important role.[10] Indeed, this treatment of NPOs is consistent with general financing practices in Japanese business, where the debt/equity ratio is much higher than that in the USA and other industrial nations. In the *zaibatsu* tradition, Japanese firms typically get 70–80 per cent of their growth capital from bank loans which are short-term but regularly rolled over.[11] Japanese business, too, pays small dividends, relying on reinvested earnings, rather than new stock issues. In this sense NPOs, which necessarily depend on retained earnings and bank loans, operate very much like the ordinary Japanese profit-maximising business. Table 5.1 shows that by the mid-1960s over 20 per cent of all private secondary and higher educational expenditures were loan-financed

Table 5.1 Debt service and debt finance as percentage of total expenditures in private educational institutions

	Debt service and capital outlay (as %)				Debt finance (as %)	
	(1)	(2)	(3)	(4)	(5)	(6)
	High schools		Higher education		High	Higher
	DS	CO	DS	CO	schools	education
1950	0	21	0	34		
1955	6	28	9	21		
1960	12	35	11	25	16	16
1963			12	33		21
1965	20	32	15	37		29
1968	18	22	16	37	18	20
1970			19	26		19
1973		40	14	36		16
1974			13	23		15

Sources: Data on debt service and capital outlays for 1950–68 is from *Educational Standards in Japan*, 1970, pp. 241–7; 1963 and 1974 data from Ken Ogata, *Introduction to Educational Economics*, pp. 25 and 227. Data on debt service and capital outlay for 1973 is from *Educational Standards in Japan*, 1975, p. 351. Debt finance for high schools in 1960 is from *Education in 1960*, pp. 194–5. Debt finance for 1960 and 1965 and all 1970 data is from S. Ichikawa in Cummings *et al.* (eds), *Changes in the Japanese University*, p. 60. Debt finance for 1968 is from *Educational Standards in Japan*, 1970, pp. 241–7. Debt finance for 1973 is from Akira Ninomiya, *Private Universities in Japan*.

(columns 5 and 6). Since the figures for capital outlays were over 30 per cent at this time (columns 2 and 4), this implies that about two-thirds of all capital outlays were debt-financed. This may be compared with debt-financing of education in most other developed countries, which is virtually nil.[12] The problem of venture capital for NPOs is relatively small in a society where that is readily supplied, on a loan basis, by banks.

To illustrate the above points: we discussed at length the funding issue with the principal and founder of a leading high school in the Yokohama area, which was started in the 1960s. 10 per cent of his venture capital came from donations by large private companies, 90 per cent from bank loans. The banks, he believed, were induced by the interest of the business community to make these loans. Since the high school was profitable and he could not distribute these profits, he used them to start a new junior high school and a new college. Thus, he is now principal and head of the board of directors of several schools, and draws a salary for these positions. He has provided the organisational and entrepreneurial ability, but has not had to donate his own time or money.

The important question then becomes: why did the banks supply such generous loans to the expanding private-school sector? As noted above, this question is particularly significant because the 1960s were a period of credit shortage, and much credit was rationed according to a set of national priorities jointly determined by the government and the banks. Thus, the ability to borrow was a privilege, not a foregone conclusion, the interest rate for many borrowers was below equilibrium levels, hence an indirect subsidy. Our interpretation is that the private-school sector had access to favourable bank loans because an implicit public-policy decision had been made to facilitate its growth, in a way which did not impose heavy direct costs on the government's budget. The creation in the 1960s of a special loan-making government foundation was further evidence of this policy.

Debts, of course, must eventually be repaid: hence debt-financing merely postponed the day of reckoning when private schools had to cover their own costs. At first, larger new loans were generated each year, to cover the payments due on old loans and the costs of capital expansion. But clearly, this pyramiding could not continue forever. By the early 1970s, new loans were barely covering the costs of debt service an old loans (see Table 5.1) and many institutions complained they were having difficulties meeting their interest payments – they could do so only by drastic increases in tuition, which student activists vigorously opposed. For several schools and universities, bankruptcy loomed. [13] The stage was set for the introduction of more direct government subsidies – to prevent student uprisings and protect the bankers' investments – a development which will be discussed in greater detail in Chapter 11.

In summary: the absence of a strong organised religion, separate from the state, has been an impediment to the growth of private education in other countries, such as Sweden. However, in Japan several major mitigating factors were present. These included the possibility of disguised profit distribution as a motivating factor, a large assured demand resulting from limited government production, and the availability of borrowed capital on favourable terms. These conditions have not existed simultaneously in other countries, nor are they all found in other Japanese social service areas. Their presence enabled the private non-profit sector to grow with unique rapidity at the secondary school and, even more so, at the university levels, in post-war Japan.

6 Private Benefits, Costs and the Pecking Order among Schools

How does the private sector behave when it is a large provider of education? And how does it affect the nature of the public sector? Are private schools in the vanguard of pedagogical innovation, or are they carbon copies of the public schools? Does the diversion of students to the private sector reduce society's willingness to spend on public education? Do private schools become the élite schools, providing selective superior education to the children of the rich, while the poor are left to receive low-quality, low-cost education in the public schools? Does this system therefore lead to a segmentation of society, by economic class, racial or social background, and does it reduce socioeconomic mobility by correlating educational opportunity with family's initial endowments? These questions are at the core of American and British concern over privatisation of education, and over public policies (such as tuition tax credits or voucher plans) that might lead to a larger private sector. What light can the Japanese experience with a large private sector throw on the answers?

Private high schools in Japan are, formally, very much like the public: the curriculum is set by the Ministry of Education (*Mombusho*), texts require *Mombusho* sanction, and required teacher credentials are the same in public and private schools. Even more important, the overwhelming pressure to prepare students for university examination forces all high schools into a uniform mould; employer recruitment patterns plus civil service examinations do the same for universities. Thus, there is little room for pedagogical innovation, or discretion about what is to be taught, in Japanese education; the deviant school or university is penalised by low examination performance and low career prospects for its students, making it more difficult to attract a clientele in the future.

Nevertheless, the public and private sectors differ greatly, with respect to cost, quality, efficiency, tuition, rate of return, and to a lesser extent, socioeconomic background of students. In Japan, the public sector is the élite sector – selective (measured in terms of examination scores required for entrance), high cost (measured in

69

terms of expenditure per student) and high quality (measured in terms of access to jobs thereafter). Thus, private education has apparently not impoverished public education, nor has it become the enclave of first choice for the rich, as it is at the secondary level in the UK and the university level in the USA. However, it does provide a 'second chance' or 'safety net' which must be paid for privately and which the rich can more easily afford.

As we shall see throughout this and the subsequent two chapters, there is great diversity within each sector, particularly the private, making it difficult to generalise. However, certain sectoral differences do clearly emerge, specifically:

1. Within secondary and higher education in Japan, the public sector is more prestigious than the private and also leads to higher lifetime earnings.
2. The private sector is cheaper than the public, in terms of real cost per student, and this shows up in various indices which indicate either lower quality or greater efficiency.
3. However, cost to the student is greater in the private sector, where most current expenditures have been covered by tuition and other fees.
4. The net outcome of this combination of factors is that, ironically, the social rate of return is higher in the private sector but the private rate of return is higher in the public sector – where students consequently prefer to go. This allows the public sector to remain more selective, more prestigious, more successful than the private.
5. Both sectors are attended disproportionately by students coming from families in the upper income group. However, the skewing is greater in the private sector; except at the university level, where the data are ambiguous.
6. Since tax shares are skewed more than enrolment shares in both sectors, it appears that the net result of any government funding of education is a transfer of real income from rich to poor, but this transfer has been concentrated in the public sector which has received a much greater subsidy per student. Thus, the decision to limit government spending and allow the private sector to grow at the expense of the public sector was also a decision to limit the redistributional impact of secondary and higher education.

PRIVATE COSTS AND BENEFITS

One of the salient differences between the public and private sectors is that cost to the student is much greater in the latter, since tuition rather than taxes is used to pay most of the bills. Data on sources of income in public and private educational institutions are reported in Table 6.1. We see there that public high schools and universities are virtually all (90–100 per cent) government-financed. Fees are charged but only to a minimal extent. However, government financing of private institutions was practically non-existent before 1970. (As discussed later, subsidies did increase after that point and now consitute about 30 per cent of current expenditures). Instead, debt-financing (column 4) and retained earnings were used to cover capital cost; and tuition plus fees, the largest source of private revenues (column 5), covered most current expenses at private schools. In fact, column 6 shows that tuition and fees have sometimes exceeded costs and have generally covered at least two-thirds of current expenditures. If 'donations', which are often required for admissions, are counted as fees, this percentage rises still further, to over 80 per cent.

The heavy reliance of private universities on fees means that tuition varies greatly by institution and also by field within a given university. Engineering, science and medical students pay higher fees, consistent with the higher cost of educating them. In contrast, tuitions and fees are low and constant across institutions and most fields at national universities. In this way, the private sector forces students to take differential real costs into account in their choice of fields, while in the public sector student decisions are independent of real costs. The latter is true, incidentally, at public universities in most countries. It is not surprising, then, that private enrolments are disproportionately high in low-cost fields such as the humanities and social sciences, while public enrolments are disproportionately high in the sciences (see Chapter 7).

On the average, Table 6.2 shows that private tuition and other fees in private schools have consistently run at least 3 times as high as public, six or seven times as high in the late 1960s. At that point, political pressure finally forced the government to intercede, provide subsidies, and reduce the private/public tuition disparity.[1] To put these numbers into international perspective: in the USA in the mid-1960s, the private/public tuition ratio at universities was much less – 2.6; and tuition and fees covered only one-third of current expenditures at private universities, which also receive donations, income from endowments and government grants.[2]

Table 6.1 Public–private differences in sources of educational revenues, percentages for 1965 and 1973

	Total (in billion yen) (1)	Government % (2)	Donations* % (3)	Loans and other** % (4)	Tuition and other fees*** % (5)	Current expenditure divided by tuition and fees (6)
1965						
High school						
Public-local****	248	91.5	8.5	0	10.8	6.8
Private	106	3.8	5.5	15.4	75.3	0.8
Higher education						
Public-national****	129	100	0	0	2.8	19.0
Private	143	2.1	8.6	32.5	56.8	1.5
1973						
High school						
Public-local	797	97.7	2.3	0	3.9	18.9
Private	253	14.8	5.4	32.8	47.0	1.3
Higher education						
Public-national	327	100	0	0	3.7	19.8
Private	513	10.8	15.3	26.8	47.1	0.9

* Part of the 'donations' are required for admission to a private school.
** Although the precise breakdown between 'loans' and 'other' is not available, other data indicated that loans constitute, by far, the larger part of this category.
*** Tuition and other fees at public institutions were paid to government, not kept by school. The number given here indicates tuition and other fees as percentage of total expenditures that were directly financed, in public schools, by other sources (mostly government). The other sources, therefore, total 100 per cent, without adding tuition and fees. For private institutions, however, tuition and other fees were spent directly by the school and are therefore included in the 100 per cent.
**** In this and many subsequent tables we refer to a subset of public high schools (local) and a subset of public universities (national). Most public high schools and local i.e. funded and run by municipalities or prefectures; however, a few are national. Most public universities are national, but a few are run by prefectures or municipalities.

Source: Educational Standards in Japan, 1975, pp. 356, 197, 351.

Table 6.2 Tuition and other fees per
student, private/public ratios, 1965–82

	High school	University
1960	n.a.	3.4
1965	6.1	7.4
1973	8.6	5.2
1977	7.6	3.2
1982	5.8	2.5

Sources: 1960 figures calculated from data in
Educational Standards in Japan, 1970, p. 250;
1965 and 1973 figures calculated from data in
Educational Standards in Japan, 1975, p. 199;
1977 and 1982 data supplied to us by the
Ministry of Education; includes all regist-
ration fees paid by first-year students.

What are the consequences for wages and employment of this
system, in which a minority of students are educated at low tuition
and a majority must pay high tuition, for university education? To
analyse this question, let us look in Figure 6.1 at the supply and
demand for educated workers under different assumptions about
tuition. The vertical axis of Figure 6.1 indicates the wages that
employers pay and the horizontal axis indicates the number of
workers that will be demanded and supplied. The demand curve for
educated workers, indicated by line DD, shows that more workers will
be hired at lower wages. Line W_1S_1 indicates the supply of educated
labour that will be available if students pay low tuition, have
unlimited (open) access to high schools and universities, and corporations and citizens at large are taxed to subsidise their education. A
large number of educated workers will then be available, at a
relatively low wage, W_1, and employers will hire L_1 people at that
wage. (To the extent that education is financed out of general income
taxes, after-tax wages will be lower yet, but we assume it is at least
partially financed by sales, excise or property taxes which do not
directly affect disposable wage income.) This is a situation that would
be favoured by employers and industries with a high demand for
educated workers, since they benefit from the low wage-structure, but
would be opposed by those who pay the taxes.

If, however, students must pay high tuition, citizens and firms have
a correspondingly low tax-burden but workers must receive higher
wages to compensate them for bearing the investment cost of their

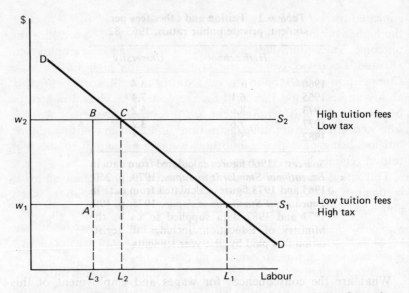

Figure 6.1   Wages and employment under high and low tuition fee regimes

own education. For simplicity we assume that the supply price of uneducated labour and the employers' demand curve for educated labour are unchanged under the two scenarios. Then, the new supply curve for educated labour is indicated by W_2S_2, the wage required to induce them to get educated is now W_2, and employers hire a smaller number, L_2, at the higher wage. This situation would be favoured by employers with a relatively low demand for educated workers, since they benefit from the low tax structure.

While some income redistribution among individuals undoubtedly takes place as a result of this change, the higher wage paid to educated workers in the second scenario does not make them better off as a group. It merely enables them to recoup education costs they would never have had to incur under the first scenario.

What we actually find in Japan, however, is neither the first nor the second scenario but a combination of both – a public education system which is low tuition, tax-supported and small, plus a large private system with high tuition, low tax support. The size of the public sector is fixed, as shown by the line L_3, while the private sector is free to expand to meet the demand. We then have a discontinuous supply curve for educated labour, indicated by line W_1ABS_2. That is, L_3 workers would be available at the low wage W_1, but beyond that educated workers are only available if the wage rises to W_2, to cover the higher tuition. In Japan demand is high enough to produce this outcome. The equilibrium is at point C, with wages and employment W_2 and L_2, respectively – the same as in the high tuition case. Competition in the labour market requires that all workers of equal ability and education receive the same wage, W_2. Thus, the greatest beneficiaries of this arrangement are the small number of workers who were educated at public institutions under the low tuition regime, but are being paid the equilibrium wage consistent with the high tuition regime.

This situation may be further illuminated by the following arithmetic example. Suppose that, in making their decisions about where and how much to work, workers care only about wages and education-training costs. Suppose further that the market wage for uneducated workers is $10 000 and each worker works for forty years. Then, if education is tuition-free and is paid for out of excise, property or non-wage income taxes, people will be willing to spend four years being educated so long as they can recoup their 'opportunity cost' (i.e. their lost wages) over the remainder of their working lives (appropriately discounted for time). Suppose, for example, that an annual wage of $12 000 for thirty-six years has the same 'present value' as a wage of $10 000 for forty years. Then, W_1 is $12 000. In terms of lifetime income, educated and uneducated workers are equivalent. But employers of educated workers pay a relatively low wage for their training.

Now, under the high tuition fee regime taxes are 0 but those workers receiving an education must pay for it. Therefore, they will be willing to incur these costs only if they recover their investment later on. Suppose that a wage increment of $2000 for thirty-six years has the same 'present value' as the initial tuition fees for education. Then, W_2 will be $12 000 + $2000 = 14 000. Again, in terms of lifetime income net of tuition fees, educated and uneducated workers are equivalent. But this time employers of educated workers pay a relatively high wage, to cover the cost of their training.

The higher wage, discounted for time, is just enough to cover the higher tuition payments. The higher labour cost is then passed on to consumers, in the form of higher prices. Taxpayers in general gain but consumers of goods with much educated labour lose, as we shift from a low tuition to a high tuition regime.

Now, in a third case approximating the Japanese system, a small group receives free (or low) tuition education in public institutions while the rest of the market demand is met by the high tuition group in private institutions. Taxes are relatively low as a result. But equilibrium wages for the educated are high – $14 000 as in the previous case. The big gainers are the workers who are eligible for the low tuition education but receive the market wages consistent with the high tuition equilibrium.

Actually, public university students gain even more than W_2. Employers are aware that the quality of students and schooling varies and must decide whether to offer superior wages and working conditions in order to attract superior educated workers. In general, government and large firms offer higher wages, but even more important, they offer greater job security and/or prestige, hire public university students who are considered better, and who therefore obtain the highest private rate of return.

THE PRIVATE RATE OF RETURN

This hypothesis is borne out by empirical studies of the private rate of return, which tells us how much extra income, after taxes, individuals get over their lifetime, as a return to their own private investment in education (the payment of tuition and loss of wages they would otherwise have earned during their college years). By comparing the rate of return to education (human capital) and other investments (physical capital) prospective students can determine whether it is worthwhile, on monetary grounds, to continue in school. (In the USA, for example, these rates of return are approximately equal, on average, and about half the high-school seniors go on to college.) By comparing the rates of return to different schools (if this information is available) students can determine which institutions they prefer to attend. Private rates of return vary by field of study, industry of employment and size of firm. However, in Japan, at both the secondary and university levels, they are generally greatest for those educated in the public sector, both because their cost is lower and because their lifetime earnings and status are higher.[3] This is demonstrated for higher education in Table 6.3, which gives the private rate of return for two fields and for six different types of universities. In engineering, for example, the private return ranges from 9.5 per cent in the top-ranking imperial universities to 6.9 per cent in the newest private universities. Even the least prestigious (youngest) public institutions are shown to yield a higher private return (8.7 per cent) than the most prestigious private institutions (7.8 per cent).

Table 6.3 Private rates of return to university education by university group

	Social science	Engineering
National universities – total	9.0	9.0
I Imperial universities	9.5	9.5
II Other old prestigious universities	9.1	9.1
III New universities	8.7	8.7
Private universities – total	7.5	7.0
I Waseda and Keio	8.4	7.8
II Old private universities	7.7	7.1
III New private universities	6.9	6.9

Notes: Foregone earnings are assumed to be the same for all groups; future earnings are broken down by university-group but not by field of study; tuition varies by field in private universities but not in public universities.
Source: Masakazu Yano, 'Rates of Return from Education and Resource Allocation' in Shogo Ichikawa, *Allocation of Educational Resources in Japan*, p. 141.

LABOUR MARKET CHANNELLING THROUGH THE EDUCATIONAL SYSTEM

The differential rates of return stem partially from cost differences and partly from benefit (wage) differences among universities. The former are due to foregone earnings during the college years, which in these calculations are assumed to be the same across university groups, and tuition and fees, which differ widely across universities, as already discussed. The latter are due to the key role of education in channelling people within the Japanese labour market.[4]

Education has a number of purposes, but in modern societies one of the most important is the function of schools in preparing students for participation in the economic system and in allocating students to jobs. Japanese high schools and universities play a central role in this allocation process and a well-defined hierarchy has developed, depending on the career tracks that are opened or closed to a student from attendance at different educational institutions.

Traditionally, the old imperial universities, led by Tokyo and Kyoto, have been the main suppliers of personnel to the élite civil-service ranks (similar to the traditional role played by Oxford and Cambridge in England). Large private employers also confine their recruitment to the national universities, plus a few of the oldest private ones. A survey of 321 members of the Japan Federation of Corporations revealed that over half considered applicants from no more than ten universities; sixty-one limited themselves to five schools or fewer.[5] In Japan, these large firms are the most remunerative places to work; they do virtually all their hiring at the college graduation level, and they hire (men) for life. Thus, the university one attends determines one's future; and, since high schools often have feeder relationships to universities, so too does one's high school.

Information about the hiring practices of major firms is widely known to the public in Japan. Books are published giving the educational backgrounds of executives in numerous firms, and universities advertise the companies that recruit their graduates. Consequently, once a student is accepted into a given university, he knows quite clearly what his employment opportunities are going to be when he graduates four years later. And when he is accepted into a given high school, he knows which set of universities he is likely to attend. It is hardly surprising, then, that we find a decided pecking order among schools, a pecking order ultimately tied to labour market recruitment practices. In principle, a similar situation exists in the UK and the USA, with Oxford and Cambridge, Harvard and Yale, and their 'feeder' secondary schools, at the top of the pecking order in their respective countries. However, labour market channelling and hence the educational hierarchy are much more firmly established in Japan (and least in the USA).

As examples of the labour-market channelling provided by the educational sector in Japan, we may cite the following:

1. In 1971 two-thirds of the Japanese Cabinet were graduates of Tokyo and Kyoto Universities.[6] (Imagine how different American politics would be if we could say the same of Harvard and Yale!)
2. Although only 5 per cent of all university students currently graduate from Tokyo (the percentage was, of course, much higher in pre-war years), 66 per cent of all executives in national ministries and agencies came from Tokyo – including 80 per cent of those in prestigious ministries such as Finance and Foreign Affairs.[7] Kyoto ranked second in these two ministries and all private universities together contributed 2 per cent.[8]
3. Over half the 14 256 successful applicants for senior civil-service positions between 1972 and 1982 were from Tokyo or Kyoto Universities. The remaining half were spread across a large number of institutions, with Waseda and Keio the only private universities to contribute more than 100 each.[9]

4. Similarly, 33 per cent of 'large company presidents' and 50 per cent of middle management in Japan's largest company, Japan Steel, came from Tokyo. Kyoto usually ranks second, followed by the other national universities; among the private universities only Keio and Waseda appear on such lists.[10]
5. National universities and older private universities are also overrepresented in 'finance and insurance' – the most remunerative industry.[11]
6. Tokyo University also provides a disproportionate number of educators, doctors, lawyers and 'opinion leaders'.[12]

One of the most significant differences between public and private universities concerns the size of firm for which their graduates ultimately work. National universities, particularly the imperial universities, will probably send their graduates to high managerial or technical positions in large firms; graduates of private universities, particularly the newer and lesser known ones, usually became middle-level 'salary-men' at medium- and small-sized enterprises. This is particularly important because wages in Japan are more closely tied to the size of enterprise than in most other countries and the rate of return to education varies more with size of enterprise than with other factors such as field of study or industry of employment. Smaller firms also offer less security, perks and prestige.[13] The following tables outline some of these differences. The data are taken from the *Japan Statistical Yearbook* which, significantly, groups workers by size of enterprise as well as education.

In Table 6.4, which shows earnings for males in different size firms and with different academic levels, the figures should be read down in columns. Each column groups together men of similar educational attainment and compares their average monthly earnings in different

Table 6.4   Index of earnings of regular workers by size of enterprise and education (males), 1981

No. of employees	Compulsory education	High school	Technical school, junior college	University
10–99	100	100	100	100
100–9999	110	105	105	105
1000 +	132	118	129	126

Source: Japan Statistical Yearbook 1983, pp. 98–9.

size firms. Thus, for men with only compulsory school education, for
every 100 yen that a man in a small firm earns, a man in a large firm
earns 132 yen. Similarly, for men with a university education, for
every 100 yen earned by those in small corporations, workers in large
corporations earn 126 yen. The wage differential between small and
large firms is much larger for Japanese males than for males in any
other countries.[14] (For women with a university degree, however, the
return to working in a larger firm is negligible: 105 versus 100 in
smaller firms. This is consistent with the point made earlier that large
corporations simply do not hire women for prestigious, remunerative
lifetime positions; the rate of return to education is much lower for
women than for men.)

In Japan it is widely recognised that monthly wages do not tell the
whole story with regard to remuneration for employment. Bonuses
and fringe benefits of a wide variety are also important. One way of
gauging their importance is to look at the total cost to employers of
employees, and to compare this for firms of different sizes. Table 6.5
shows that the cost of an average employee in terms of all cash
earnings is 58 per cent higher for the largest firms than for the smallest
firms. But other labour costs increase even more steeply, more than
doubling from the smallest to the largest firms.

Another factor which affects lifetime earnings is stability of employment and in larger firms employees have much longer periods of
uninterrupted service, about twice as long as in small firms. It is the
larger firms that offer the lifetime job security for which Japan is
famous, since they have enough flexibility and diversity within their
various units to keep their core group of workers fully employed.

Table 6.5 Index of average monthly labour cost
per employee by size of enterprise, 1981

No. of employees	Cash payments	Other labour costs
30–99	100	100
100–299	108	112
300–999	125	132
1000–4999	143	171
5000 +	158	209

Source: Adapted from *Japan Statistical Yearbook
1983*, pp. 120–1.

Workers in smaller firms (and women) do not receive the benefits of 'lifetime employment'.

Still another advantage of large firms is less easy to document. It concerns the options that long-term employees have at retirement age. This age is 55 or 60 for most employees, and it is at this age that the term of 'lifetime employment' is over, for those workers fortunate enough to have been hired on that understanding. Companies benefit from this early retirement age because it gives them a chance legitimately to reduce the pool of employees at the highest levels, since only a few of the most valuable ones need be offered post-retirement jobs with the firm. While promotions, salary increases and rank have been most heavily influenced by seniority until this time, this is the only opportunity the company has to divest itself of less productive employees. For employees hired under the 'lifetime' system, their security between the ages of initial hiring – 19 or 24 – and retirement at 55 is paid for in two ways: by low wages at the beginning of their career (to be compensated for as their seniority increases) and by forced retirement at the age of 55 or 60. But at 55 most Japanese men are in good health and in no way anxious or financially able to retire. Pensions are generally low, and children are not able to support both their own young families and their retired parents very well. Large companies can more often find temporary post-retirement jobs for their employees, because of their control over subsidiary companies, and because they have more connections than smaller firms.

In general, the work organisation is extremely important for a Japanese man, because it is usually the only organisation to which he will have ties. Competition for organisational loyalty from church, lodge, voluntary organisations, union, professional associations, even family, is much less in Japan than in many other countries, including the USA and UK. Instead, the employment organisation is likely to subsume many of the functions we associate with such organisations, including sports, recreation and welfare. Not only does a man spend his important working hours there, he also spends the major portion of his leisure hours within the sphere of the same organisation. And the larger it is, the more it has to offer.

There are many reasons, then, why employment in a large firm should be a career goal for Japanese. But not many people can actually achieve this goal. Tables 6.6 and 6.7 show the distribution of the Japanese working force over firms of different sizes. According to Table 6.6, only 15 per cent of the entire Japanese labour force works for firms with more than 1000 workers. On the other hand, according

Table 6.6 Size of firms and percentage of work-force engaged, 1981

Size of firm by number of employees	Percentage of work-force engaged
<10	31
10–99	37
100–999	16
1000+	15

Source: Adapted from *Japan Statistical Yearbook 1983*, pp. 120–1.

to Table 6.7, about 30 per cent of private university graduates and 60 per cent of national university graduates work for these prestigious, remunerative companies, and for Imperial university graduates this proportion rises to over 75 per cent. It is unclear whether graduates of top universities get these coveted jobs because they have learned more at school or simply because they were more capable to begin with; these two effects are difficult to disentangle in any system where the initial student intake is different for different schools. It may be that a marginal student who just happened to get into a good university would not profit much from that experience, either in terms of learning or earning, so these figures may not accurately represent his employment chances. But it is probably true that a good student who had a bad examination day, and therefore got into an inferior university, would suffer from that for the rest of his life because he

Table 6.7 Size of company which new university graduates enter – percentages

	<499	500–999	1000–4999	>5000	Unknown
Total	40.5	10.9	18.1	16.1	14.4
National – total	11.6	8.7	21.8	36.8	21.0
Imperial	4.5	5.9	16.6	57.2	15.8
Other old	10.9	7.6	16.6	38.5	26.3
New	15.5	10.8	27.0	25.7	21.0
Private – total	47.7	11.4	17.1	11.0	12.7
Started before 1939	38.7	11.9	21.1	14.9	13.5
Started after 1945	63.6	10.7	10.1	4.2	11.4

Source: *Social Framework of Private Universities*, p. 125.

simply would not be considered by the best employers; Table 6.7 accurately tells us that for him, there are practically no second chances. At any rate, the Japanese believe that once you are admitted to a university you become an average member of the group, so the goal is to enter the institution with the highest average chance of employment success. The recruitment patterns of employers, then, determine the segmented nature of the labour market and the hierarchical nature of the educational system, as well.

STUDENT SELECTIVITY AND SCHOOL RANKINGS

A key feature of the Japanese educational system is the fact that all schools, public as well as private, are selective, at the secondary as well as the university level, and they all select according to uniform objective criteria. In contrast to the USA, where a student who remains within the public sector must attend the neighbourhood school (or state university) and the neighbourhood school must accept him or her, choice exists on both sides of the market in Japan. A student may travel to another part of town, even to another prefecture, to attend a better high school; and high schools may refuse to accept students living next door. In contrast to the UK, where state secondary schools (comprehensives) are precluded from selecting on grounds of ability (except for the few remaining grammar schools), in Japan selection on grounds of prior academic achievement is universal. (The key exceptions, the cities of Tokyo and Kyoto, will be discussed in Chapter 11). Similarly, the university market is nationwide, and features selection by both students and institutions.

Moreover, there is remarkable agreement on the criteria to be used in ranking students and schools: universities are ranked according to the job prospects they bring, high schools according to their ability to gain access to (top) universities, and students according to their performance on key (entrance and civil service) examinations – tests which stress memory and detail rather than aptitude and general understanding. This agreement on goals seems to be characteristic of Japanese society, stemming, perhaps, from its cultural homogeneity and long-time isolation. Within the educational sector it leads to a pecking order among schools which maintains itself until the equilibrium is disturbed by some exogenous force. Schools which place their students well attract better students and this in turn helps them to place their students well, etc. As demand has grown, the newer untested schools take their place at the bottom of the hierarchy; only a strong shock, such as the 1967 Tokyo reform (discussed in Chapter 11), produces large changes in the ordering.

Universities

If we rank higher educational institutions according to minimum test scores needed for entrance, Tokyo and Kyoto, the two old Imperial universities, are on top, and almost all public universities rank above the median in most subjects. A minority of private universities are also above the median, Waseda and Keio leading the list.

These rankings are published periodically by *Obunsha*, a commercial firm which supplies information eagerly purchased by prospective students, and they tend to be stable across fields and time. *Obunsha* bases its estimates on mock exams it gives which simulate actual examinations. A selection from the *Obunsha* of August 1983 is presented in Table 6.8, for illustrative purposes. Note that the number of public universities is relatively constant across fields whereas private universities are concentrated in low-cost areas such as economics and literature, which they consequently dominate. The range of scores is obviously greater in the private than the public sector, indicative of the greater diversity there. Some private institutions rank close to the top. Nevertheless, even though private universities constitute 70 per cent of the total, the percentage of private universities above the median is always less than 50 per cent (usually less than 30 per cent), and the percentage of public universities above the median is always above 50 per cent (usually more than 70 per cent). In the two areas where most private universities are found, many of them new small specialised institutions, the disparity between the two sectors is the greatest. Tokyo and Waseda consistently head the list for their respective sectors.

Along similar lines, Table 6.9 shows that if we measure the 'success rate' of applicants to universities (i.e. the proportion of applicants admitted), it is greater in private universities, indicating that selectivity is greater in the public sector.[15] In education-oriented prefectures such as Tokyo and Kyoto, almost 25 per cent of those wishing to go to national universities ended up in the private sector, while only 1 per cent of those aiming at private universities ended up in the public sector (about half of both groups entered the labour force or became *ronin*).[16]

As other evidence of the stable pecking order among universities,

Table 6.8 Minimum entrance examination scores, public–private, by field, 1983

	Economics and business	Literature and education	Law	Science	Engineering	Medicine
Number of public universities	42	46	25	37	57	49
Number of private universities	100	117	28	25	55	28
Total	142	163	53	62	112	77
Number and percentage of public universities above median	42 (100%)	45 (98%)	14 (56%)	21 (57%)	41 (72%)	35 (71%)
Number and percentage of private universities above median	30 (30%)	36 (31%)	12 (43%)	10 (40%)	15 (27%)	3 (11%)
Public range of scores	77–52	75–55	76–53	71–47	71–44	77–58
Private range of scores	72–38	69–38	73–38	68–38	65–39	72–46
Top public universities and scores	Tokyo (77)	Kyoto (75)	Tokyo (76)	Tokyo (71)	Tokyo (71)	Tokyo (77)
Top private universities and scores	Waseda (72)	Waseda (69)	Waseda (72)	Waseda (68)	Waseda (65)	Waseda (72)

Source: Our calculations from Obunsha, August 1983.

Table 6.9   Success rate among new applicants, 1974

	Public %	Private %
Humanities	13	19
Social science	15	19
Science and engineering	19	18
Medicine and dentistry	8	15
Agriculture	19	29
Education	21	30

Source: *Educational Standards in Japan*, p. 268.

we note that only 5 per cent of all teachers at national universities got their degrees from the private sector, while at private universities 40 per cent were trained in the public sector.[17] This, of course, is due largely to two facts: the public universities are older, and they are more likely to offer graduate degrees – two indicators of relative prestige. Also, private universities are more likely than public universities to base some of their admissions on letters of recommendation (from feeder schools), for students who do not have sufficiently high test-scores (50 per cent of the private universities do so as against 16 per cent of the public universities).[18] This indicates that private universities are being less selective than public ones, searching for criteria which are not universally accepted, as a basis for accepting students.

By making special efforts a university can, however, raise its ranking. For example, the Jesuit-run Sophia University decided to do so during the 1960s and 1970s. It actively recruited top high school seniors, admitting the best without an entrance exam, thereby saving them the traumas of 'Examination Hell'. It recruited famous professors by paying high salaries, but kept its payroll balanced by also using large numbers of low-paid priests. It went to great lengths to secure jobs for its students at large prestigious firms. These efforts did indeed raise Sophia's standing; it now ranks among the top ten in the private sector.[19]

High Schools

We find a similar preference for public over private at the high school level. In a recent survey asking students how they chose their high school, many students in private schools indicated they preferred a public one but had failed the entrance examination, and those with better grades in junior high were more likely to get their first choice – a public high school.[20] Moreover, some public schools are much preferred to others. It is interesting to note that within the public high school sector in Japan, teachers are periodically rotated among schools. Thus the ranking of the school, which is relatively stable through time, must depend upon the quality of its students, not the quality of its teaching staff.

Detailed evidence of the hierarchical nature of high schools was presented in 1975 in a study by Masaharu Hata. This study was based on a sample of fifteen prefectures in Japan, and looked at the proportion of students from public and private high schools who gain entrance to public and private universities.[21] (Tokyo is not included in the sample; this aberrant case will be discussed in detail later on.) In almost every prefecture, students from public high schools are more likely than students from private high school to go on to the university, indicating that the former are·drawing from the top group of students. The advantage of public high schools is even greater when one considers the probability of entrance to national universities – the top of the pinnacle. Among schools sending more than 20 per cent of their graduates to national universities, only 11 per cent are private. The top schools are likely to be old, for boys only, established during the Meiji Period – and public.

To give a more detailed picture, Figure 6.2 divides all high schools in the sample into five categories, based on the percentage of graduates who enter (four-year) colleges or universities (both public and private). Schools in Category V send 80–100 per cent of their graduates to college, those in Category IV 60–79 per cent, and so on down to Category I, where no more than 19 per cent of the graduates enter university. It is immediately apparent that almost half (41.1 per cent) of the high schools fall into Category I, which send only a few students to university each year. If the schools in each class are roughly equal in size, these figures imply that over half the entrants to colleges and universities come from the top quarter of institutions which are in Categories IV and V. It will obviously seem important to prospective college students that they attend one of these high schools, especially if they believe that the school average accurately predicts their chances. This chart also indicates the percentage of schools in each category that are private schools. Since 30 per cent of all the schools in the sample are private schools, their representation

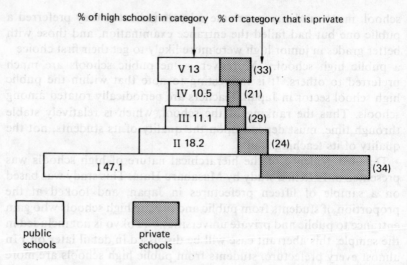

% of high schools in category   % of category that is private

V 13	(33)
IV 10.5	(21)
III 11.1	(29)
II 18.2	(24)
I 47.1	(34)

public schools   private schools

Source: Masaharu Hata, *Journal of Education Department , Nagoya University*, vol. 1, p. 241.

Figure 6.2 High schools classified by college entrance rates of graduates

in the different categories does not appear very skewed, although Categories I and V were slightly overrepresented.

A more revealing look is given in Figure 6.3, however. Here, the high schools in the sample are divided into categories based on the percentage of their graduates who enter national universities. As we have seen, national universities tend to be ranked above private, and so constitute the goal of most students. Here the most striking feature is the huge proportion (82.1 per cent) of all schools that fall into Category I. While most schools are in Category I, the majority of students in national universities come from the small group in Categories II to V. When we look at the proportion of private high schools in each category in Figure 6.3, it is clear that they are concentrated at the bottom. The number of public schools in the upper ranks is small; the relative number of private schools in the upper ranks is much smaller.

For reasons discussed in Chapter 11, in Tokyo this situation is reversed and private schools are at the top of the hierarchy. As we shall see there, the reason is simple: public high schools are less selective, hence private schools are more selective, and more preferred.

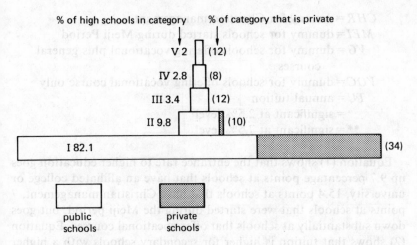

Source: Masaharu Hata, *Journal of Education Department , Nagoya University*, vol. 1, p. 242.

Figure 6.3 High schools classified by national university entrance rates of graduates

Within the private sector, the importance of historical factors and vertical integration (affiliated institutions) are indicated by the following regression analysis, which we ran for all 91 private high schools in Tokyo. This statistical technique shows how the percentage of graduates entering higher education (denoted *ER*) from different private high schools depends upon certain characteristics of the high schools, such as its age, religious management, and academic affiliations.

$$ER = 68.4 + 9.7\ AFFHI + 15.4\ CHR + 7.0\ MEI - 15.8\ VG - 32.9\ VOC$$
$$(2.1)^* \qquad (2.4)^* \qquad (1.5)^{**} \qquad (2.0)^* \qquad (5.0)^* (1)$$
$$R^2 = 0.39$$

$$TU = 194.5 + 0.72\ ER \qquad\qquad\qquad\qquad\qquad (2)$$
$$(4.4)^*$$
$$R^2 = 0.18$$

where:

ER = entrance rate to higher education, i.e., % of high school graduates continuing to higher education

AFFHI = dummy for high schools affiliated with higher educational institutions

CHR = dummy for Christian management
MEI = dummy for schools started during Meiji Period
VG = dummy for schools offering vocational plus general
       courses
VOC = dummy for schools offering vocational course only
TU = annual tuition
   * = significant at 2.5% level
 ** = significant at 7.5% level

Equation (1) shows that the entrance rate to higher education goes up 9.7 percentage points at schools that have an affiliated college or university, 15.4 points at schools that have Christian management, 7 points at schools that were started during the Meiji period, but goes down substantially at schools that offer vocational courses. Equation (2) shows that tuition is higher for secondary schools with a higher university entrance rate.[22] The numbers in parentheses are t-statistics that tell us whether these results could have occurred by chance. Most of these results are so consistent that there is only a very small chance (2.5 per cent or less) that they could have occurred accidentally – they are statistically significant.

7 Quality, Efficiency and Social Returns

We have thus far established that, within the rigid Japanese hierarchy, the top-ranking institutions (in terms of consumer choice, hence selectivity) are likely to be public, those at the bottom will be private and there is a mixture in between. We now look in Table 7.1 at data on social costs in these two sectors from 1950 to 1980. While private tuition is much higher in the private sector, expenditure per student has consistently been lower there, ranging between 50 and 90 per cent of public expenditures at the secondary level, 30 and 40 per cent at higher levels. In terms of international comparisons, costs per student in Japanese public universities are comparable to those in American or German universities, but private university costs are lower than in other OECD countries.[1] A key question is: should the Japanese public–private differential be interpreted as evidence of lower quality in the private sector (consistent with consumer rankings) or higher

Table 7.1 Annual expenditures per student, 1950–80 (000s yen)

	Secondary school[1]			Higher education[2]		
	Public	Private	Private/ public ratio	Public	Private	Private/ public ratio
1950	11.9	2.3	0.19	94.2	22.3	0.24
1955	19.4	9.6	0.49	120.4	41.1	0.34
1960	32.1	20.5	0.64	196.6	73.3	0.37
1965	73.0	63.9	0.87	517.6	179.4	0.35
1973	275.0	196.9	0.72	909.4	343.5	0.38
1980	599.0	546.0	0.91	1982	848.0	0.43

[1] Data are for upper and lower secondary schools 1950–60, upper secondary only (high schools) thereafter.
[2] Data are for universities plus junior colleges 1950–60, universities only thereafter.
Sources: Data for 1950–60 from Educational Standards in Japan, 1964 (White Paper), pp. 204–5. Data for 1965–73 from Educational Standards in Japan, 1975, p. 354. Data for 1980 provided by Foundation for the Promotion of Private Schools (Shinko–Zaidan).

efficiency? Much of the debate about the future of private education that raged in Japan in the late 1960s and early 1970s presumed the former. Analysis of this issue, however, is complicated by differences among schools in their student inputs, as well as ambiguities concerning the appropriate measure of output.

The output of education has been variously interpreted as amount earned (i.e. incremental lifetime earnings), amount learned (e.g. incremental scores on achievement tests), or willingness to pay (i.e. the consumer's subjective evaluation of all the investment and consumption benefits of education). To ascribe differential output effects to a school requires us to control for student input, so that we are measuring 'net value added' and not 'gross value of output'. That is, we must subtract the educational background that a student brings to a school to get a true measure of the value added by the school itself; otherwise, we would be giving the school credit when it simply takes in brighter students. Lower quality, then, should mean less value added, using one or more of these measures. 'Greater efficiency' means a higher ratio of benefits to costs, i.e. the value added is high, compared with the costs. Unfortunately, data on output measures are often unavailable, and hence the assumption is made that input measures can be used as a proxy for output. That is, higher costs are taken to mean higher value added. This procedure, which implicitly assumes full and equal efficiency for all systems, makes it impossible for us to test whether lower costs imply lower quality or greater efficiency.

In Japan, fortunately, considerable evidence on output is available. We have already seen that in general students at public schools and universities achieve higher test scores and lifetime earnings, suggesting that the 'gross output' is indeed greater there. However, we have also seen that the student input is superior at these schools, and that employers may use them for their screening function rather than their function of building human capital. Both these observations suggest that incremental earning or learning may overstate the true social value added by the public schools and universities, making it unclear whether their 'quality', or value added, is truly greater.

In this section we adopt a different approach. We examine exactly how private schools have managed to operate at lower cost, and evaluate whether these actions are likely to imply lower quality or greater efficiency. Four forces are seen to be operating: economies of scale, different product-mix, different input/output ratios, and different prices paid to factors of production, particularly teachers. It turns out that while lower quality at private institutions cannot be ruled out as a partial explanation, higher efficiency is also probably present. Consistent with this analysis, other studies have shown that the social rate of return is higher in private than public institutions. Even if their quality is less, their efficiency is greater, measured in these cost–benefit terms.

ECONOMIES AND DISECONOMIES OF SCALE

The average size of private high schools and universities is greater than that of public institutions, suggesting that economies of scale may be at work. That is, larger schools may be more efficient, partially explaining the cost advantage of private institutions. To examine this hypothesis, Tables 7.2 and 7.3 present comparative data on size distribution of high schools and universities, respectively. Examination of these data provides little support for believers in either economies or diseconomies of scale in education.

If we look at the distribution of public and private high schools (Table 7.2) we find most of them uniformly distributed over the range 200–1400 students (and some even larger), with only a small peak between 800 and 1000. The general literature on existence of scale

Table 7.2   Size distribution of high schools, number and percentage, 1975

Number of students	Public %	Private %
0	0.0	6.3
1–200	25.5	7.5
200–400	11.4	8.0
400–600	11.3	10.9
600–800	11.5	11.9
800–1000	14.6	12.2
1000–1200	12.9	9.1
1200–1400	10.1	9.5
1400–2000	2.7	16.1
2001 and over	0.0	8.5
Total number of high schools	4724	1339

Source: *Educational Standards in Japan*, 1975, pp. 172 and 339.

economies in education is inconclusive. However, since private schools are not constrained as to size (i.e. they are free to choose their most preferred size), the maintenance of this broad distribution over long periods in Japan suggests there are no strong economies or diseconomies of scale over a wide range. On the other hand, it is consistent with some cost disadvantage to very small schools; e.g. schools with fewer than 165 students may not be able to fill three classes (tenth to twelfth grades) to capacity in a system where typical class size is 50–55. Thus, the fact that public schools are clustered in the lower part of the range, 25 per cent of them having less than 200 students, may account in small part for their higher average input–output ratio and cost per student. Public authorities, unlike private, may be pressured to operate schools in sparsely populated rural or suburban areas. While this may lead to higher costs, the marginal social benefit may also be high; hence, *a priori*, this is evidence neither of lower efficiency or higher quality.

Among universities, too, we find a wide range in size distribution, from 100 to 80 000 (Table 7.3).[2] Here, however, the private sector predominates at both ends of the spectrum, the national institutions clustered towards the centre. In contrast, in the USA public universities are generally larger than private, political pressures pushing them towards quantity rather than selectivity – but they rarely get as large as 80 000.

To analyse the issue of scale economies, it is important to recognise that students in Japan enter a particular faculty or field, rather than the university as a whole. Moreover, the term 'university' includes what we would call liberal arts undergraduate colleges and polytech-

Table 7.3   Size distribution of universities, number and percentage, 1975

Number of students	National		Private	
Less than 500	4	(4.9%)	35	(11.5%)
500–1000	4	(4.9)	60	(19.7)
1000–5000	48	(59.3)	142	(46.6)
5000–10 000	17	(21.0)	36	(11.8)
10 000–20 000	8	(9.9)	17	(5.6)
20 000–85 000	0		15	(5.0)
Total	81		305	

Source: *Educational Standards in Japan*, 1975, p. 343, and our own calculations from data supplied by the National Institution for Educational Research.

nics. Specialisation in institutions by field and level is possible and frequently occurs in Japan; i.e. there are many small 'social science', 'humanities', or 'management' undergraduate 'universities'. This minimises their size and the start-up costs for private enterprise. Under such circumstances, scale economies are probably largely absent, as again suggested by the continued survival of many small institutions.

On the other hand, a few very large Japanese universities dominate the scene, indicating that diseconomies of scale also are negligible. These have multiple faculties existing side by side almost as separate colleges, a kind of horizontal integration. Fifteen private universities, or 5 per cent of the total (ten of them in Tokyo), have over 20 000 students each and, all together, one-third of total private enrolments.[3] The private sector in higher education is thus both more dispersed in size distribution and more concentrated in student enrolments than the public; economies of scale are probably not a major factor in explaining their lower costs.

PRODUCT-MIX DIFFERENCES

The first and simplest explanation for cost differences in public and private institutions is their difference in product mix. Product-mix differences are much greater at the university than at the high school level, corresponding to the fact that cost differentials are much greater there. By this interpretation, public universities are neither more efficient nor higher quality than private universities; they are simply providing a different service, which happens to require more inputs.

As we saw above, public universities in Japan are likely to be medium-size multi-purpose training institutions, providing research and graduate as well as undergraduate training in many fields, whereas many private universities are small undergraduate teaching institutions, concentrating on a few low-cost subjects. Table 7.4 shows that if we break down the universities into 'research', 'graduate', and 'undergraduate', we find that the research institutions, which cover most major fields, are predominantly public, while the undergraduate institutions are predominantly private. Along similar lines, a large number of faculty members at national universities have zero or very low teaching loads, enabling them to devote most of their time to research, while this practice is much less frequent in the private sector.[4] Teaching services can be sold to students at a fee, but it is

Table 7.4 Public–private division of research, graduate and undergraduate universities

	Public	Private	Total	Private %
Research	19	5	24	20
Graduate	83	158	241	66
Undergraduate	23	145	168	80
Total	125	308	433	71

Source: Calculations made by authors from data supplied by Shogo Ichikawa, National Institute of Educational Research.

much harder to find a buyer for basic research, whose benefits are very diffuse. Hence private universities around the world rarely have a large research component, unless supported by the government, and this emphasis on teaching also keeps their costs down.

Similarly graduate education, especially at the Ph.D. level, is expensive and few students would be willing to pay the real costs. Therefore, this too is not a viable activity for private universities unless they are subsidised. Thus, while the total number of graduate students in Japan is small (most firms hire at the B.A. level and provide on-the-job training or send their managers for further education abroad) the vast majority of domestic graduate students attend public institutions, in contrast to the 78 per cent of university undergraduates who are found in private institutions.[5]

The undergraduate universities, moreover, specialise in a small number of low-cost liberal-arts subjects. For example, Table 6.8 showed that the number of private faculties in the humanities and social sciences exceeds those in the public sector, while the opposite is true in science, medicine and engineering.[6] Almost 66 per cent of all students enrolled in private colleges and universities but only 25 per cent of those in public institutions, were in the former low-cost fields.[7] Even among graduate institutions, the proportion of humanities and social-science students is much higher in the private than the public sector (78 per cent versus 44 per cent, respectively).[8] At both the graduate and undergraduate levels, most students would probably be unwilling to pay the high cost of science education. Hence, this again is an area that private universities in many countries minimise unless they are subsidised by government or industry. Indeed, the predominance of the private sector may help to account for the low proportion of Japanese students in science and engineering – 25 per cent – in comparison with 40–50 per cent in countries such as the UK and the USSR which have predominantly public university systems.[9]

Product-mix differentials, therefore, account for part of the cost differential. However, even when we control for field of study, most of the cost disparity remains, suggesting that we must look for other explanations as well. For example, an OECD study of Japan in 1971 showed that private university costs per student were 62 per cent of public university costs in language departments, 20 per cent in commerce departments.[10] Data supplied to us by the Foundation for the Promotion of Private Schools (*Shinko-Zaidan*), a quasi-governmental organisation, showed private–public cost ratios of 91 per cent, 37 per cent and 48 per cent in medicine, dentistry and natural sciences, respectively. How, then, can we account for these differences?

INPUT–OUTPUT DIFFERENTIALS

The second ingredient in our explanation is the smaller use of inputs per student in the private sector. Private high schools and universities simply have less space, fewer library books, and higher student–faculty, student–staff ratios than do public institutions. Administrative costs per capita, too, are lower; for example, in private high school the principal often teaches as well.[11]

Tables 7.5, 7.6, and 7.7 show that inputs per student at private high schools are only 70–80 per cent of those at public high schools. For example, in 1975 there was one teacher for every eighteen students in public high schools, but only one for every twenty-six students in private high schools in Japan. (This may be compared with one teacher for every seventeen, eighteen and twenty-two students, respectively, in state-run secondary schools in France, the UK and Germany in 1973, and with one teacher for every twenty-one and seventeen students, respectively, in public primary plus secondary schools in the USA and the USSR.)[12] At private high schools in Japan more students are squeezed into smaller classrooms, with less ancillary space and equipment. That is one way they keep their costs down, to compete with public schools. It is interesting to note that the large religious (Catholic) component of the private secondary sector in the USA keeps its costs down in a similar way. On the other hand, the much smaller élite part of the private sector in the USA, and the independent schools in England, compete in quite a different way – by

Table 7.5 Public and private student/faculty ratios*

	1960	1965	1970	1975	1980	1982
High schools						
Public–local	22.9	23.6	19.1	17.6	17.6	17.2
Private	30.6	34.0	26.8	25.7	23.9	23.1
Private/public	1.3	1.4	1.4	1.5	1.4	1.3
University						
Public–national	11.0 (10.3)	11.2 (10.2)	11.9 (10.6)	11.7 (10.0)	8.5	8.1
Private	34.8 (24.0)	37.3 (25.8)	40.1 (26.4)	41.0 (26.8)	27.9	25.6
Private/public	3.2 (2.3)	3.3 (2.5)	3.4 (2.5)	3.5 (2.7)	3.3	3.2

*This is the number of students divided by the number of full-time teachers. Numbers in parentheses include part-time teachers, who are more numerous at private institutions.
Sources: Data for 1960–75 from Educational Standards in Japan, 1975, pp. 316–17. Data for 1980 from Mombusho, 1981, pp. 15–18. Data for 1982 supplied to us by the Foundation for the Promotion of Private Schools. Since 1980 and 1982 data were supplied by different sources it is possible that their definitions and measurement methods are different from 1960–75. However, this probably affects comparability between absolute numbers, not private–public ratios.

Table 7.6 Public and private student/staff ratios*

	1960	1965	1970	1975
High schools				
Public–local	86.1	95.8	71.1	63.1
Private	118.7	126.0	91.0	91.1
Private/public	1.4	1.3	1.3	1.4
Universities				
Public–national	6.0	5.0	5.9	6.7
Private	27.7	28.3	32.0	27.3
Private/public	4.6	5.7	5.4	4.1

*This is the number of students divided by the number of non-teaching staff.
Source: Educational Standards in Japan, 1975, pp. 316–17.

featuring smaller classes, better facilities, and higher cost per student. Since they do not face an excess demand, they can compete with state schools only be offering higher 'quality'.

The 'inferiority' of the private sector in Japan is even greater at the higher educational level where the competition from the public sector

Table 7.7   Public and private floor space and school site per student

	Floor space per student			School site per student	
	1965	1974	1981	1965	1974
High schools					
Public–local	8.2	10.0	11.5	38.0	73.1
Private	7.1	7.6	9.2	31.7	33.5
Private/public	0.9	0.8	0.8	0.8	0.5
Universities					
Public–national	25.8	26.4	24.1	85.3	83.4
Private	8.2	8.7	9.2	30.2	29.5
Private/public	0.3	0.3	0.4	0.4	

Sources: Data for 1965 and 1974 from *Educational Standards in Japan*, 1975, pp. 344–5. Data for 1981 supplied to us by the Foundation for the Promotion of Private Schools.

is much less; the 'left-overs' simply have nowhere else to go. At private universities, inputs per student are only 30 per cent that of public universities, as demonstrated for teachers, staff and space in Tables 7.5, 7.6 and 7.7. Books are an essential ingredient in a university education by most standards, particularly in the humanities and social sciences. Yet, in 1978 private universities on average had only twenty-seven books per student in their libraries, compared with 109 in national universities, and many had virtually no libraries at all.[13]

Moreover, the public–private disparity increased as the private sector accommodated the enrolment expansion of the 1960s by decreasing its input–output ratios and the government, which supposedly set minimum standards for recognition, simply looked the other way.[14] In 1960 there were eleven students for every faculty member at national universities, thirty-five students per faculty member at private universities. By 1975 the situation at national universities was roughly unchanged but the number at private institutions had risen to forty-one. (In contrast, the average student/faculty ratios for universities in the USA, the UK, France and Germany were 17, 8, 18, and 12 to one, respectively, in 1972–3.)[15] A statistical (regression) analysis of the sources of growth in university expenditure, 1959–74, showed that the impact of quality improvement was greater than that of student growth in the public sector, while the opposite was true in the private sector. In both sectors, expenditures increased greatly over this period, most of the increase (79 per cent) due to rising prices for supplies, utilities, teachers and other factors of production. The remaining 21 per cent was divided into two parts: that due to larger enrolments and a residual, interpreted as higher quality. In the public sector larger enrolments accounted for only 7 per cent of the increase, quality improvement 14 per cent, while these percentages were roughly reversed in the private sector. According to this analysis, the quality gap between the two sectors widened during this period.[16]

It is instructive to compare this with the situation at the elementary level, where public supply is great enough to accommodate everyone. There, the small private sector can compete with the public only by offering superior service, superior student/faculty ratios (twenty-five as against twenty-two to one, 1982) and higher expenditures per student (555 000 yen versus 434 000 yen, 1980).[17] This suggests that large 'inferior' private sectors exist mainly where there is excess demand, where the government schools are not 'open access', as at the secondary and higher levels in Japan. For the same reason, in the USA and the UK, which have open-access public systems, the private sectors are generally considered superior; they could not survive otherwise.

The higher student/faculty ratio in private schools and universities is especially noteworthy. While each sector exhibits considerable dispersion, there is practically no overlap between them in this respect. For example, among ninety-five doctorate-granting institutions which had two or more divisions or schools, the number of students per faculty member ranged from eleven to nineteen in the public sector (five to ten if part-time faculty are included), twenty-two to seventy-seven in the private sector (ten to thirty-eight with part-timers) in 1981.[18]

Japanese classes are large by international comparison (over fifty students in a typical high-school class, over 500 in a typical university class) and they are larger still in private schools. American and British consumers tend to assess this as 'low quality', but Japanese do not seem to make the same subjective valuation. Class sizes are large even in the most élite schools. For example, at Nada, a private high school which consistently places more students in Tokyo University than any other high school in Japan, the average class size is fifty-five.[19]

Private schools, after all, do have the option of charging higher tuition fees and offering smaller classes, but their assessment is that most consumers would not be willing to pay the price. If they are correct in their assessment, this would imply that consumers prefer the low-input technology prevailing in the private sector over the high-input technology in the public sector, once they have to take account of the greater cost of the latter. While the public sector may be higher in quality than the private, it is also higher in real cost to society. The evaluation of Japanese consumers seems to be that the cost–benefit ratio is more favourable in low-input institutions, which is why most private schools choose that technology. In that sense, the private sector has chosen a more efficient technology than the public.[20]

Are consumers misinformed about educational technology? Would students really learn much more in smaller classes? Despite the tendency of many academics and parents to believe that, and despite numerous attempts by researchers to test this hypothesis, the evidence is inconclusive. As we have already observed, the Japanese seem able to obtain unusually high scores on international achievement tests in mathematics and science, despite their large classes.[21] Thus the Japanese consumer may be more correct than the British or American consumer and we are left in doubt about whether to interpret the higher public sector inputs as evidence of higher quality or lower efficiency.

SALARY DIFFERENTIALS

While differences in product-mix and input–output ratios thus account for much of the cost differential, an additional explanation is the lower salaries which private teachers receive, as well as their longer working hours. In many countries, private schools survive by keeping their costs low, usually by paying lower wages to their workers. Volunteer labour and quasi-volunteer labour by members of religious orders are extreme but not uncommon examples, in the West. In Japan there is little volunteer labour and few priests or nuns but the use of low-wage educated workers is facilitated by enclaves of underemployed workers who do not have full access to the labour market, namely, young women and retired men. The disproportionate presence of these groups in the private sector keeps wages low there, despite the fact that formal credentials of teachers are quite similar to those in the public sector (e.g. in private high schools 83 per cent of the teachers are university graduates, 16 per cent junior college graduates, as compared with 78 per cent and 20 per cent in public high schools).[22]

Labour market participation for women is still very restricted in

Japan, since large companies as well as the civil-service bureaucracy
are unwilling to hire them during their pre-child-bearing years for the
lifetime career ladders available to educated men. Similarly, most men
(including professors at the national universities) face compulsory
retirement from their lifetime jobs at a relatively early age, usually 55
or 60, with only a small pension. Both groups seek short-term
employment opportunities, which are limited, and hence yield a lower
equilibrium wage. And the private schools have availed themselves of
these low-cost services. We see from Table 7.8 that women and older
men are hired disproportionately by private high schools and
universities (where they constitute over 30 per cent of the faculty, as
compared with less than 15 per cent in the public sector); this is even
more true of junior colleges. In fact, if one analyses the teaching staff
by age, the peak occurs at 'over 70' in private education.[23] Many of
these older workers are teachers who have retired from public schools.

The benefit to the private sector of hiring women is magnified since
most of them work during their pre-child-rearing years, and hence are
paid at the low end of the steeply rising age–earnings profile characteristic of Japan.[24] As for the older men, the private sector offers them
relatively low wages too; the age–earnings profile in the private sector
is flatter and peaks earlier than that in the public sector. Thus, public

Table 7.8   Use of females, retired men and part-timers by public and private
schools, 1974 and 1980

	% Female		% Men over age 60		% Part time	
	Public	Private	Public	Private	Public	Private
1974 Data						
High school	14	25	2	12		
Junior college	21	36	11	28	51	59
University	5	11	6	18	38	51
1980 Data						
High school	16	25	1	8		
Junior college	30	40	8	28	58	61
University	5	11	5	16	41	52

Sources: Educational Standards in Japan, 1975, pp. 322, 330. 1980 data
supplied by Ken Ogata from Mombusho, *Report on Statistical Survey on
School Teachers*, 1980; and *Report on Fundamental Survey on Schools*, 1980.

and private school salaries are very similar for ages 18–50, where the market is most competitive, but by the age of 60 a teacher in a public high school earns 84 000 yen ($350) more each month than a teacher in a private school; a teacher in a public university earns 52 000 yen ($200) more than a teacher in a private university.[25] However, the teacher in the public school is forced to retire at that point. The fact that private institutions do not require retirement at the age of 60 gives them a competitive advantage, enabling them to attract high-quality younger teachers, as well as retired teachers, without having to pay a higher wage.

At private universities, as Table 7.8 indicates, these groups are heavily supplemented (over 50 per cent) by part-timers, often people with regular positions at national universities.[26] The hiring of part-timers is a common mode of behaviour in private universities around the world. Moreover, the average part-timer teaches more classes per week in the private than the public sector. Receiving their pension and welfare benefits from their regular jobs, they do not require this from the private universities, and the moonlighting wage-rate tends to be lower as well.

Table 7.9 allows us to disaggregate the cost differences in public and private institutions, between capital costs, expenditures on teachers, and other current costs. In 1973, for example, total cost per student in private universities was only 37 per cent that in public universities. Capital costs per student were only slightly lower in the private sector (82 per cent). But teacher-cost per student in private universities was 25 per cent that in public universities, accounting for most of the public–private cost differential. According to Table 7.5, in 1975 each faculty member at national universities taught the equivalent of ten full time students which meant, in effect, that each student utilised 1/10 of a full-time equivalent faculty member, while at private universities each student utilised 1/26.8 of a faculty member. Thus, the fraction of a teacher per student was only 39 per cent as large in private as in national universities. But teacher costs per student at private universities were only 25 per cent the public rate (Table 7.9). In effect, private universities spent 25 per cent of the money public schools spent (per pupil), to buy 39 per cent of the public teaching staff. They hired fewer staff and also paid each teacher less, thereby saving considerable money.

In high schools, the differences were similar in direction but smaller in magnitude. Private school costs per pupil were 72 per cent of public school costs in 1973, and all of this was accounted for by differential

Table 7.9 Private/public ratios in capital, current and teacher costs per student, 1965–80

	High school	Junior college	University
1965			
Total costs	0.88	0.94	0.35
Capital and debt service*	1.70	2.09	0.50
Current costs	0.57	0.49	0.26
Teacher costs	0.48	0.38	0.25
1973			
Total costs	0.72	0.56	0.37
Capital and debt service*	1.07	1.01	0.82
Current costs	0.59	0.41	0.25
Teacher costs	0.52	0.34	0.25
1980			
Total costs	0.91	n.a.	0.43
Current costs	0.80	0.47	0.34

*While capital and debt service are grouped together in this table, other data (*Educational Standards in Japan*, 1970 pp. 241–2) indicates that approximately one-third of this expenditure was for debt service in the private sector while in the public sector it was almost all capital outlay.

Sources: Data for 1965 and 1973: *Educational Standards in Japan*, 1975, p. 354. Data for 1980 provided by Foundation for the Promotion of Private Schools.

current expenditures, particularly teacher expenditures. Their teacher-costs per student were 52 per cent that of the public schools, although the fraction of teacher utilised per student in private schools (Table 7.5) was 69 per cent that in public schools. They used 52 per cent the money public schools had (per pupil) to purchase 69 per cent as much teacher staff. Thus, salary differentials apparently explain 20–30 per cent of the teacher-cost gap between the two sectors, although the credentials of the teachers in the two systems are comparable.

GREATER EFFICIENCY OR LOWER QUALITY?

Is this evidence of greater efficiency or lower quality? Do the lower wages available to these groups stem from their lower productivity, or simply from an artificial segmentation of the labour market, which arbitrarily makes different opportunities available to different kinds of people? By the former interpretation, the private sector is offering lower quality teaching. By the latter interpretation, the private sector is able to take advantage of these labour market imperfections and hire equivalent services at lower cost, while the public sector is proscribed by custom and law from doing so.

In either case, it is clear that without this labour market segmentation the private sector in education would have found it more difficult to survive and grow. Higher costs would have had to be passed on to the consumer, with a corresponding cut in quantity demanded and, probably, with increased pressure for state subsidy at an earlier date. The availability of low-wage workers, resulting from a segmented labour market, meant that they, rather than consumers or taxpayers, would bear much of the cost, and is an important factor in explaining the large size of the private non-profit-making sector in Japan.

In summary, we have shown that the cost differentials between the public and private sectors in education stem partially from product-mix differences (which are independent of quality and efficiency), partially from a lower input–output ratio at private schools and partially from lower wages paid to their workers, the two latter probably due to a combination of lower quality and greater efficiency (i.e. a lower value added per pupil but higher value added per unit of expenditures). While the quality gap may have increased during the 1960s, the recently instituted government subsidies have narrowed the cost differential by improving facilities but especially by raising teacher salaries, as we shall see in Chapter 11. By the same reasoning, this probably implies, simultaneously, a rise in quality and a decline in efficiency in the private school sector.

SOCIAL RATE OF RETURN AND SOCIAL EFFICIENCY

An alternative way to evaluate efficiency is to examine the social rates of return in the public and private sectors. The social rate of return tells us how much extra individuals produce, as indicated by their additional pre-tax income, as a return on the investment in their education, where all costs paid by them personally as well as those paid by the rest of society are considered part of the investment. While individuals care primarily about the private returns to their own

educational costs, as members of society we care about the total social
returns, particularly if taxpayers are carrying part of the cost. Social
rates of return to education will be high when productivity gains
(value added) are great and total costs are relatively low.

The higher quality education in public schools may lead to higher
lifetime production and earnings, and rate-of-return calculations
enable us to compare these returns for the public and private sectors.
Data for this purpose are available only at the university level;
however, since students at national universities come disproportionately from public high schools, and private high schools are more likely
to supply students to private universities (as shown in the previous
chapter), to some extent inferences can be drawn about relative high
school rates of return as well.

Social rates of return, by field and university group, calculated
under the strong assumptions that lifetime earnings indicate social
productivity, are presented in Tables 7.10 and 7.11. These tables are
based on cost figures which vary by field and university group, and
earnings figures which vary only by university group. They show that,
within each sector, there is considerable diversity in social rates of
return, depending on field of specialisation and which university one
attends. In general, within each sector, the older universities spend
more per student. For example, within the public sector in 1975
Tokyo and Kyoto Universities had 9 per cent of the students at
national universities but 15 per cent of total expenditures; the five
other Imperial universities had 15 per cent of the students, but 21 per
cent of total budgets; eleven other older universities had 21 per cent of
students, 24 per cent of budgets; while sixty-four new colleges and

Table 7.10   Social rates of return to higher education, 1978

	Social science	Engineering
National universities – total	7.6	6.6
I Old Imperial universities	8.0	6.9
II Prestigious national universities	7.6	6.6
III New less prestigious universities	7.2	6.2
Private universities – total	7.8	7.1
I Waseda and Keio	8.6	8.0
II Old private universities	7.9	7.3
III New private universities	7.0	6.5

Source: Masakazu Yano, 'Rates of Return from Education', in Shogo
Ichikawa, *Allocation of Educational Resources in Japan,* pp. 138, 141

Table 7.11   Comparison of social, private and public rates of return to higher education, 1978

	Humanities	Social science	Science	Engineering
Social rate of return				
National universities	6.3	7.1	5.1	6.1
Private universities	7.3	7.6	6.5	7.1
Private rate of return				
National – average over fields	8.4			
Private	7.2	7.4	6.9	6.8
'External' rate of return				
National	4.6	5.9	3.0	4.3
Private	7.3	7.5	6.9	7.2

Note: Numbers for social rate of return are slightly different in Tables 7.10 and 7.11 because method of aggregation differed.
Source: Same as Table 7.10.

universities had 55 per cent of the students and 41 per cent of total expenditures.[27] But the older universities also produce an earnings premium which exceeds their higher costs, so they yield a higher social rate of return.

These tables make it clear, however, that the rate of return to society is greater in the private than the public sector for every field and overall. Even though the public sector generates higher lifetime earnings, it also costs much more than the private sector, so, on balance, it apparently is not a good investment for society.

Note that the social rate of return is highest in the social sciences and humanities, because their cost is low. The data used in these calculations assume that earnings are as high in these fields as in the sciences. In the USA this would not be an accurate assumption, but in Japan it probably is, because of different employer hiring practices. American employers often expect workers to get some of their specialised training in school or college before acquiring a job. In Japan, on the other hand, large corporations prefer a 'general' education for their managerial élite, with managers frequently shifted across jobs and specialised training provided later on by the company as needed. A low rate of labour mobility in Japan assures that companies investing in worker training will benefit from that training. Thus, initial employment opportunities are high for 'liberal arts' graduates. Since, as we have seen, the private sector specialises in these low-cost, high-yield, liberal arts fields, this increases its average social rate of return, which is over 7 per cent in private universities, about 6 per cent at national universities.

Of particular interest in Table 7.11 is the 'external' rate of return, i.e., the higher income-tax revenues received by the rest of society other than the individual directly involved, compared with the educational costs paid by society through the public treasury. As we have seen, the treasury bears most of the cost at national universities but gets relatively little return because of the low tax rates in Japan, so the average 'external' rate of return barely exceeds 5 per cent there. However, it is over 7 per cent at private universities. Ironically, the advantage of the private sector is the greatest for this group–society at large.

There is some reason to believe that these figures understate the true social rate of return to the public sector. Perks and bonuses, which may not be fully counted in this data, are probably higher in the large corporation, and intangible benefits may be greater in the civil service. Also, these employers pay their workers partially in the form of prestige, so that real productivity may exceed the monetary wage. If that is so, using wages as an index of productivity, as was done in these calculations, would understate the true social rate of return at public universities, which train the personnel for civil service and large corporate bureaucracies. Including these factors would raise the social returns closer to that of the private sector.

However, even more compelling are arguments that Tables 7.10 and 7.11 overstate the social return at public universities. First, the pattern of lifetime hiring at the age of 22, when there is still much uncertainty about the future productivity of a person, means that the lifetime earnings stream may be a less accurate measure of individual productivity than in systems where greater turnover and wage-adjustment is the rule; thus, productivity of individuals coming from public and private universities may overlap more than their wages.

Second, and more important, the student input is not the same for all schools. Rather, as we have noted, students are tightly segmented into different high schools and universities, according to examination scores. Hence, when we observe a higher output for a school, this may simply reflect its better student input, not the value added by the school itself. Public high school and university students are more likely to have had higher scholastic achievement in the past, and it may be this which accounts for their later success. In addition, if students learn from each other, the 'peer-group effect' may be more positive at public schools. That is, a typical graduate of a public high school or university may have higher lifetime earnings because he (or she) is brighter than private school graduates and because he (she) has been in the same class with other bright students, not because the school inputs or teaching technology is superior.

Closely related, the Japanese education system is often said to operate as a huge screening device, funnelling the brightest people in the country to the top employers. Indeed, the universities are popularly known as 'leisure centres' where students spend four years relaxing and recovering from 'examination hell'.[28] By this interpretation, relative wages paid to students from different schools mainly reflects their innate ability, little learning has gone on, and the real (productivity-enhancing) returns to higher education are very low. This effect would be greater for public universities which attract the smartest students, strengthening our conclusion that the social rate of return, a proxy for social efficiency, is higher in the private sector. The new programme of government subsidies was designed to equalise education in the two sectors by permitting the private sector to raise its costs. Paradoxically, unless lifetime productivity and earnings were to rise by an equivalent amount (with interest) this would imply a reduction in the social rate of return, especially the 'public' or 'external' return to society at large.

8 Socioeconomic Distribution and Redistributional Effects of Education: Japan

Chapters 6 and 7 have demonstrated that the public educational sector in Japan is characterised by higher entrance standards, lower tuition and greater lifetime earnings than the private sector, hence a higher private rate of return. Clearly it is the élite sector, in the sense of being preferred and selective. Do the various socioeconomic classes get equal access to it? Who benefits most – the rich, who usually consume a disproportionate share of higher education or the poor, who pay low taxes which may give them inexpensive access to an élite school system? Relatedly, which sector is more income-biased, the private or the public? Which has the greater impact: the price barrier that keeps the lower classes out of the private sector or the barrier stemming from cultural disadvantage, which may keep them out of the élite public sector? These turn out to be difficult and ambiguous issues to analyse.

We start by presenting data on the socioeconomic distribution of the student body, removing distortions in these data that are due to the steep age–earnings profile and the age of child-rearing in Japan. These data allow us to compare the income bias of enrolments in the public and private sectors for different levels of education. Next, we add data on the distribution of the tax burden in Japan, which, together with the enrolment data, allow us to calculate how education redistributes real income: certain groups gain and others lose as a result of public spending on education. These results on distribution of education and income redistribution through education are then compared with similar data from the USA and the UK. Finally, we analyse the policy variables that have a key effect on these outcomes.

Our main conclusions are that the private sector is income-biased at every level but in the public sector the bias is heavily concentrated at the higher education level. Hence, in universities, where access is most unequal over-all, the degree of inequality is roughly the same in the public and private sectors; apparently at this level one sector cannot

110

be preferred to the other on distributional grounds. We discuss these results at some length because they are counter-intuitive in some respects, contrary to the American experience and different from what some scholars believe is the case for Japan.

We also find that at the university level tax-shares are even more skewed than enrolment shares, which implies that government spending on education (whether in public or private institutions) leads to a net redistribution of income away from the rich and towards the poor. Comparable data, presented in the next chapter, indicate that the enrolment bias is larger and the redistributive effect smaller in the UK; and results for the USA vary greatly depending on which state system is under discussion. We argue that differences in the degree of selectivity and the quantity–quality choice in the public system are important policy variables that determine the distribution of education and the redistribution achieved through education in all these cases. We also suggest that a long-run political coalition of top business executives, small shopkeepers and agricultural interests, led to this particular pattern of educational distribution and income redistribution in Japan.

SOCIOECONOMIC DISTRIBUTION OF ENROLMENTS

Ideal Data and Available Data

In order to decide if access to education in Japan is greater for some socioeconomic groups than for others, we would like to examine each age group or cohort separately. We would like to know the distribution of lifetime incomes for the entire cohort and for the families of students coming from that cohort. Then we could tell whether or not students come disproportionately from the wealthier parts of the cohort. We would prefer to have these data broken down by institution so that we could determine whether there is an income bias at academic versus vocational schools, high versus low-ranking universities, etc.

Unfortunately, the data available to us from Japan (or indeed, from any other country) are not categorised in this way. Therefore we encounter problems in interpreting the data that are available, and we need to manipulate the data to make them more appropriate to our purposes. In this chapter we spell out some of the problems we have faced, the steps taken to overcome them and the conclusion we have finally drawn.

We start out with data on the current income distribution of the entire population and the current family income of each student, collected periodically by the Prime Minister's Office. These data are disaggregated by sector but not by institution. This information is presented in Table 8.1, which shows us the proportion of students coming from each quintile in the population. Since each quintile, by definition, contains 20 per cent of the families in the population, the difference between these numbers and 20 per cent should inform us in a preliminary way about the income bias in enrolments.

The data are immediately puzzling because they conflict with other information we have about access to education in Japan. For example, we know that virtually all Japanese children in the relevant age group attend school for the nine years of compulsory education, and 99 per cent of them are in public schools. Thus, there can be no income bias operating at the primary or junior high school levels, over-all or in the public sector. Yet, Table 8.1 appears to show an income bias. How do we explain this contradiction? Our explanation focuses on two factors: the life cycle of earnings and the timing of marriage and child-bearing in Japan. These two factors explain the discrepancy at the compulsory level and require us to reinterpret the data for the high school and university levels, as well.

Adjustment for Age–Earnings Profile

First, kindergarten and primary school children have young parents, whose current income understates their lifetime income, while the opposite is true at the university level. This would pose an analytic problem in any country but especially so in Japan, where earnings rise steeply with age. The earnings of a 55-year old male may be four times that of a 20-year old male, especially in large firms and government employment, in comparison with the USA, where the older worker typically earns only double the entrant's wage. Similarly, the age–earnings profile in Japan is twice as steep as that of European countries such as France, Germany and the UK.[1] This means that if we examine the data in Table 8.1 casually it may appear that poor or middle-income families are heavily represented in kindergartens, rich families in universities, but this will simply be telling us about the relationship between income and age, not about the educational access of different lifetime groups.

One way to circumvent this problem is to consider only the age group or cohort relevant to each level of education. According to

Table 8.1 Distribution of students by national family income quintiles, 1976

	I	II	III	IV	V
Kindergarten					
Public	21.6	23.5	24.8	18.8	11.1
Private	13.8	22.9	25.8	21.6	15.9
Total	16.3	23.1	25.5	20.7	14.4
Primary					
Public	14.7	19.4	23.9	23.9	18.2
Private	17.5	11.1	17.5	19.0	33.3
Total	14.7	19.3	23.8	23.8	18.4
Junior high school					
Public	12.9	15.6	20.9	25.3	25.2
Private	7.2	2.4	13.3	21.7	54.2
Total	12.7	15.0	20.5	25.1	26.6
High school					
Public	13.8	14.9	17.4	25.1	28.7
Private	9.2	11.6	18.2	24.3	36.8
Total	12.4	13.9	17.6	24.9	31.1
Junior college					
Public	16.7	25.0	8.3	25.0	25.0
Private	7.1	9.5	11.9	28.6	42.9
Total	8.3	11.5	11.5	28.1	40.6
University					
Public	7.4	12.3	7.4	29.6	43.2
Private	8.9	8.3	12.6	23.4	46.6
Total	8.6	9.0	11.6	24.6	45.9

Sources: Office of Prime Minister, *Annual Report on the Family Income and Expenditure Survey*, 1976, as quoted by Jyoji Kikuchi, 'Access to Education and the Income Redistributive Effects', in Ichikawa, *Allocation of Educational Resources in Japan*, pp. 152–7.

Jyoji Kikuchi, who has written the most detailed paper on this topic, most kindergarten and primary students have fathers aged 25–44, junior high school students have fathers aged 30–49, fathers of high school students are aged 35–54 and fathers of junior college and university students are 40–59.[2] Table 8.2 presents data on the current income distribution of households whose heads fall into each of these age groups or cohorts and Table 8.3 juxtaposes data from Tables 8.1 and 8.2.

Table 8.2 confirms our suspicion that families with younger heads will be underrepresented in the top income quintile while those with older heads will be overrepresented. For example, the proportion of

Table 8.2   Distribution of households by national income quintiles for
selected age groups, 1976

Age of head of household	Relevant education level	I	II	III	IV	V
25–44	Kindergarten and primary	17.9	24.9	24.9	20.0	12.7
30–49	Junior high school	15.1	21.0	23.2	22.4	18.3
35–54	High school	14.0	17.0	20.7	24.0	24.1
40–59	University	14.7	14.7	17.7	24.2	28.7

Source: Same as Table 8.1.

families in quintile V is less than 20 per cent in younger age groups associated with primary and junior high school, more than 20 per cent in older age groups associated with high school and university.

Table 8.3 shows that, by taking into account this age factor and the differential wages that accompany age (i.e. the life cycle of wages), we narrow the apparent income bias of education but we do not completely eliminate it. To some extent, the high enrolment quintiles are those with a high proportion of households. However, the proportion of students still exceeds the proportion of families in Quintiles IV and V, and vice versa in Quintiles I and II, at all levels. Yet, as noted above, we know that at the compulsory level an income bias does not exist. This brings us to our second explanation – the timing of child-bearing and its impact on the number of schoolchildren within each age group.

Allowance for Age of Child-bearing and Number of Children

Because of the pattern of child-bearing, younger and hence poorer families *within the 'relevant' age group* will tend to have fewer children of primary school age, while the opposite is true of the older (hence richer) families who consequently appear to 'overutilise' the schools. Looking at 'relevant' cohorts, then, eliminates some but not all of the distortion due to age–income profiles. We really need much smaller age categories, but these are not available.

This point is made clearer if we reconstruct the marriage and child-bearing cycle of the typical Japanese family.[3] Cultural homogeneity makes this pattern quite uniform. In the modal family the marriage occurs when the groom is aged 25–9, the bride aged 20–4. The first

Table 8.3   Distribution of students compared with distribution of households for relevant age groups, 1976

	I	II	III	IV	V
All households, 25–44	17.9	24.9	24.9	20.0	12.7
Primary pupils					
Public	14.7	19.4	23.9	23.9	18.2
Private	17.5	11.1	17.5	19.0	33.3
Total	14.7	19.3	23.8	23.8	18.4
All households, 30–49	15.1	21.0	23.2	22.4	18.3
Junior high school pupils					
Public	12.9	15.6	20.9	25.3	25.2
Private	7.2	12.4	13.3	21.7	54.2
Total	12.7	15.0	20.5	25.1	26.6
All households, 35–54	14.0	17.0	20.7	24.0	24.1
High school students					
Public	13.8	14.9	17.4	25.1	28.7
Private	9.2	11.6	18.2	24.3	36.8
Total	12.4	13.9	17.6	24.9	31.1
All households, 40–59	14.7	14.7	17.7	24.2	28.7
University students					
Public	7.4	12.3	7.4	29.6	43.2
Private	8.9	8.3	12.6	23.4	46.6
Total	8.6	9.0	11.6	24.6	45.9

Source: Tables 8.1 and 8.2

baby is born soon after the marriage, and the second baby three to five years later. This means that the first child is in primary school when the father is aged 32–42, the second child when the father is aged 36–46. Thus, within the 'relevant' age category (25–44), men who are younger than 36 are likely to have no children in primary school or only one, while those who are older than 36 are likely to have at least one and probably two children in primary school. These more senior fathers are also in a higher income group. Since they contribute more children to the primary schools they create the appearance of an income bias (overrepresentation of Quintiles IV and V, underrepresentation of Quintiles I and II) in enrolments, just as we find in Table 8.3, when other data assure us that everyone has equal access. A similar distortion appears at the junior high school level. This effect would be eliminated if we could look at households with heads aged 25, 26, . . . 44, each year taken separately. Thus, the apparent over- and underrepresentation of some income quintiles that we observe in Table 8.3 at the primary and junior high school levels stem from the way our data have been collected and categorised, and not from an inherent inequality in access to compulsory education.

Our real problem arises, not at the compulsory level where we know the attendance rates are 99 per cent, but at the non-compulsory levels where education is not universal. These data are subject to the same sorts of distortions we have just outlined, but we have no other independent source of information on income bias. Fortunately, the demographic patterns described above imply that the relative share of the top-income quintiles is most overstated for the primary and junior high school levels; this overstatement is much less and possibly zero at the high school and university levels.[4] Moreover, these distortions, which are related to the age of parents, probably do not affect the relative degree of bias in the public and private sectors. Thus, they do not greatly affect the areas in which we are most interested.

As we will discuss at greater length below, these data make it clear that income bias exists in the private sector at all levels. Our interviews confirmed that scholarships and other efforts to 'balance' the student intake are virtually non-existent in Japan. However, at the higher educational level the public sector also becomes heavily biased and the two sectors display a very similar income distribution of their student populations.

Importance of Disaggregating by Institution

The data we have just given confirm that the private sector is income biased but obscure what we believe to be an important bias in the public sector. That is, the public sector includes both the most desirable high school places – those in academic (university-track) schools and courses – and the least desirable high school places – those in vocational or night schools, which are at the bottom of the pecking order. About one-third of all public high school students, including many of the poorer ones, are in the latter group.

A recent study of five high schools in Kobe suggests that at the élite public schools, which send most of their students to university, most students have fathers with college education, in managerial positions, and attend expensive private cram schools, whereas the vocational schools draw from a lower-class clientele.[5] Similarly, data available from Tokyo University, the most élite public university, show that in 1970, 81 per cent of its students had fathers who were salaried employees or managers in public service or private enterprise and only

19 per cent came from agriculture, self-employed or 'other' groups. In 1976, 43 per cent of the entering class were from families with fathers in private enterprise management. Practically none came from blue-collar working-class families.[6] Since the university attended is so tightly correlated with the high school attended (see Chapter 6), we can read backwards from income-biasing in public universities to similar biasing in public high schools. And in the private sector we can similarly separate competitive high schools such as Nada or universities such as Waseda or Keio from others which demand and offer relatively little in the way of educational or employment prospects.

Thus within each sector it appears that certain schools cater heavily to the upper classes and others to the working classes. This stems not from residential segregation and neighbourhood schools, as in the USA, but from the opposite – choice by students and schools which allows both self-selection and exclusion according to academic, hence socioeconomic, criteria. (Varying combinations of these mechanisms are also found in other countries such as the UK where residential segregation plus parental choice also produces income differences among users of different schools, even though selection of students on academic grounds has largely been ruled out.)

It would be useful to have data on family background at top- and bottom-ranking high schools and universities in both the public and private sectors. In a situation where public schools are selective, the most important bias may occur in the schools attended by different income groups within each sector, rather than across sectors. However, such data are unfortunately not available on a systematic basis, so we are left with our oversimplified sectoral averages.

COMPARISON OF PUBLIC AND PRIVATE SECTORS

Enrolment Shares by Lifetime Income within a Cohort

We now proceed to compare in greater detail, the socioeconomic background of students in public and private schools.[7] As we stated at the beginning of this chapter, we wish to base this analysis on lifetime income distribution but unfortunately we only have data on current income. Furthermore, Tables 8.1 and 8.2 divide students and households into quintiles for the population as a whole, which is different from quintiles for their own cohort. We have devised a method to 'redistribute' these households and the enrolments they generate,

118   *The Public and Private Sectors*

dividing them into quintiles based on their expected lifetime income
within a given age cohort. That is, each quintile contains 20 per cent
of the families from a given cohort, ranked according to estimated
lifetime income. This method is described in detail in Appendix 1.
Here, we simply present the results of this procedure, in Table 8.4,
which gives us the enrolment shares for each cohort quintile, for each
educational level.

In general, enrolment shares in Table 8.4 are less skewed than those
in Table 8.1, because they partially remove age as a source of
distortion. In fact, at the high school and university levels more than
half the income bias is removed as we shift to Table 8.4, which is based
on lifetime income standing with a given cohort. This is consistent

Table 8.4   Enrolment shares by lifetime cohort quintiles

Cohort quintiles	I	II	III	IV	V
Kindergarten					
Public	23.6	18.9	20.0	19.3	18.0
Private	15.7	18.4	20.7	21.4	23.8
Total	18.2	18.6	20.5	20.7	22.0
Primary					
Public	16.3	15.6	19.0	23.3	26.9
Private	18.4	9.0	13.5	17.3	39.9
Total	16.3	15.5	18.9	22.2	27.1
Junior high school					
Public	16.5	15.5	18.2	22.6	27.1
Private	7.8	4.0	11.8	19.4	55.8
Total	16.2	15.0	17.8	22.4	28.5
High school					
Public	19.1	17.2	18.4	21.4	23.8
Private	13.3	15.4	18.6	22.3	30.5
Total	17.3	16.7	18.4	21.7	25.8
Junior college					
Public	25.7	21.0	16.6	19.3	17.4
Private	10.5	13.2	20.0	26.4	29.9
Total	12.4	14.3	19.6	25.4	28.3
University					
Public	11.8	12.3	18.8	26.9	30.1
Private	11.9	12.8	17.6	25.0	32.5
Total	11.8	12.7	17.8	25.4	32.0

Source: Our calculations, based on method described in Appendix I and
data in Tables 8.1 and 8.2.

with our earlier observation that the age–earnings profile has accounted for much of the skewing in Table 8.1. Thus, this adjustment is extremely important to make, if we wish to understand how education is distributed among different socioeconomic groups, rather than among different age groups.

The distortion stemming from child-bearing patterns and number of children within the relevant age group remains, since we have been unable to account for that in a systematic manner. As noted above, this effect is probably relatively weak at the secondary and higher levels and there is no reason to believe that it affects one sector more than the other. In the following discussion we use both cohort (age-adjusted) data based on lifetime income (Table 8.4) and data based on current income which is not age-adjusted (Table 8.1). While recognising the weaknesses of each of these, we assume that these weaknesses do not influence the relative position of public and private sectors in which we are primarily interested.

Quintile Ratios

Two methods are used to summarise the income bias implied by Tables 8.1 and 8.4. The first and simpler method is to calculate the 'quintile ratio', i.e. the enrolment representation of quintile V divided by that of quintile I. If both groups have an equal chance to attend school, this ratio will be 1.0. On the other hand, if the rich are overrepresented relative to the poor, the quintile ratio will be greater than 1 (and vice versa). Unfortunately, this index tells us nothing about the representation of the middle class (quintiles II–IV). We have calculated the age-adjusted and unadjusted quintile ratios based on current and lifetime income from data given in Tables 8.1 and 8.4, and they are presented in Table 8.5. Both ratios are clearly larger for the private than the public sector, until we reach the university level.

Gini Coefficients

The second method of measuring inequality is the Gini coefficient. This is more complicated but preferred because it includes the middle classes. The educational Gini coefficient may be described in the following way. Suppose we rank families by income quintile on the horizontal axis and indicate the cumulative enrolment share of each quintile on the vertical axis. Then, we obtain a 'Lorenz curve' for education, such as curve OCB in Fig. 8.1 based on data in Table 8.1

Table 8.5   Quintile ratios

	Current income (Table 8.1)	Lifetime income (Table 8.4)
Kindergarten		
Public	0.51	0.76
Private	1.15	1.52
Total	0.88	1.21
Public/Private	0.44	0.50
Primary school		
Public	1.24	1.65
Private	1.90	2.17
Total	1.25	1.66
Public/Private	0.65	0.76
Junior high school		
Public	1.95	1.64
Private	7.53	7.15
Total	2.09	1.76
Public/Private	0.26	0.23
High school		
Public	2.08	1.25
Private	4.00	2.29
Total	2.51	1.49
Public/Private	0.52	0.55
Junior college		
Public	1.50	0.68
Private	6.04	2.85
Total	4.89	2.28
Public/Private	0.25	0.24
University		
Public	5.84	2.55
Private	5.24	2.73
Total	5.34	2.71
Public/Private	1.12	0.93

Source: Tables 8.1 and 8.4.

for all high school students. Now, under a system of perfect equality (and if all families have the same number of children) each income quintile will supply 20 per cent of the enrolments and the 'Lorenz curve' will coincide with the (dotted) 45° line. Under a system of perfect inequality, where only rich families are educated, the Lorenz curve will lie along the horizontal axis (at 0) until the top quintile is reached, at which point it becomes very steep (vertical). Under an in-

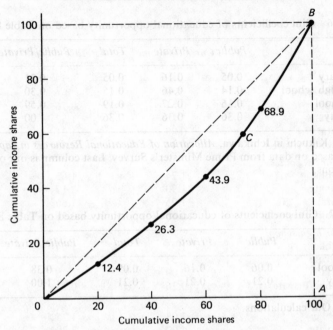

Note: Gini coefficient equals $OBCD/OBA = 0.19$

Figure 8.1   Educational Lorenz curve and Gini coefficient – high-school level by current income.

between system of partial inequality, the Lorenz curve lies beneath the 45° line and the area between the Lorenz curve and the 45° line is a measure of the degree of inequality. The Gini coefficient is the ratio of this area to the total area under the 45° line (area OBCO/triangle OBA). Under perfect equality the Gini coefficient is 0, under perfect inequality it is 1 and therefore it ranges between 0 and 1, the smaller the more equal. A study by Kikuchi calculates Gini coefficients based on data in Table 8.1 (unadjusted for age) and these are reproduced in Table 8.6. Our calculations based on Table 8.4 (adjusted for age) are presented in Table 8.7. While the absolute values of the Gini coefficients are questionable for the reasons given above, the relative value of the coefficients in the public and private sectors may be more reliable.

As expected, the skewing towards the wealthy is greater in the private sector at the pre-university levels. Also as expected, the inequality increases with the level of education, both in the public sector and overall. This effect would be even more pronounced if the

Table 8.6   Gini coefficients of educational opportunity based on Table 8.1

	Public	*Private*	*Total*	*Public/Private*
Elementary	0.05	0.16	0.05	0.31
Junior high school	0.14	0.46	0.15	0.30
High school	0.16	0.27	0.19	0.59
University	0.36	0.36	0.36	1.00

Source: Kikuchi in Ichikawa, *Allocation of Educational Resources in Japan*, p. 172, based on data from Prime Minister's Survey. Last column is our own calculations.

Table 8.7   Gini coefficients of educational opportunity based on Table 8.4

	Public	*Private*	*Total*	*Public/Private*
High school	0.06	0.16	0.09	0.38
University	0.21	0.21	0.21	1.00

Source: Our calculations.

data problems discussed above had been solved, since the Gini coefficient for primary school and junior high school would be much smaller, that for university only slightly smaller. Thus, we find larger Gini coefficients (Tables 8.6 and 8.7) and quintile ratios (Table 8.5) in the private sector generally and at higher educational levels in the public sector as well. Clearly, the private sector draws students from a higher socioeconomic background than the public sector, at the early levels of education. And the income bias increases in the public sector at higher levels of education.

However, within the private sector the income bias does not invariably increase at higher levels of education. Consequently, if we calculate the Gini coefficient in the public and private sectors, and take the ratio between the two, we notice that this ratio becomes larger as we move to higher educational levels, reaching unity at the university level, where the two coefficients are identical.

How do we explain this phenomenon? We would expect the income bias within the public sector to be larger at higher levels of schooling as age–enrolment ratios decline because of drop-outs and excluded students who are more likely to come from poor backgrounds, and this indeed seems to be the case. Declining enrolment ratios will also tend to make the private sector more income-biased, but a counteracting force is at work as well in Japan, stemming from the increased market share of the private sector at higher levels. Large private school sectors are not likely to be the exclusive preserve of the rich and may, indeed, be considered inferior to small public sectors. That is, the public sector is likely to be considered élite and the private sector aimed at the masses, if the former is relatively small and the latter relatively large. Large private sectors in Japan and many other countries stem from excess demand by those who cannot get into the preferred public schools, and often these students come from poorer backgrounds. Since the relative size of the private sector in Japan rises as we move from elementary to high school to university, so the private Gini coefficient or quintile ratio does not increase nearly so much as the public and the two become virtually identical. Apparently the cultural barrier to superior performance keeps the poor out of the public universities and the price barrier keeps them out of private universities to the same extent, so the socioeconomic distribution of the student body is approximately the same in both sectors.

Given the over-all enrolments in public and private universities relative to size of age group (5.4 per cent and 19.4 per cent, respectively, in 1975) the attendance probabilities that are implied by Table 8.4 for each cohort quintile are given in Table 8.8. The proportions of the relevant age group attending university range from 40 per cent for families in the top quintile to 15 per cent for those in the bottom quintile, the percentage of the total attending private institutions is very similar in all quintiles and the skewing towards upper income groups is the same in both sectors.

Table 8.8 University enrolment probabilities, age group 18–22, 1975

| | \multicolumn{5}{c}{Cohort Quintile} | | | | |
	I	*II*	*III*	*IV*	*V*	*Total*
Public	3.2	3.3	5.1	7.3	8.1	5.4
Private	11.5	12.4	17.0	24.2	31.5	19.4
Total	14.7	15.7	22.1	31.5	39.6	24.8
% Private	78.2	79.0	76.9	76.8	79.5	78.2

Sources: Our calculations based on Table 8.4 and *Educational Standards in Japan*, 1975, pp. 265, 270–7, for cohorts graduating from junior high school in 1969–72 and university enrolments in 1975.

INCOME REDISTRIBUTIONAL EFFECTS OF PUBLIC SPENDING ON EDUCATION

Methodology

Moving beyond the question of the socioeconomic background of students, we would like to understand the redistributional effects of the Japanese educational system, i.e., which groups gain and which groups lose, as a result of the public–private division of responsibility for financing education. This topic has been a controversial one in the USA, with different studies giving different distributional consequences of public spending for higher education.

When government subsidises or completely finances education, some people obtain goods for which they have not paid, while others pay for goods they have not received. Thus real income, i.e. the ability to consume goods and services, gets redistributed. Some groups favour a public education system precisely because they see this as one way of redistributing real income to the poor. Other people maintain that it is the rich who will avail themselves of the good public universities, so public higher education ends up as a redistribution to the wealthy. If this is true, a privately financed and managed university system such as that in Japan may be more egalitarian than a public system because then the upper-income classes will be paying for the goods they consume rather than receiving services at the taxpayer's expense.

There are several alternative ways of conceptually defining the redistributional effects of education and other collective goods. For example, we might compare the total benefits received by different groups with their total taxes; using this method, if a good is very 'beneficial' relative to costs, it might be that everyone receives a 'redistribution' in the sense that benefits exceed taxes for each group. Of course, some groups may receive a smaller redistribution than others, in the sense that their share of benefits is less than their share of taxes. This benefit-based method of measuring redistribution would require us to know the distribution of benefits as well as taxes.

Another definition of redistribution would have us compare share of taxes paid with share of educational resources used by different groups. A group has then received a redistribution if its tax share is less than its share of educational resources, regardless of the size of the benefits received therefrom. This 'cost-based' approach is easier to apply, since it does not require us to place a value on the benefit received.

In this study, we adopt the latter approach. We compare each group's tax share with its enrolment share, which is a proxy for its resource share; we say a group has received a redistribution if its relative contribution to the relevant government budget is less than its share of enrolments, and vice versa. In some countries specific taxes, such as sales taxes or property taxes, have been designated for education. If these taxes would be reduced were educational spending to be decreased, we would measure the redistributional effects of education by focusing on the contribution of each income group to these specific taxes. However, in Japan there is no reason to believe that certain taxes have been earmarked for education more than others and there is no way of knowing which taxes would be cut if educational spending declined. Therefore, the following calculations assume that education is financed out of general (national and local) tax revenues (i.e. that the same fixed proportion of each tax is contributed to education) rather than out of some specific tax or alternative government project foregone.

We also assume it is the past and future taxes of the student's parents that are paying for his education, rather than future taxes paid by the student himself. Similarly, in the previous section we displayed enrolment shares according to parental income, not students' future income. We use this approach for two reasons: from the conceptual viewpoint, we are interested in whether public spending on education has been used to raise the real incomes and prospects of today's lower income families and from the practical viewpoint this is the only precise data we have available. We do know, however, that university students will subsequently receive high incomes and will be overrepresented in quintiles IV and V in the future. If this overrepresentation is greater than that of their parents, it is possible that our measure will show a redistribution to the present poor, but it may also be a redistribution to the future rich.

As before, we would like to confine our analysis to redistributions within a given cohort, based on lifetime income and tax shares. That is, we would like to compare the enrolment shares of each quintile within a given cohort, with the lifetime tax shares paid by that cohort quintile. Otherwise, we will be mixing inter-generational with intra-generational effects. For example, many parents of primary school pupils have low incomes and do not pay enough taxes to cover their child's current education. Some of them will always be poor and will never repay society for their children's education, but most will have higher incomes, and will pay higher taxes, later in life. For them, society's outlays should be thought of as a temporary loan which they will repay later on, not as a gift or permanent redistribution.

We already have the enrolment share of each cohort quintile, from Table 8.4. We now need the lifetime tax share of each cohort quintile. Unfortunately, we only have, as before, the current tax share, by national income quintile, for each age group, and these are presented in Table 8.9. For example, we know that, within age group 35–44, those families falling into national quintile I pay only 3.2 per cent of the total national tax bill for their cohort. But we also know, from Table 8.2, that this low number results partially from the fact that relatively few people aged 35–44 are 'poor' at that point in their life. To convert to cohort quintiles, based on lifetime income, we follow the same procedure that we used for shifting enrolment shares, as described in Appendix 1. Table 8.10 displays the distribution of lifetime national and local taxes within each cohort, as it appears from these calculations.

Now, approximately one-third of all primary and junior-high-school bills are paid directly by the central government, the rest by localities. Localities are responsible for most public high school expenses. Approximately 40 per cent of the general revenue of

Table 8.9   Tax shares by national income quintiles for each age group

	I	II	III	IV	V
National Taxes					
Parental Age Group:					
(1) 25–34	8.8	19.4	23.3	24.1	24.4
(2) 35–44	3.2	8.5	16.0	28.3	44.0
(3) 45–54	1.8	3.6	6.9	20.9	66.8
(4) 55–64	4.3	4.7	8.4	18.7	64.0
(5) Total	4.2	8.6	13.4	23.8	50.0
Local Taxes					
Parental Age Group:					
(6) 25–34	12.7	22.7	23.6	20.7	20.2
(7) 35–44	5.1	10.8	17.6	26.5	39.9
(8) 45–54	3.0	4.8	8.1	20.6	63.6
(9) 55–64	6.9	6.2	9.5	18.0	59.4
(10) Total	5.6	10.9	14.9	22.4	45.3

Source: Kikuchi in Ichikawa, *Allocation of Educational Resources in Japan*, pp. 89–190.

Table 8.10 Tax shares by lifetime cohort quintile

	I	II	III	IV	V
National taxes (for universities and junior colleges)	5.1	9.9	14.1	24.0	46.9
Local taxes (for kindergarten)	7.6	11.9	15.3	22.5	42.6
0.5 National + 0.5 local (for primary, junior high and high)	6.4	10.9	14.7	23.3	44.8

Source: Our calculations, based on method described in Appendix I.

Table 8.11 Income redistributive effects of education

School level/ cohort quintile	I	II	III	IV	V
Kindergarten					
Public	16.0	7.0	4.7	−3.2	−24.6
Private	8.1	6.5	5.4	−1.1	−18.8
Total	10.6	6.7	5.2	−1.8	−20.6
Primary school					
Public	9.9	4.7	4.3	0.0	−17.9
Private	12.0	−1.9	−1.2	−6.0	−4.9
Total	9.9	4.6	4.2	−1.1	−17.7
Junior high school					
Public	10.1	4.6	3.5	−0.7	−17.7
Private	1.4	−6.9	−2.9	−3.9	11.0
Total	9.8	4.1	3.1	−0.9	−16.3
High school					
Public	12.7	6.3	3.7	−2.6	−21.0
Private	6.9	4.5	3.9	−1.7	−14.3
Total	10.9	5.8	3.7	−2.3	−19.0
Junior college					
Public	20.6	11.1	2.5	−4.7	−29.5
Private	5.4	3.3	5.9	2.4	−17.0
Total	7.3	4.4	5.5	1.4	−18.6
University					
Public	6.7	2.4	4.7	2.9	−16.8
Private	6.8	2.9	3.5	1.0	−14.4
Total	6.7	2.8	3.7	1.4	−14.9

Source: Tables 8.4 and 8.10.

localities also comes from the central government, the rest from their own tax sources, but these proportions vary greatly among prefectures, the central government share being higher in prefectures with large public high school sectors – as discussed in greater detail in Chapter 10. For illustrative purposes, we have assumed that kindergartens are funded primarily out of local taxes, universities and junior colleges out of national taxes, and other public schools out of an equal combination of the two. Then, by subtracting the cohort tax shares (Table 8.10) from the enrolment shares (Table 8.4), we derive the redistributional effects of the Japanese educational system, as presented in Table 8.11. That is, we say an income group has 'received a redistribution' (e.g. of 6.7 per cent) if its share of total enrolments (e.g. 11.8 per cent) is greater than its share of total taxes (e.g. 5.1 per cent), and vice versa. Negative numbers in Table 8.11 indicate 'redistributions away from', positive numbers indicate 'redistributions to'.

Results

In the public schools, at all levels, we observe a redistribution of real income from rich (quintile V) to poor (quintile I) families, who use the system but pay little taxes. The same can be said of public subsidies to private kindergartens, primary and high schools – albeit less so, because enrolment patterns are more skewed there. And at the university level we must conclude that government funding of the public and private sectors will have exactly the same redistributive effect. (A contrary view and data sources are, however, discussed in Appendix 2 to this chapter.) Based on these data one cannot favour government expenditures in public rather than private universities on equity groups in Japan, although the opposite is true at the high school level. In fact, higher subsidies to private universities, if tied to a policy of tuition restraint, might enable more of the poor to attend, making them more redistributive than they are now and more redistributive than the public sector. Nevertheless, the low level of public subsidies to private schools and universities means that relatively little redistribution has taken place through this mechanism, in the past. (Note that both in the public and private sectors, redistribution to or from the middle classes is small.)

Within the public sector, skewing of enrolment shares is greater at university than at lower levels. Relevant tax shares are also more progressive at higher levels, since national rather than local funding is used and national taxes are more progressive than local ones. Thus, the net aggregate redistributive effect is not very different for different levels of education.[8]

However, at the university level the aggregate redistributive benefits are highly concentrated, a large per capita subsidy received by a small number of students. That is, only a small number of students get into the prestigious public universities, from any income group. Only 10 per cent of male and 3 per cent of female secondary school graduates enter public universities; public universities spend three times as much per student as private but enrol only one-third as many students. If the poor are more risk-averse than the rich, the poor would rather take their subsidies in a more equally distributed form which reached a larger proportion of the population. Subsidies to the private sector, where expenditures per student are much lower and enrolments much higher, would accomplish this.[9] Still more redistribution would be achieved by charging higher fees combined with means-tested grants, in both sectors. For any given government budget this would minimise the enrolment bias and maximise the redistributive effect of educational expenditures. However, the bulk of Japanese public higher educational spending goes to the small number of students in the public sector, and it goes to them regardless of family income.

Thus, the allocation of public educational resources in Japan, which is weighted towards the primary and junior high school levels, may be in the interest of the lower working class. But this class would have benefited still more from a larger government budget devoted to education, which would have permitted more public or low-tuition private high schools and universities and more means-tested aid, a greater redistribution from rich to poor. The political economy of this result, placed within a broader international context, is discussed in the next chapter.[10]

APPENDIX 1: LIFETIME COHORT ENROLMENT AND TAX SHARES

This Appendix presents our efforts to adjust the available Japanese data in order to disentangle the effects of inter-generational and intra-generational redistribution of resources through the education system, public and private, in Japan. To measure a student's or a family's income at one moment in time may (particularly in Japan) give a misleading impression of that family's place in the socioeconomic or class structure. The major reason for this is the strong relationship between age and earnings discussed in the text. Ideally, we would like to examine each age group or cohort separately, and we would want to study distributional effects defined by lifetime income, not by the income class into which a family happens to fall in a given year. To do this we would need to know the distribution of lifetime income for each cohort (e.g. for the group of people born, say, in the year 1950, what their lifetime incomes will be, what the incomes corresponding to the first and last quintiles in this distribution are, etc.). We would also need to know the lifetime income of each student (or each student's family) so that we could determine how many students are from each quintile in the lifetime income distribution of the relevant age cohort.

In reality, we only know the *current* family income of *each student* and the *current* income distribution of the *entire population* (i.e. the incomes corresponding to each quintile in the distribution). These are the data presented in Table 8.1 in the text, which shows us the proportion of students coming from each quintile in the population. We also have limited data on the current income distribution of different cohorts, grouped into broad age categories. These data were presented in Table 8.2.

Our object is to redistribute all households and the enrolments they generate, as they would appear if we were dividing them into quintiles based on rankings of their expected lifetime income within their given cohort. In this Appendix we describe the method we have devised to accomplish this.

First we divide *all* households in the population into groups or cohorts, according to the head of household's current age. For this purpose we use Table 8.2, in which each such group corresponds to the 'relevant' age cohort for a different level of education. As expected, households with younger heads have stronger representation in the lower income quintiles, those with older heads are disproportionately found in upper income quintiles.

Next we shift households from the national quintiles given in Table 8.2 to cohort quintiles, based on their current income. We construct this shift so that each cohort quintile contains 20 per cent of the households in that age group (generation), as it should by definition. For example, we see that only 17.9 per cent of the families in age group 25–44 are in quintile I for the entire national population, but 24.9 per cent are in quintile II. This means that some families (20 per cent − 17.9 per cent = 2.1 per cent) at the bottom of national quintile

Table 8.12 Distribution of households by national income quintiles for selected age groups, 1976: with adjustments to obtain cohort quintiles

Parental age	Relevant education level	I	II	III	IV	V	$\overset{K}{\underset{1}{\sum}}$
25–44	Kindergarten and primary	17.9	24.9	24.9	20.0	12.7	100
	Adjustment to obtain cohort quintiles	+2.1	−2.1	+2.8	+7.3	+7.3 }	0
			−2.8	−7.3	−7.3		
30–49	Junior high school	15.1	21.0	23.2	22.4	18.3	100
	Adjustment to obtain cohort quintiles	+4.9	−4.9	−3.9	−0.7	+1.7 }	0
			+3.9	+0.7	−1.7		
35–54	High school	14.0	17.0	20.7	24.0	24.1	100
	Adjustment to obtain cohort quintiles	+6.0	−6.0	−9.0	−8.3	−4.1 }	0
			+9.0	+8.3	+4.1		
40–59	University	14.7	14.7	17.7	24.2	28.7	100
	Adjustment to obtain cohort quintiles	+5.3	−5.3	−10.6	−12.9	−8.7 }	0
			+10.6	+12.9	+8.7		

Source: Same as Table 8.2. Adjustment to obtain cohort quintiles is ours, by method described in text.

II really belong in quintile I, compared with their own cohort; quintile I should be increased and quintile II decreased by 2.1 percentage points. Another 2.8 per cent that appear to be in quintile II really belong in quintile III, but 7.3 per cent of those now in quintile III really belong in IV, etc. Table 8.12 shows the adjustments we have made, moving households from one quintile to another, in order to shift from a national quintile concept to a cohort quintile concept. The additions and subtractions are designed to assign 20 per cent of the cohort to each quintile and sum to zero overall.

We also assume that relative standing remains unchanged through life, so that ranking households within a cohort by current income at one age also ranks them correctly by lifetime income. While such an assumption may not be true of younger age groups, given the possibility that they may be investing in human capital (i.e. accepting lower wages plus training initially in order to receive a return later on), it is probably more true of the older age groups (with children of high-school or university age), whose current income reflects these higher returns and their consequently higher lifetime incomes. Under this strong assumption, then, Table 8.12 also tells us what shifts are necessary to rank households according to their lifetime income, within their own age cohort.

We are now in a position to shift the enrolments which these families are generating. We know that some of the primary school enrolments attributed to quintile II in Table 8.1 really belong to quintile I, i.e., they belong to families that will always be in the bottom 20 per cent of their own age group. Specifically, the enrolment share of quintile I should be augmented by 2.1/24.9 of the enrolment share attributed to quintile II, i.e. (2.1/24.9) (19.3 per cent) or 1.6 per cent. Thus, the new enrolment share for quintile I is 14.7 per cent + 1.6 per cent = 16.3 per cent. Similarly, quintile V is augmented by (7.3/20) (23.8 per cent) or 8.7 per cent, etc. More generally, if national quintile I has an enrolment share of b_1 the adjusted enrolment share $\tilde{b}_i$ for each cohort quintile i becomes:

$$\tilde{b}_1 = b_1 + \frac{2.1}{24.9} b_2$$

$$\tilde{b}_2 = b^2 - \frac{2.1}{24.9} b_2 - \frac{2.8}{24.9} b_2$$

$$\tilde{b}_3 = b_3 \qquad + \frac{2.8}{24.9} b_2 - \frac{7.3}{24.5} b_3$$

$$\tilde{b}_4 = b_4 \qquad\qquad +\frac{7.3}{24.5}b_3 - \frac{7.3}{20}b_4$$

$$\tilde{b}_5 = b_5 \qquad\qquad +\frac{7.3}{20}b_4$$

We use this procedure, in conjunction with data in Tables 8.1 and 8.2, to obtain the enrolment shares for each cohort quintile, based on lifetime income, presented in Table 8.4.

A similar procedure is used to derive cohort tax shares. Starting with Tables 8.2 and 8.9, we need to 'augment' quintile I so that it has 20 per cent of the families in the age group, and we need to augment the tax-share of cohort quintile I by a similar proportion. The first step gives us quintiles which reflect positions in the cohort rather than the national income distribution and the second step gives us the corresponding tax shares. In this way we obtain the share of the current cohort tax bill paid by each cohort quintile.

Of course, taxes are not only paid by this group during the years when their children are in school. It is possible, for example, that quintile I paid a different share of the total cohort tax bill when the cohort was younger, or will when it is older. To test this possibility indirectly, we did a similar calculation for other age groups. We found that, within each age group, cohort quintile I currently pays 4–6 per cent and cohort quintile V 45–50 per cent of the total tax bill for that cohort. This suggests that, as age group 35–44 moves through life, the tax-shares of each quintile will be roughly unchanged, so these shares also give us the distribution of lifetime taxes within that cohort if underlying conditions (e.g. the aggregate tax structure) remain constant. It also suggests that the lifetime tax shares of each quintile will be the same for all cohorts, *ceteris paribus*. The resulting distribution of lifetime national and local taxes within each cohort was given in Table 8.10.

APPENDIX 2: CONFLICTING DATA SOURCES AT THE UNIVERSITY LEVEL

This chapter has used data collected by the Prime Minister's Office. For universities there is an alternative data set collected by the Ministry of Education, which shows much less income bias in the public sector, much more in the private, hence a greater disparity between the two. The top panel of Table 8.13 gives the probability

Table 8.13 University enrolment probabilities in public institutions by income quintiles for parental age group 40–59

National income quintiles	I	II	III	IV	V	V/I
Prime Minister's Data						
1972						
Public	3.2	2.1	2.4	5.0	6.9	2.2
Private	6.9	11.1	14.9	15.7	28.0	4.1
Total	10.1	13.2	17.3	20.7	34.9	3.5
1976						
Public	2.8	4.7	2.4	6.8	8.5	3.0
Private	13.2	12.1	15.3	21.0	35.0	2.7
Total	16.0	16.8	17.7	27.8	43.5	2.7
Ministry of Education Data						
1961						
Public–National	1.9	2.5	2.2	2.5	3.0	1.6
Private	1.2	1.8	2.3	4.4	11.3	9.4
Total	3.1	4.3	4.5	6.9	14.3	4.6
1972						
Public–National	5.5	4.9	2.9	3.1	3.7	0.7
Private	9.1	13.7	10.7	13.4	25.0	2.7
Total	14.6	18.6	13.6	16.5	28.7	2.0
1976						
Public–National	4.3	4.2	4.3	5.1	6.2	1.4
Private	8.2	11.2	13.0	22.7	38.2	4.7
Total	12.5	15.4	17.3	27.8	44.4	3.6

Source: Prime Minister's *Income and Expenditure Survey*, 1972 and 1976, and Ministry of Education, *Report on University and College Life*, 1961, 1972, 1976, as quoted by Kikuchi in Ichikawa, *Allocation of Educational Resources in Japan*, pp. 177–8.

that a student will attend the university, varying with his parents' income quintile, for 1972 and 1976, according to data collected by the Prime Minister's Office; the bottom panel does the same for 1961, 1972 and 1976, according to Ministry data. (Both sets of data use current income with national population quintiles, not lifetime income with cohort quintiles.)

The Prime Minister's data tell us that in 1976 the proportion of age-eligible poor students attending public universities was only 2.8 per cent, while for age-eligible rich students the attendance proportion was 8.5 per cent. These proportions were much higher, 13.2 per cent and 35 per cent, at private universities, corresponding to the fact that there are many more places in the private sector. A family in the top quintile is roughly three times more likely to send a student to university than is one coming from the bottom quintile. Most interestingly, this bias is slightly greater for the public sector. Moreover, the bias in the private sector has been growing smaller as it has expanded (consistent with the hypothesis already set forth), while the bias in the public sector has been increasing slightly through the 1970s as it became more selective, enrolling a smaller proportion of the total university student body. The Education Ministry's data tell us that in 1976 the range was 4.3 per cent to 6.2 per cent at national universities, 8.2 per cent to 38.2 per cent at private universities. The average quintile ratio overall is still approximately 3, but the bias is much greater in the private than the public sector, with both increasing through the 1970s. This obviously contradicts the conclusions drawn earlier.

Which of these data are more accurate and more consistent with theoretical expectations? The Prime Minister's data suggest that the primary forces keeping the poor out of higher education are their social disadvantages (leading to low examination scores), combined with their reluctance to bear the costs of foregone earnings (which are the main cost of attending college) and extra instruction in *juku* (private for-profit academies) which coach students for entrance exams. These costs must be incurred for attendance at both public and private universities; indeed, they are even more necessary for admission to the élite public institutions. Also, the poor are less able to serve as *ronin*, i.e. the teenagers who, having failed the entrance exam to the national university on their first try, spend a year or two in full-time study, hoping to pass subsequently. *Ronin* have constituted approximately 30–40 per cent of all university applicants and entrants through the 1960s and 1970s. The cost, in terms of foregone earnings, is obviously high, and more easily borne by the rich.[11]

The Ministry data suggest, on the other hand, that tuition fees constitute the primary barrier, hence the private sector serves as a haven primarily for the wealthy who are unable to gain admission to the élite public institutions. The national universities seem equally accessible to all groups, even those whose parents are uneducated and who can barely afford *juku*, *ronin* status or foregone earnings.

Obviously, the choice between these two measures is a critical one. Many studies use the *Mombusho* data without even mentioning the contradictory picture posed by the Prime Minister's data.[12] On the other hand, most Japanese experts we have consulted believe that the Prime Minister's data are more accurate, since they are based on a more carefully collected source.[13] This is consistent with evidence from specific national universities, which shows an overrepresentation of families from the high-income group; we have already cited such data from Tokyo and other national universities. In 1974 the average family income of Tokyo University students was over 4 million yen, compared with almost 3 million for all public and 2.4 million for the rest of the population, numbers which are compatible with the Prime Minister's but not the Ministry's data.[14] The Prime Minister's data are also consistent with the observation that low income students are less likely to attend private high schools if they do not secure one of the scarce places in academic public high schools, and hence they are more likely to be excluded from the university race at an early stage. Moreover, since foregone earnings plus *juku* costs far exceed tuition fees, from a theoretical and common-sense point of view they should logically play a more important role than that implied by the Education Ministry's data. For all these reasons, we place more credence in the Prime Minister's data and have utilised it in this chapter.

9 The Distribution of Education and Redistribution Through Education: Comparisons with the USA and the UK

How does the distribution of enrolments and the redistributional effects of education in Japan compare with that in other countries? Comparable data are difficult to obtain for the public sector and are practically non-existent for the private sector in most countries. However, for England and Wales we do have data on comparative enrolment probabilities in state schools for different socioeconomic groups, which may be compared with relative tax shares paid by different income groups. And for the USA we have detailed analyses of the redistributional effects of public higher education in several states. The first section deals with the case of England and Wales, while the next section discusses the US situation at greater length, followed by a general discussion of the relationship between quantity, quality and the redistribution of income and opportunities through education.

COMPARISONS WITH ENGLAND AND WALES

Table 9.1 presents estimates for 1973 of the relative probabilities of enrolling in public institutions at various levels, for persons in the relevant age category, broken down by four main socioeconomic groups: semi- and unskilled workers; skilled manual workers; intermediate non-manual, and professionals and managers. The first and last groups correspond roughly to lifetime cohort quintiles I and V, respectively; the others comprise the middle-income quintiles. For each level, we depict the probability that a child from a given socioeconomic group will attend a public institution relevant for his

137

Table 9.1   Relative enrolment probabilities in public institutions by socioeconomic group, England and Wales, 1973

	I Semi- and unskilled	II Skilled manual	III Other non-manual	IV Professional and managerial
Primary	1	1	1	0.9
Secondary (under 16)	1	1	1	0.9
Secondary (over 16)	1	0.7	1.5	1.8
Further education*	1	2.3	3.1	3.5
University	1	0.7	3.4	5.4

*Polytechnics, institutes of further education, colleges of education
Source: Calculated from data provided in Julian Le Grand, 'The Distribution of Public Expenditures on Education', pp. 63–8.

or her age, using an index of 1 for the lowest class. Thus, we observe that the probability of enrolment during the compulsory school years (up to age 16) is virtually the same for all socioeconomic groups, except that the top class is slightly less likely to attend a state school, because it is more likely to use a private school. At this stage, public expenditures on education are clearly redistributive, since the lower classes pay less taxes but receive roughly equivalent access to publicly provided benefits. (Attendance at private schools is small and heavily skewed towards the rich but these do not receive public subsidies except for implicit tax subsidies).

At the post-compulsory stage, however, differences begin to appear in access within the public sector. Thus, a child from the top class is 1.8 times more likely to stay in secondary school after age 16, and is 3.5 times more likely than one from the lowest class to attend a polytechnic or institute of further education. And at the selective university level, the relative enrolment probability of an upper class child is 5.4, a much more skewed distribution than we find in Japan.[1] (Except for one small institution, there are no private universities in England.)

How do we explain this strong income bias in England and Wales? Public universities in Japan and England both enrol approximately the same small percentage of the relevant age group and in that sense are equally élite. However, in England the secondary school lasts seven or eight years, instead of six as in Japan, and students face a double examination barrier: ordinary 'O' levels at age 16 and advanced 'A' levels at age 18 or 19. A study of educational achievement among cohorts attending secondary school between 1925 and 1970 showed that the probability of staying on past age 16 was the major determinant of examination success, which in turn determined admissability to higher education. It is hardly surprising that these obstacles had the greatest deterrent effect on these most easily discouraged, i.e. those from the lower classes. For example, 93 per cent of those staying on till age 18 obtained one or more A-levels, regardless of class; but an upper class child was 9 times more likely to stay on than a lower class child (28.2 per cent versus 3.0 per cent).[2]

In addition, unlike Japan, the élite secondary sector in England is private, posing a high price barrier as well as academic barrier to potential students. The concentration of élite schools in the private sector was true before the elimination of selective grammar and direct grant schools in the 1970s and is even more true now. These private schools select an academically able student body, gear their training to the 'sixth form', the O-level, A-level and university entrance examinations, and they secure a disproportionate number of university places. For example, in a regression analysis which controlled for family background variables, before the comprehensive reform attendance at élite private schools raised the school-leaving age by 1.67 years, raised the probability of obtaining O-levels 63 percentage points and the probability of obtaining A-levels 39 percentage points, compared with nonselective public secondary schools (secondary moderns) which enrolled the vast majority of students. A lower tier of private schools also improved the success rates, albeit not quite as much.[3] A level success in turn corresponds to likelihood of university enrolment, which was 8 (and 3) times the average probability, for élite (and nonélite) private schools respectively. The children attending these schools, needless to say, are drawn heavily (more than 50 per cent) from the top class, less than 10 per cent from the bottom class.[4] Thus, families that can afford the high private tuition at the secondary level are more likely to obtain free public education at the higher level; the winners in this system, as we have seen, come heavily from the upper classes.

It is possible, of course, that tax shares are also heavily skewed toward the upper classes, in which case higher education might still be redistributive in England and Wales. To investigate this question we utilised data published by the Central Statistical Office for 1972, averaged over all households. Again using an index of 1 for the tax share of quintile I, relative (direct plus indirect) tax shares for quintiles II, III, IV and V were 2.7, 4.2, 5.8 and 9.6, respectively.[5] Thus, the distribution of taxes by income quintile is not very different from that in Japan. Since the relative taxes of quintile V exceed the relative enrolment probability of the professional and managerial class, it appears likely that there is a redistribution through higher education from the top to the bottom income group in England and Wales; however, because of the very skewed enrolment shares, this redistribution is considerably less than in Japan.

COMPARISONS WITH THE USA

Considerable work has also been done on the redistributional effects of public higher education in the USA, with which it is instructive to compare these results.[6] For this purpose, we have adapted data presented in Hight and Pollock, who analyse tax and public university enrolment shares in the mid-1960s of different income groups in California and Florida.[7] Families are grouped in Hight and Pollock according to absolute incomes; we have extrapolated from these data the enrolment shares of each quintile, to facilitate comparability. These figures, based on state-wide quintiles, are presented in Table 9.2.

We then converted the US data to cohort quintiles. Unfortunately,

Table 9.2   Distribution of students for selected US state systems, 1960s, by state-wide family income quintiles

	I	II	III	IV	V	V/I
Florida	8.9	13.9	20.1	26.2	30.3	3.4
California	8.7	21.0	26.0	22.5	21.8	2.5
University of						
California	8.3	14.3	17.8	22.4	37.2	4.5
State colleges	7.9	17.8	23.9	26.6	23.9	3.0
Junior colleges	9.0	23.0	27.7	21.2	18.9	2.1

Source: Our calculations, by method described in the text, based on data in Joseph Hight and Richard Pollock, 'Income Distribution Effects of Higher Education Expenditures in California, Florida and Hawaii', pp. 318–30; and *Census of the Population*, vol. I, Characteristics of the Population, 'Detailed Characteristics', Table 198 for Florida and California.

cohort data were not available for the precise income definition used by Hight and Pollock (and, indeed, they point out that this definition may be somewhat different for Florida and California). Instead, we derived cohort data in the following way. We used census data for 1969, and found the ratio between (a) proportion of families in the cohort (heads aged 45–64) and (b) proportion of families in the state as a whole, for various income categories.[8] The relevant ratios were then applied to the state-wide percentages given in Hight and Pollock (for 1968) to derive the corresponding cohort distribution. For example, according to Hight and Pollock, the lowest income category presented had 28.1 per cent of all families in Florida. From census data we found the closest corresponding income range, which contained 26.4 per cent of all families; however it contained only 19.6 per cent of families with heads aged 45–64. The ratio between these two, 0.74, was then applied to 28.1 to derive the cohort proportion in the lowest Hight and Pollock income category. That is, 20.8 per cent of families with heads aged 45–64 had that low income. We followed this same procedure for all income categories given in Hight and Pollock. These figures and the enrolment shares that go with them were then reshuffled into quintiles according to the method described for Japan in Appendix 1, Chapter 8. Our results, giving the enrolment shares of each cohort quintile, are presented in Table 9.3. If we make the strong assumption that relative position in the income distribution is unchanged through life, this also represents enrolment shares according to cohort quintiles based on lifetime income.

Table 9.3 Distribution of students for selected US state systems, 1960s, by cohort quintiles

	I	*II*	*III*	*IV*	*V*	*V/I*
Florida	11.9	16.7	22.4	25.4	23.5	2.0
California	14.8	26.4	23.4	20.3	14.9	1.0
University of California	12.6	17.5	18.1	20.0	30.4	2.4
State colleges	13.0	23.1	24.2	24.0	15.8	1.2
Junior colleges	15.6	28.9	23.7	19.2	12.4	0.8

Source: Our calculations, by method described in the text, based on data in Joseph Hight and Richard Pollock, 'Income Distribution Effects of Higher Education Expenditures in California, Florida and Hawaii', pp. 318–30; and *Census of the Population*, vol. I, Characteristics of the Population, 'Detailed Characteristics', Table 198 for Florida and California.

It can immediately be seen that this life-cycle adjustment substantially decreases the apparent income bias in enrolments (measured according to the deviation of the quintile ratio from 1), almost as much as it did for Japan. Thus, this is an extremely important correction to make for the USA as well. We also observe that the Japanese public university system has approximately the same degree of income bias as the University of California (UC) system; as expected, degree of income bias corresponds to degree of academic selectivity, when price barriers are low. The greatest income bias would be at Tokyo and Kyoto in Japan, Berkeley and UCLA in California. On the other hand, the private university system in Japan is much more income-biased than the California state college system, which is its academic counterpart, because of the relatively high tuition fees which private institutions must charge to cover costs. These comparisons thus allow us to separate the distributive impact of rationing by price and by academic criteria.

Unfortunately, data on cohort tax shares in the USA were not available for the relevant time period. We reorganised the Hight and Pollock tax data according to state-wide income quintiles and these are presented in Table 9.4. These give the proportion of state and local taxes paid by each quintile within the state as a whole; it corresponds to line 10 in Table 8.9. Under certain conditions these data (which aggregate taxes across age groups at a given point in time) may approximate the lifetime tax shares of different quintiles within a given cohort (i.e. the aggregation of taxes within a given cohort as it ages through time). In Japan, for example, Table 8.10, lines 1 and 2, are almost the same as Table 8.9, lines 5 and 10.

If we use Table 9.4 as an approximation of lifetime tax shares for the relevant cohorts in Florida and California, we obtain the redistributive effects of public higher education presented in Table 9.5. The redistribution from rich to poor is much more marked here than in previous studies, because some of the enrolments which appeared to

Table 9.4　Tax shares by state-wide family income quintiles

	I	II	III	IV	V
Florida	14.2	15.2	18.0	22.0	30.7
California	10.5	13.4	16.9	23.4	35.8

Source: Calculated by us from data in Joseph Hight and Richard Pollock, 'Income Distribution Effects of Higher Education Expenditure in California, Florida and Hawaii'.

Table 9.5 Income redistributive effects of public education

	I	II	III	IV	V	$\sum_i^V$
Florida	−2.3	1.5	4.4	3.4	−7.2	0
California	4.3	13.0	6.5	−3.1	−20.1	0
University of California	2.1	4.1	1.2	−3.4	−5.4	0
State colleges	2.5	9.7	7.3	0.6	−20.0	0
Junior colleges	5.1	15.5	6.8	−4.2	−23.4	0

Source: Calculated from data in Tables 9.3 and 9.4.

come from families in the high-income group are now seen to come from families in the middle or low income groups, relative to their cohorts. Nevertheless, comparing the USA with Japan (Table 8.11), we observe that the University of California and Florida systems are much less redistributive, because the state tax systems which are used to finance higher education in the US are less progressive than the national income tax system which is used to finance universities in Japan. In fact, given our margin of error there may be virtually no redistribution in these systems. On the other hand, the California state and junior college systems, which have neither high academic nor price barriers, are the most redistributive of all. Government spending in the latter, which serve roughly the same academic function as the private universities in Japan, makes the higher education system in California (and similar states) less income-biased and more redistributive than the Japanese system, overall.

QUANTITY, QUALITY AND THE REDISTRIBUTION OF INCOME AND OPPORTUNITIES

We can now set forth a general relationship between educational quantity, quality, and the redistribution of income and opportunities through the public sector, when the possibility exists of opting out to the private sector. This will help to illuminate the choices available to a society as far as quality and equality in its educational system are concerned.

Suppose, in Case I, a government opts for quality over quantity in its public system, that is, for a small number of student places, each funded at a high level. This system will, by definition, be selective overall, and its selectivity will be augmented if academic criteria are used as a rationing device for each institution, as in Japan, where there is a well-defined hierarchy among public secondary schools and universities. A large non-selective private sector may then develop to accommodate the excess demand. However, both the high spending per student as well as the selectivity and consequent high peer-group ability would lead the public sector to be considered the high-quality, preferred sector. Since upper-class students are more likely to pass through the academic (admissions) barrier, they are disproportionately represented in the public sector. Since they are also more able to pass through the price barrier they will also be disproportionately represented in the private sector. If the tax system is sufficiently progressive public education will be redistributive, but this effect is moderated by the limited size and the strong selectivity of public universities. This is the system we find in Japan and in selective American universities such as the University of California system.

Suppose, in Case II, a government decides to spend its given educational budget on high-quantity–low-quality, that is, on many student places, each funded at a relatively low level. Since this system is geared to accept large numbers of students, by definition it will not be very selective overall. This lack of selectivity is augmented if random assignment (e.g. open access to neighbourhood schools or state colleges) is used as a method of matching students to institutions. The low spending per student in the public schools means that some parents will opt out to the private sector for reasons of quality. The lack of selectivity in the public schools will have the same effect: in the presence of a peer-group effect, adverse selection takes place in the public sector while private schools can decide to remain academically selective, hence to have a better learning environment. Since the rich are better able to pass through the price and academic barriers to admission, both of which are now concentrated in the private sector, they will be greatly overrepresented there. In contrast, the public sector now has neither a high price barrier nor a strong academic barrier to keep out the poor, so it is much less income-biased than the private sector and more redistributive than in Case I. This is the situation we find in many Latin American higher education systems and in some non-selective state university systems within the USA.

We get a different picture, however, when we consider the influence of educational variables on the distribution of opportunities. Significantly, the choice of quality over quantity, which is less redistributive in the short run, may be more redistributive in the long run, because of its impact on intergenerational social mobility. To illustrate this point, let us make the strong assumption that access to élite positions depends on access to élite education. That is, the best jobs go to those who have attended the best universities, which serve as a screening device.[9] In the case of countries which have opted for high quantity public systems (case II), the élite institutions are private and, as discussed above, they are likely to be most heavily skewed towards the rich, who therefore have preferential access to the best jobs. Let us assume more precisely that, in such a system, the enrolment probabilities of quintile IV and V in private universities would be 50 per cent greater than currently in Japan and the enrolment probabilities of quintiles I, II and III would be correspondingly less (see Table 8.4). This would imply that 85 per cent of the élite university places and élite jobs would go to students whose families were in quintile IV and V and only 15 per cent would go to those having backgrounds in quintiles I, II or III. Such a system redistributes substantial current educational resources to the lower classes through its large public sector, but does not redistribute the opportunity to become part of the future élite. Those who end up in quintiles IV and V later in life are those who came from quintile IV and V backgrounds and therefore attended superior private universities.

In contrast, countries which have chosen high quality public systems (case I) only moderately redistribute current resources to the lower classes but may be more generous in their redistribution of future opportunities. For example, in Japan, where the public universities are highly selective, enrolments are more skewed towards the upper classes than in most American public universities, hence their redistribution of current resources is limited. However, 43 per cent of their enrolment are from quintiles I, II or III (see Table 8.4), much more than we would find in élite private sectors. Many of these students later in life move into quintiles IV and V, partially as a consequence of their *élite public* education. Intergenerational social mobility is enhanced. Thus, the assessment of the relative equity of these systems depends on which measure of redistribution one choses to use.

A third case, which is typified by the three-tiered California system, offers both the redistribution of current resources through a quantity-oriented track and the redistribution of future opportunities through a quality-oriented track, thereby leaving relatively little scope for the private sector. However, it requires a larger public budget than is needed by a less comprehensive system and much more than is allocated to education in Japan.

THE POLITICAL ECONOMY OF EDUCATION

These observations enable us to throw some light on the questions: why was this particular size and allocation of education budget adopted in Japan? Who benefited the most?

In order to gain and retain power political parties in democracies must come up with a package of collective goods and taxes that appeal to a majority of people, drawn from various classes. The group in power uses the government as a mechanism for maximising the income redistribution to it (or minimising the redistribution away from it). However, the desire to constrain the popularity of the opposition group ultimately limits this process and leads to an equilibrium amount of redistribution. We now inquire to what extent the Japanese educational system is consonant with the interests of the group in political power and in what ways the opposition has been appeased.

Recall that the Japanese government has been controlled by the LDP, the Conservative Party, since the end of the Second World War. The LDP is viewed as the party of 'big business', small shopkeepers and agriculture. For example, LDP support in the 1975 general election was strongest among managers of large companies, owners of family business and family farms, weakest among white- and blue-collar workers and professionals.[10]

If we ask what kind of educational policy would be preferred by the leaders of modern industry, the following elements emerge: corporations need a large literate labour force, hence a high quality mass educational sector at the lower, compulsory, levels. They also need a small highly trained managerial élite. They would prefer that these groups be trained at government expense; otherwise wages would have to rise to induce private educational expenditures and/or many able prospective employees would be excluded from the market. On the other hand, they would prefer to limit government responsibility for higher education, to keep taxes low. These are, after all, the groups that lose by redistribution when government spends on post-compulsory education. A small number of high quality public universities are sufficient to train the managerial élite, allowing the upper classes to buy further education in the private sector for their own children, if necessary, without having to subsidise those less well-off.

Similar preferences would exist among the many families with low income in rural areas and among families in small businesses where demand for secondary and higher education is limited; they would lose by redistribution if more government funds were spent on education. Data comparing educational attainment and occupation show the lowest educational levels for workers in agriculture and fisheries; less than 10 per cent have post-compulsory education.[11]

These groups are very large in Japan, much more so than in most advanced industrial states. In the period 1955–60, when the educational policy we have described was being formulated, 40 per cent of Japan's population was officially classified as 'farm population', 31 per cent of the Japanese labour force was engaged in agriculture and another 18 per cent was either self-employed or family-employed in small non-agricultural family businesses. Only half the labour force was employed outside agriculture and outside their own family business. In contrast, during the same period only 3–4 per cent of the labour force in the USA and the UK was engaged in agriculture.[12] Additionally, the rural areas are overrepresented relative to population in the Japanese Diet (legislature), while urban workers are underrepresented and their ability to organise and gain political power has been limited by law. As will be shown in the next chapter, the limited demand for secondary and higher education in the low-income rural areas is fulfilled by the public sector. It is in the wealthy urban prefectures that demand is high and not satisfied by public spending, so that students must resort to private schools and universities.

Even in the cities, the salaried middle class would be relatively indifferent to public school expansion, since they neither gain nor lose by redistribution. Indeed, given the fact that private schools cost less per student in real terms than do public schools and that even if the public system were somewhat expanded it would not accept all students (hence would be risky), the salaried middle class is probably not inclined to press for higher taxes that would support more public schools and universities. On the other hand, the working class would clearly benefit therefrom.

It should come as no surprise that the educational policy adopted by the LDP was consistent with the preferences of its supporters. The basic ingredients were limited government spending on a high quality-low quantity academically selective secondary school and university system. For the reasons we have given, this was the preferred educational system of the majority of voters in Japan, who supported the LDP. On the other hand, the differing occupational structures in the USA and the UK led to different political coalitions and therefore very different educational policies.

Political entrepreneurs who want to remain in power must also appease the opposition, just enough to keep them from gaining strong support. One pay-off to the opposition in the Japanese equilibrium is the progressive tax system, which did indeed yield net redistributive benefits to the urban working class. However, the redistribution was not nearly as much as a larger government budget (more public schools and/or more subsidies to private schools) would have implied. (Indeed, the progressivity of the tax system may be one reason for the limited government spending. Given the high tax price to the politically powerful upper classes, they opt for a low quantity of government-financed education and other public goods.)

A second important 'opposition' element in the political equilibrium is the opportunity for upward mobility of the lower classes into the élite. As we have seen, the choice of a public system oriented towards quality rather than quantity meant less redistribution of current resources to the urban workers but greater redistribution of future élite opportunities. This effect is enhanced by a public primary system which offers both quantity and quality and by a quality-oriented public secondary system which therefore gives the lower classes access to the universities. (For purposes of contrast, university access is much more problematic for the lower classes in England, where the élite secondary schools that secure large numbers of university places are independent.)

A third pay-off to the opposition was the decision to grant a partial subsidy to private schools and universities. This decision was made in the late 1960s, at a point when the private educational sector was in severe financial difficulty and the electoral majority of the LDP had fallen to its lowest post-war level, as the population shifted from rural to urban areas and the agricultural labour force decreased. The subsidy enabled private institutions to survive without massive tuition increases – and the LDP survived as well.

These policies, we have seen, did indeed yield net benefits to the urban working class – but the redistribution was not nearly as much as a larger government budget (more public schools and/or more subsidies to private schools) would have implied. Apparently, the pay-off to the lower income group was just sufficient to stifle the opposition and to help to keep the LDP in power for over thirty years.

10 Analysis of Prefectural Differences[1]

To throw further light on the determinants of the size and nature of the private sector, a statistical analysis was performed using prefectural data. There are forty-seven administrative units, or prefectures, in Japan, which have very different public/private divisions of responsibility for education. While elementary and junior high school levels are almost completely public everywhere, the percentage of high school enrolments in private schools varies from 2.2 per cent in Tokushima to 55 per cent in Tokyo. Similarly, the proportion of private university enrolments ranges from zero to 91 per cent. How do we explain these large differences across prefectures?

Our hypothesis is that the private sector in education arose in response to excess demand, which varied across prefectures. First and most important, demand is higher in high income prefectures; at the secondary level, these differences in demand were even greater in earlier years, when the development of the private sector took place. Supply of public school places, on the other hand, is not higher in wealthier prefectures, and may even be lower, for reasons we shall give below. Hence, we predict that excess demand and the relative role of private schools will be a positive function of prefectural income per capita, and a negative function of public sector size. Differences in the supply of entrepreneurship, particularly religious entrepreneurship, to the private non-profit sector are seen as another important explanatory factor.

This situation is depicted diagrammatically in Fig. 10.1, where we show demand for secondary education (line AA) as a positive function, supply of public school places (line BB) as a negative function of prefectural per capita income. That is, we expect that demand for education increases with income while, conversely, the size of the public system decreases with income. For prefectures with per capita incomes greater than PCI^*, the public schools do not provide a space for everyone who wants secondary education and the resulting excess demand is partially met by the private sector, particularly in prefectures where the supply of non-profit entrepreneurship is high.

Our empirical findings are consistent with this hypothesis. As we develop this model further we shall note the current influence of

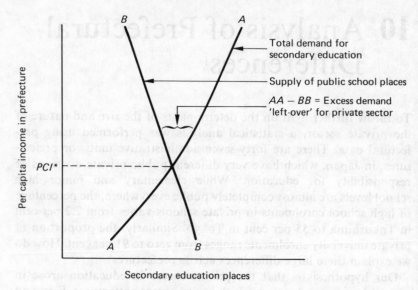

Figure 10.1   Total demand and public supply of secondary education

historical forces and also consider the political economy of public spending and production.

This is the most technical chapter in the monograph, and uses a statistical technique known as regression analysis. This technique tries to show how different variables are related to each other. For example, it allows us to ascertain whether the private sector is larger in wealthier prefectures, by how much, and whether this apparent relationship could have occurred by chance. By using this method we are able to establish that:

1. While demand may be higher in wealthy prefectures, the funds available to finance public education are not greater, because of the particular method of local finance used in Japan.
2. Wealthy prefectures prefer high quality education (as measured by high cost per student).
3. Therefore, they supply fewer public school places, because their funds are used to produce quality rather than quantity.
4. Consequently, excess demand is greater and the private sector plays a larger role in these wealthier prefectures and in prefectures which, for other reasons, have small public sectors.

5. The private sector is also larger in prefectures that had a large availability of non-profit entrepreneurs, as indicated by the presence of Christian missionaries before the Second World War.
6. The redistribution implied by this pattern of public and private schools is consistent with the interests of the supporters of the Liberal Democratic Party, which has been in power in Japan for the past thirty years.

Readers wishing to skim the more technical parts of this chapter are advised to move quickly to the section on 'Regression results'.

THE MODEL: DEMAND

We focus on explaining prefectural differences in the relative size of the private sector in secondary education. This level was chosen because elementary and junior high schools are almost completely public while the university level is characterised by substantial inter-prefectural mobility; i.e. higher education operates in a national, not a local, market, and we are looking for local explanations and differences.

We hypothesise that demand for secondary education from the individuals in a prefecture is a positive function of their per capita income (*PCI*). Our reasoning is that education has a positive income elasticity of demand: *ceteris paribus*, the more income people have, the more they are willing to expend on education. In addition, per capita incomes are higher in urban prefectures with a larger proportion of the labour force in secondary and tertiary industries, hence a greater rate of return to education and more incentive to acquire it. We conjecture that these differences in demand were particularly great in earlier years, e.g. the 1950s and 1960s, when government spending on education was low, and private schools filled the gap, developing their present configuration.

The demand for higher education is also positively related to income, if higher education is a normal good. In this chapter we do not attempt to explain prefectural differences in university, or private university, enrolments. Here we simply note that since part of the motivation for attending a private high school is to be able to attain college admission, this demand for university education translates into a demand for private secondary education in high income prefectures.

PUBLIC QUANTITY AND QUALITY

Decisions about spending in secondary schools in Japan are left largely to the prefectures, although the central government controls matters such as curriculum, texts, and teacher qualifications. The question is: how do prefectures make decisions regarding the supply of public school places? If all prefectures made the same decisions – e.g. if the quantities supplied were imposed by central government and were uniform for all (relative to population) – then we would simply expect the prefectures with higher incomes to have more students left out of public schools, hence larger private school sectors. On the other hand, if prefectures were responsive to local conditions, we might expect those with higher demands to have a larger public supply, hence the proportion left over for the private sector would be the same across prefectures. In fact, we find considerable variation across prefectures in percentage of enrolment in private schools, the implication being that different prefectures have different kinds of responsiveness to the demands of their constituents, and that is what we must explain on the supply side of the model.

We hypothesise that the supply of public school places is not a positive function of income and may, in fact, be negatively related. Our reasoning is that:

1. Prefectural budgets are independent of prefectural income, because of the particular method of public finance in Japan;
2. While the proportion of prefectural budgets spent on all education is also independent of income, per capita spending on secondary education actually declines with income, indicating that high income prefectures prefer to spend their public budget on primary education and other public goods;
3. However, the quality of public secondary education (as measured by expenditure per student) is higher for high income prefectures;
4. Therefore, because of the quantity–quality trade-off in the face of fixed local budgets, the supply of public school places is a negative function of prefectural income.

1. Prefectural budgets versus prefectural income

As noted above, one might expect supply to be positively related to per capita income (PCI) in the prefecture, since PCI determines its local tax base. However, this relationship may not hold because of the method of local funding in Japan. Basically, prefectural funds come from two sources: local taxes and central taxes which are 'shared' with prefectures, on the basis of 'need'. The latter constitute almost 40 per cent of total prefectural budgets over-all and go mainly to low-income prefectures. Thus, the supply of public goods, including educational expenditures, depends on local tax plus shared tax, the former positively, the latter negatively related to per capita income, so the net impact of per capita income on educational expenditures depends on the relative strength of these two factors. This is largely an empirical question, since there is no strong theoretical reason to predict on *a priori* grounds which of these two effects will be larger.

We depict this situation in Fig. 10.2, where we show the trade-off between public and private goods faced by a prefecture. Lines *AA*, *BB* and *CC* represent the public–private budget constraints faced by three prefectures with different incomes, in the absence of shared taxes. These lines show the different combinations of public and private goods that each prefecture can purchase with its total income. All prefectures are presumed to have the same population size and tastes, but different incomes, hence a different local tax base. With the given utility function (see $U_A U_A$, $U_B U_B$ and $U_C U_C$, which depict utility as depending on consumption of public and private goods), the equili-

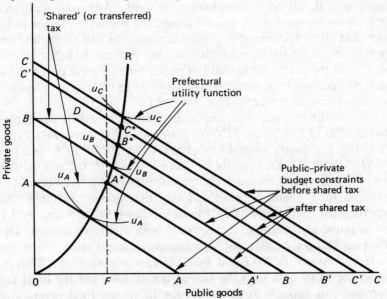

Figure 10.2 Trade-off between public and private goods

brium points lie along OR. Each point on OR gives us the combination of public and private goods that allows some prefecture to achieve the highest possible level of utility, given its income. As we move north-east along OR, we move to prefectures with higher incomes, hence higher utility levels.

Now suppose shared taxes are instituted. Rich prefectures such as C pay taxes to the central government, which shrinks their own budget constraint to the left, e.g. to $C'C'$. This prefecture now consumes at point C^*, less public and private goods than it did previously. On the other hand, poor prefectures such as A and B receive positive transfers, which can only be spent on public goods. Since this gives such prefectures a free gift of public goods, it moves their budget constraint to the right. For example, if the tax share is amount AA^*, the budget constraint for prefecture A become AA^*A'. This prefecture can still have, at most, OA of private goods, gets a free gift of AA^* of public goods, and can trade off private goods for public beyond that if it wants more. In this case it does not do so and instead stops at point A^*. Prefecture B, which gets a shared tax of BD, does supplement this up to point B^*, in order to reach its highest possible utility level. Thus prefectures A, B and C end up consuming almost the same amount of public goods A completely out of transfers, C completely out of local taxes, and B out of a combination of both. Although wealthier prefectures consume more private goods, the shared tax seems to be such that all prefectures spend approximately the same amount (per capita) on public goods, regardless of their income. In other words, because of the particular method of public finance, local government budgets and supply of public services appear to be largely independent of prefectural per capital income (PCI).

To examine this question empirically, we regressed (i) per capita shared taxes ($PCSHT$) on PCI; (ii) per capita local taxes ($PCLT$) on PCI; (iii) per capita shared + local taxes (PCT) on PCI, and (iv) $PCSHT$ on $PCLT$. Our results are given in Table 10.1. The numbers in Column B tell us how much the 'dependent variable' rises or falls in response to a one-unit change in the 'independent variable'. As expected, the coefficients of PCI in determining $PCSHT$ and $PCLT$ are negative and positive, respectively, both highly significant. The effect of PCI on PCT is not significantly different from 0 and the trade-off between $PCSHT$ and $PCLT$ is approximately -1. That is, as per capita income rises the shared tax declines but the local tax increases just enough to substitute for it, so the total prefectural budget, hence the supply of public goods, is largely independent of per

Table 10.1   Shared and local taxes as dependent variables

Dependent variable	Independent variable	B	t*	R²
PCSHT	PCI	− 0.13	8.3*	0.69
PCLT	PCI	0.11	12.8*	0.78
PCT	PCI	− 0.01	0.6	0.01
PCSHT	PCLT	− 1.1	8.9*	0.64

*Indicates significant results at 0.1 per cent level.

capita income. In other words, wealthier prefectures will not, in general, have a larger budget for public goods, despite the greater demand there. The high significance of our results (see Column *t**) indicates it is unlikely they could have occurred by chance.

2.   Relative income elasticity of public education

Of course, if higher income prefectures spent a higher proportion of their public budgets on education, this could still imply a higher educational budget per capita (*EDBUDG*) and a positive relationship between prefectural income and supply of public school places. On *a priori* grounds, there is no reason to expect such an effect. We tested it empirically by regressing % *EDBUDG* (percentage of local government budgets spent on elementary plus secondary education) on *PCI* (per capita income – the total income constraint) and *PCT* (per capita shared plus local taxes – the public goods constraint) which, as we know from the above analysis, is independent of *PCI*. Our results showed that % *EDBUDG* is negatively related to *PCT* (indicating a higher 'public budget elasticity' for other services), while the impact of *PCI* was not significant.

We also regressed *HSEDBUDG* (public high school spending per capita) on *PCI* and *PCT*. Our results are given below.

$$HSEDBUDG = 2945 - 0.816PCI + 0.027PCT \qquad R^2 = 0.36$$
$$\quad\quad\quad\;\; (7.6)* \quad\; (4.93)* \quad\quad (0.02)$$

(Numbers in parentheses are *t*-statistics and * indicates coefficients are significantly different from 0 at 0.1 per cent level in all equations.)

While this equation only explains about one-third of the variance in *HSEDBUDG*, it appears that spending at the secondary level actually declines as *PCI* rises. Evidently, high income prefectures choose to spend more on elementary education and other public services, consistent with the hypothesis that they leave secondary education to the private sector.

3.   Supply and the quantity–quality trade-off

Even if they had the same *HSEDBUDG*, we might expect wealthier prefectures to spend more on each child in a secondary school, and to supply places for fewer children. This is because the demand for quality education is likely to be higher in prefectures with higher per capita incomes (a positive income-elasticity of demand for quality) and because at the same time, the private sector can be utilised to provide more spaces for all who are excluded from the public schools. Because the public sector need not provide space for everyone, it can choose to provide fewer and more expensive places, and wealthier prefectures will often do this. In that case, the supply of public school places will be negatively related to prefectural income and demand for private school places positively related to prefectural income. In other words, higher quality in public schools (measured, e.g., by expenditures per student), in the face of inflexible government budgets and declining high school budgets, leads to a smaller public educational sector, hence a larger private sector, in Japan. (Note that this is the opposite of the situation in open-access school systems with zero excess demand, such as are found in the USA, where higher quality may attract more people to the public schools, hence may lead to a larger public school budget and a smaller private sector.)

To test empirically the relationship between prefectural income and school quality, we regressed *PSS* (per student expenditures in public high schools, a proxy for quality) on *PCI*, *PCT* and *HSEDBUDG*. The results, presented below, indicate that *PSS* is independent of *PCT* but positively related to *PCI* and *HSEDBUDG*. That is, the income elasticity of demand for quality leads high income prefectures to spend more per student, hence to provide fewer public school places, than poorer prefectures, a negative income elasticity of supply.

$$PSS = -17.16 + 0.22PCI - 0.225PCT + 0.173HSEDBUDG \qquad R^2 = 0.45$$
$$\quad\;\; (0.14) \quad\; (5.04)^* \quad\;\; (0.73) \qquad\; (5.42)^*$$

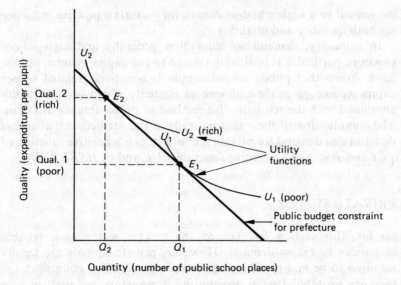

Figure 10.3 Quantity–quality trade-off in public education

This situation is depicted diagrammatically in Fig. 10.3, which shows the quantity–quality trade-off faced by prefectures with the same *PCT* and *HSEDBUDG* but different *PCI*s. We are arguing, and the regression above confirms, that these prefectures will have different preferences about public quantity and quality, the poor prefecture operating on indifference curve U_1U_1 and choosing point E_1, the rich prefecture choosing E_2, or higher quality but correspondingly lower public school quantity.

Further confirmation is provided by regressing the number of public school places per hundred population (*PUB*), the public supply variable, on *PCI*, *PCT* and *HSEDBUDG*.

$$PUB = 3.12 \quad -0.001PCI \quad +0.001\ PCT \quad +0.001HSEDBUDG$$
$$\quad\quad (4.9)^* \quad (5.04)^* \quad\quad (0.81) \quad\quad\quad (4.94)^* \quad\quad R^2 = 0.75$$

While public school quality is positively related to *PCI*, public school quantity is negatively related. (Not surprisingly, *HSEDBUDG* – a movement to a higher budget constraint – exerts a positive influence on both quantity and quality.)

In summary, demand for education generally and high school places in particular is positively related to per capita income, but we have shown that public school supply is negatively related to per capita income, given the high income elasticity of demand for quality combined with the redistributive method of public finance in Japan. The combination of these factors leads to the prediction that excess demand and demand for private school places is a positive function of *PCI* and *PSS* and a negative function *PUB* and of *HSEDBUDG*.

PRIVATE SUPPLY

So far, this section has viewed the private sector as a reliable responder to excess demand. However, private schools are legally required to be non-profit in Japan (as in many other countries); i.e. they are prohibited from distributing a monetary residual to their owners and ownership cannot be sold for monetary returns. Therefore, the private sector will respond only if there are sufficient entrepreneurs willing to start schools for motives other than dividends or capital gains. Not only does the presence of such entrepreneurs increase private supply, it also diminishes the pressure on local government to increase public supply. We therefore considered the possibility that the availability of non-profit entrepreneurship varies among prefectures, helping to explain the variation in the role of the private sector. How can we measure this potential entrepreneurship?

We have observed that in other countries organised religion, particularly Christianity, plays an important entrepreneurial role in the non-profit sector, and that appears to be true in Japan also. Christianity has typically used education as an instrument of taste-formation, an important proselytising tool. Christian missionaries have historically provided the capital, cheap labour, and organising skills necessary to start private schools, at low cost, and have also served as role-models for indigenous educational entrepreneurs. Approximately one-third of the private schools and universities in Japan have been started by religious organisations, most of them Christian. We would, therefore, expect the private educational sector to be larger in prefectures with a large Christian-missionary influence, and in our final regressions we included variables to measure this. As we show below, these were generally significant.

REGRESSION ANALYSIS

Thus, the equations estimated had 'percentage of total high school enrolments in the private sector' (%*PVT*) as the dependent variable, per capita income (*PCI*) as a major independent variable. It has been suggested that private schools are more likely to develop in urban areas, where demand is concentrated, tastes and income are diverse and entrepreneurship prevalent. To test for this possibility, two alternative exogenous 'urbanisation' variables were included: population per square kilometre (*DENS*) and percentage of population in dense areas (%*DENS*). To measure the impact of private (religious) supply, two alternative measures of missionary influence were used: percentage of Christian clergy relative to population (*CHRCL*), and a dummy for the presence of two or more Christian higher schools prior to the Second World War (*CHRSCH*).

In some equations *PSS* and/or *HSEDBUDG* were added as independent variables indicating the educational budget constraint and the quantity–quality trade-off in the public sector. In other equations PUB was added, to show directly how excess demand declines as PUB increases. Finally, we have argued that the private sector arises mainly from excess demand for pre-university education. If this is so, %*PVT* should be smaller when the academic share of public school places (%*ACPUB*) is high, the vocational share low, and we test this by including %ACPUB in our full equations. Appendix 2 gives some comments on our statistical methodology. What did we find? The key results are presented in Table 10.2.

First, per capita income is indeed positive and significant in all formulations. In the two-variable equation with *PCI* and *CHRSCH* or *CHRCL*, a high *PCI* signifies a high demand for education and also serves as a proxy for a low public supply stemming from a choice of quality over quantity. When we add *PUB*, *PSS* and *HSEDBUDG* as explanatory variables, only the demand function remains for PCI and its size and significance therefore decline.

Relatedly, the 'urbanisation' variables are significant when added as a second variable (to *CHRSCH*) but not when added as a third variable (to *CHRSCH* and *PCI*). One may infer, then, that density and urbanisation do help to explain the development of a private sector in education but much of this operates through their correlation with per capita income – which also appears to be true of other countries we have studied.

As expected, *PUB* is always negative and highly significant.[2] The

Table 10.2 Percentage of secondary school enrolments in private schools (%PVT) as dependent variable

Adj R²/F	Const	PCI	DENS	%DENS	CHRSCH	PSS	HSEDBUDG	PUB	%ACPUB
.64 (42.51)**	-16.7 (2.72)**	0.026 (5.89)*			6.1 (2.95)**				
.5 (24.34)*	18.0 (15.23)*		0.004 (3.54)*		8.7 (3.7)*				
.49 (22.7)**	9.9 (3.27)**			0.25 (3.25)**	5.7 (1.88)***				
.64 (27.75)***	-18.1 (2.06)***	0.027 (4.12)*	-0.0003 (0.23)		6.2 (2.93)**				
.64 (27.84)***	-16.0 (2.49)***	0.025 (4.39)*		0.03 (0.38)	5.6 (2.21)**				
.64 (27.7)*	-17.0 (1.88)	0.026 (5.79)*			6.1 (2.82)**	0.001 (0.04)			
.73 (41.45)*	17.2 (1.64)	0.017 (3.61)*			6.1 (3.36)*		-0.01 (3.75)*		
.8 (60.55)*	47.4 (3.95)***	0.008 (1.69)***			3.7 (2.27)***	0.05 (4.21)*	-0.02 (6.14)*		
.81 (39.9)*	23.0 (2.54)*	0.01 (2.22)*			4.9 (2.99)*			-11.8 (5.8)*	-0.15 (2.34)***
.81 (41.15)*	60.3 (4.45)***	0.01 (2.17)*			4.8 (2.95)**	-0.008 (0.87)		-12.4 (6.3)*	-0.14 (2.24)***
Sample means	%PVT = 22.7	1442	594	45.4	.3	563	1761	3.1	64.7

* = significant at .1% level; ** = significant at 1% level; *** = significant at 5% level
One tail tests were used, except for constant

same is true (but to a slightly lesser extent) of %*ACPUB*. *HSED-BUDG*, too, is significant and negative, consistent with our prediction that a larger *HSEDBUDG* implies a larger supply of public school places, hence a smaller left-over demand for the private sector. The impact of *PSS* is somewhat more complicated. To the degree that some people opt for the private sector because of low quality in the public sector, we would expect *PSS* to exert a negative influence on %*PVT*. This appears to be the case, for example, in regressions we have run for the USA.[3] On the other hand, it was argued above that the public sector in Japan is generally considered the high quality sector and is usually filled to capacity; people do not opt out to get higher quality. Moreover, we have seen that higher public quality is associated with lower public quantity, ceteris paribus. If this is so, we would expect %*PVT* to be a positive function of *PSS* if *HSEDBUDG* is controlled. But if *HSEDBUDG* is not controlled, a high *PSS* could either be a proxy for a high *HSEDBUDG*, or could signify a choice of quality over quantity along a given *HSEDBUDG*, the former leading to a low %*PVT*, the latter leading to a high %*PVT*, so if these two effects cancel each other out, the impact of *PSS* would not be significantly different from 0. Also, once *PUB* is controlled *PSS* should not have a significant effect. Our results were consistent with these expectations. When *HSEDBUDG* was in the model, PSS was significantly positive but when *HSEDBUDG* was taken out, and/or PUB was put in, PSS became insignificant – as expected.[4]

As for the two 'religion' variables, *CHRCL* and *CHRSCH*, these were considered as alternatives. *CHRCL* was usually significant, *CHRSCH* always significant, and their quantitative effects were very similar. In the two-variable models *CHRSCH* yielded the highest R^2 but in the three- or four-variable models *CHRCL* gave the best fit. *CHRSCH*, the existence of at least two Christian higher schools before the Second World War, explicitly captures and emphasises an historical element, suggesting that the private sector tended to perpetuate itself, if started early, before the rapid growth of government schools. We also experimented with 'percent of the population that is Christian' as the 'religion' variable. This did not turn out to be significant, while the presence of Christian clergy or early Christian schools was significant. Also, %*PVT* enrolments is a much larger number than 'percentage of the population that is Christian' (about 1 per cent). Both these observations are consistent with our interpretation that in Japan religion is operating as a supply-side rather than a demand-side variable. Several results with CHRSCH are presented in Table 10.2.

The two equations with CHRSCH and CHRCL that are most enlightening and consistent with our model are:

$$\%PVT = 23.0 + 0.01PCI + 4.9CHRSCH - 0.02HSEDBUDG$$
$$(2.54)^{***} \quad (2.22)^{***} \quad (2.99)^{***} \quad (6.14)^*$$

$$+ 0.05PSS - 0.15\%ACPUB \qquad R^2 = 0.81$$
$$(4.21)^* \quad (2.34)^{***}$$

$$\%PVT = 59.2 + 0.01PCI + 224CHRCL - 13.9\,PUB$$
$$(4.73)^* \quad (2.4)^{***} \quad (4.1)^* \quad (7.75)^*$$

$$- 0.005PSS - 0.11\%ACPUB \qquad R^2 = 0.84$$
$$(0.62) \quad (1.98)^{***}$$

*For significance see Table 10.2.

These equations demonstrate that high demand (from *PCI*), low public supply (from a combination of *PUB* and *%ACPUB* or from *HSEDBUDG* and *PSS*), and a large supply of non-profit entrepreneurs (from *CHRSCH* or *CHRCL*) all lead to a large private sector, as predicted. These results are also consistent with similar regressions we have run for the USA, Holland and India, in which per capita income and religious variables always play a major role in explaining why the size of the private sector varies across states, and with cross-national regressions in which stage of development, religious heterogeneity and public supply explain differences among countries.[5]

THE POLITICAL ECONOMY OF SHARED AND LOCAL TAXES

We return now to the crucial questions of (i) why the rich prefectures do not raise their taxes, thereby providing more public quantity as well as quality, and (ii) why the poor prefectures are able to get so much in transferred taxes for public goods from the central government. Several explanations are possible, the main ones consistent with the collective choice model presented in Chapters 4 and 9 which argues that public–private outcomes are consistent with the interests of the dominant political group.

On the first question: the 'shared tax' being transferred away from wealthy prefectures of course limits their ability to spend on public or private goods. Moreover, wealthy prefectures may fear that a rise in local taxes and expenditures would increase the defined level of 'need' elsewhere, hence would increase the 'shared tax' they would have to pay others. The early development of the private sector may have served as an escape valve in these prefectures, providing an alternative to and therefore diminishing the political pressure for more public spending and production. (Also, inter-prefectural mobility may limit the ability of one prefecture to raise its taxes relative to others; people in high tax-brackets may simply be driven out of the prefecture if they value low taxes more than public goods. This certainly occurs in the USA; it may, however, be less likely to occur in Japan.)

Most important, as we have seen in Chapter 8, educational expenditures in Japan represent a redistribution from the rich to the poor, i.e. the tax share of the rich is high and far exceeds their enrolment share. The upper classes, therefore, would resent higher local taxes that would permit both quantity and quality. This group gains if taxes, hence subsidies to others, are kept low, even if this means they must buy their own education (and other services) privately. The fact that wealthier prefectures do not have a larger public budget than poor prefectures suggests that the upper classes have enough political power to prevent large-scale income redistribution within their own localities. The fact that quality rather than quantity is chosen in these prefectures is also consistent with their preferences; it enables the upper classes to use the public schools. This is similar to our finding in Chapter 8, that the limited spending for education nationally implies limited income redistribution, political power for the upper classes.

In contrast, our analysis of shared taxes shows that the poor prefectures, which tend to be rural, have enough political power to secure a redistribution from rich urban prefectures; their ability to do so is enhanced by the fact that they are large in size (compared with other modern countries) and overrepresented (relative to population) in the powerful Japanese Diet (Parliament). This redistribution allows them to provide education and other public goods publicly, at no cost to themselves, rather than privately. Conversely, having obtained the redistribution one would expect them to be pleased with the central government. Therefore, we would expect support for the ruling party, the Liberal Democratic Party (LDP) to be negatively correlated with prefectural income and with percentage of private education, but positively correlated with per capita shared tax, and indeed, this is the case. Regressions with 'percentage of voters supporting LDP in the

1980 elections' as the dependent variable, *PCI*, %*PVT*, and *PCSHT* as the independent variables, have coefficients which are negative, negative and positive respectively. When all three variables were included in the same equation, they had the right sign but none was significant, although the combined R^2 was 0.44 and the *F* test indicated that the results as a whole were significant ($F = 11.36$) – a finding that is associated with collinearity, or high correlation among the independent variables. When they were run in three separate equations, each coefficient was highly significant – consistent with our view that these effects are strong, not additive, but simply different ways of saying the same thing (see Table 10.3).

Thus, the wealthy urban prefectures satisfy their demand for education and other public goods privately, to limit redistribution within their borders, while the poorer rural districts provide their education publicly, with 'free' funds supplied by others, a beneficial arrangement which is consistent with their support of the party in power, the LDP.[6]

Table 10.3 Dependent variable: percentage support for LDP

Independent variable	Constant	B	t*	R^2
PCI	104.0	−0.04	5.4*	0.39
%PVT	70.1	−0.76	4.7*	0.33
PCSHT	34.6	0.20	5.0*	0.36

*Indicates significant results at 0.1 per cent level.

APPENDIX 1: LIST OF SYMBOLS AND DATA SOURCES

(all data are averages denoted by prefecture)

PCI   per capita income, 1979, in thousand yen (*Japan Statistical Yearbook*, 1982, p. 545)

PCSHT   per capita shared tax, 1979, in thousand yen (*Japan Statistical Yearbook*, 1982, pp. 520–2)

PCLT   per capita local tax, 1979, in thousand yen (*Japan Statistical Yearbook*, 1982)

PCT   per capita shared plus local tax, 1979, in thousand yen (*Japan Statistical Yearbook*, 1982)

%EDBUDG   percent of prefectural and local budgets spent on education, 1979 (*Japan Statistical Yearbook*, 1982)

HSEDBUDG   spending in public high schools per hundred population, 1979 (*Japan Statistical Yearbook*, 1982)

PSS   per student spending in public high schools, 1979, in thousand yen (*Japan Statistical Yearbook*, 1982, p. 644)

%PVT   percent of total high school enrollments in private schools, 1980 (*Summary of Educational Statistics*, 1982, pp. 126–81)

CHRCL   percentage of Christian clergy relative to population, 1980 (*Japan Statistical Yearbook*, 1982, pp. 16, 670–71)

CHRSCH   dummy for presence of two or more Christian schools at junior high school level or above, prior to the Second World War (*Christian Education in Japan*, 1932)

DENS   population per square kilometre, 1981 (*Japan Statistical Yearbook*, 1982)

%DENS   percentage of population in densely populated areas, 1980 (*Japan Statistical Yearbook*, 1982)

PUB   number of public school students (1980) per hundred population (1979) (*Japan Statistical Yearbook*, 1982, p. 6; and *Summary of Educational Statistics*, 1982, pp. 120–3)

%ACPUB   proportion of public school places in academic rather than vocational course, 1981 (Report on Survey of School Standards, 1982, pp. 200, 201, 243, 250)

%LDP   percentage of voters supporting LDP in 1980 elections (*Japan Statistical Yearbook*, 1982)

APPENDIX 2: STATISTICAL METHODOLOGY

One theoretical problem with estimating *%PVT* directly, using a linear probability model, is that the predicted value of *%PVT* may be >1 or <0 for some prefectures, even though the acutal value can never be >1 or <0. In reality this did not turn out to be a problem for us since it only occurred twice in all our regressions, and then only by very small negative amounts.

Because of this possible problem another technique known as logit analysis is sometimes used in situations where probabilities are being estimated. In logit analysis we estimate the log of the odds of *%PVT*, $LOP = \ln[\%PVT/(1 - \%PVT)]$. Then, the predicted value of $\%PVT = 1/[+e^{-E(LOP)}]$, which can never be >1 or <0. We used both methods and found they gave very similar results.

We also found that a statistical problem known as heteroscedasticity was present in the logit model, and this we corrected for using weighted least squares. This changed the coefficients slightly but it did not change any of our results regarding statistical significance. Heteroscedasticity was not present in the linear probability model.

In this chapter we present the results of our estimation of *%PVT* using the linear probability model. This is the most direct method and it happens to give the best fit in this case. Since practically none of the predicted values were out of bounds and since heteroscedasticity was not present, this method seems superior to the logit method for our purposes – but our basic conclusions would not be changed if we used the logit model, with either weighted or unweighted data.

11 Recent Government Reforms – Two Case Studies

In the 1960s and 1970s two important reforms were instituted in Japanese education, designed to make the public schools more egalitarian and the private sector more like the public. A system of random assignment to Tokyo high schools was introduced in the 1960s, and substantial subsidies to private schools and universities were granted in the 1970s. As is often the case, the results of these reforms differed considerably from their intent – and in ways from which important lessons are to be learned.

THE INTRODUCTION OF GOVERNMENT SUBSIDIES TO PRIVATE SCHOOLS

In the late 1960s a wave of student unrest swept Japan – especially unsettling in a country which prides itself on common goals and cooperative behaviour. At the same time, the LDP electoral majority decreased to its lowest point since the Second World War; the LDP's agricultural stronghold was declining and it was particularly weak among the growing urban middle class. In effect, the 'median (or "typical") voter' had shifted from countryside to city and to stay in power the LDP had to respond to a new set of political preferences. Spurred by these developments, the government undertook a major re-examination of its policies in the fields of education and social welfare, culminating in a decision to increase expenditures in both areas.[1] In a major deviation from past policy, substantial subsidies were granted to private high schools and colleges. (At the same time, ironically, the opposite was happening in England: government payments to 'direct grant' schools were being phased out, forcing them to rely completely on private funding. The direct grant schools, of course, were highly selective and élite, quite different from the private schools in Japan).

The main reason given for the subsidies was the desire to improve quality in the private sector, by raising expenditures per student. Also

166

to be noted was the strong student resistance to increases in tuition fees, hence the inability of the schools to repay the huge bank loans upon which their expansion of the 1960s had been based. As shown in Table 5.1, debt service had caught up to debt finance by 1970. Many universities were reporting deficits rather than the surplus to which they had been accustomed, and the banks were worried.[2] The initiation of subsidies by the government at this crucial time is consistent with the premise of implicit insurance: if the banks would provide the loans when they were needed (in the 1960s), society at large would see to it that the schools had the wherewithal to repay.

Large private sectors are rarely found in modern countries without subsidies, but which is cause and which effect is less clear. In the case of Japan the subsidies were a consequence of a large private sector, which the country could not afford to lose, but they also served to keep the private sector large at a point when it might otherwise have failed.

A new quasi-governmental organisation, the Foundation for the Promotion of Private Schools (*Shinko–Zaidan*), was created to distribute the grants and subsidised loans. Tables 11.1 and 11.2 demonstrate that between 1970 and 1982, the amounts of such subsidies rose from 8.3 billion yen (5 000 per student) to 300.8 billion yen (140 000 per student), at the high school level. For higher education, the subsidies rose from 20.5 billion yen (15 000 per student) in 1971 to 371.6 billion yen (224 000 per student) in 1981. Almost 30 per cent of

Table 11.1 Subsidies to private high schools

	Local government		National government*		Total	
	Total (in bn yen)	Per student	Total (in bn yen)	Per student	Total (in bn yen)	Per student
1970	8.3	5 000			8.3	5
1972	23.5	14 000			23.5	14
1974	70.5	38 000			70.5	38
1976	109.1	51 000	18.0	10 000	127.1	60
1978	154.9	69 000	44.1	24 000	198.0	93
1980	189.1	84 000	70.0	37 000	259.1	121
1982	220.3	99 000	80.5	41 000	300.8	140

* Began in 1975
Sources: Japan National Federation of Private Junior and Senior High Schools Assoc., 1982; and *Mombusho*, 1981, p. 44.

Table 11.2 Subsidies to private higher education

	Total (in bn yen)	Grants	Loans*	Donations**	Total subsidies per student
1971	20.5	20.1		0.4	15 000
1972	62.8	30.3	30.0	2.5	44 000
1974	117.9	71.3	37.4	9.2	75 000
1976	193.4	129.5	55.9	8.1	117 000
1978	277.9	197.7	74.0	6.2	163 000
1980	339.1	260.3	71.8	7.0	199 000
1981	371.6	284.1	80.5	7.0	224 000

*A small portion of these loans went to private high schools.
**These are private donations, mainly from large corporations, that were eligible for tax deduction if funnelled through the Foundation for the Promotion of Private Schools.
Source: Data on subsidies was provided to us by the Foundation for the Promotion of Private Schools. Subsidies per student are our calculation.

current private educational expenditures are now covered by government subsidies.[3] How were these subsidies allocated and what were the consequences?

High school subsidies are provided and disbursed by the prefectures, with the amount and mechanism varying from one prefecture to another. In a typical prefecture near Tokyo which we examined in some detail, the subsidy increases per pupil for schools that charge lower tuition fees and have lower student/faculty ratios. Although the Ministry of Education sets a recommended subsidy level, prefectures may deviate from this, but the variation across prefectures has been narrowing since the subsidy programme began. Our prefecture stuck closely to the Ministry guideline, since they would have to bear most of the additional cost.

At the university level, the basic ingredient is a subsidy per student of up to 50 per cent of operating expenses. In an attempt to control total enrolments, hence to limit government outlays, an enrolment quota is set for each university and the subsidy per student declines if the quota is exceeded (the allowable subsidy is multiplied by the ratio of authorised to actual students).[4] In order to encourage schools to increase their revenues from sources other than fees (e.g. income from endowments, gifts or business activities) the subsidy rate is higher for schools with a low ratio of tuition fees to expenditures. To encourage quality improvements, the subsidy is greater for schools with a lower student-faculty ratio, and with higher research expenditures.[5] This has also meant that the 'better' schools, such as Waseda and Keio, have been the largest recipients of subsidies – consistent with the general hierarchical pattern in Japanese education.[6]

What were the consequences? If entry of private schools and expansion of old ones were permitted, we might have expected an increase in private sector size and a decrease in its price, because of the subsidy. This has occurred in many other countries when subsidies were introduced. However, this did not occur in Japan. Price did not fall in the private sector, students did not flow out of the public sector, and market shares remained roughly constant.

We observe from Tables 11.3 and 11.4 that the public to private tuition fee differential decreased substantially, both at high school and university levels. This, however, was the result of huge increases in tuition fees in the public sector rather than cuts in tuition fees in the private sector, where fees have continued to rise in real as well as nominal terms. Between 1973 and 1982, average tuition and other fees rose fourfold in private high schools, sixfold in public high schools. In universities these numbers were five and ten, respectively.

The failure of the private sector to cut tuition and other fees and increase enrolments has several plausible explanations. First, the initial point may have been below long-run equilibrium levels at which all costs were covered; as we have noted, many schools were on the verge of bankruptcy. Second, aggregate demand to the private sector may have been viewed as inelastic, given that most students would have preferred the more prestigious public institutions, if admitted, and private schools may have communicated with each other about the disadvantage of price wars. Third, there may have been an implicit market-sharing agreement between public and private sectors, i.e. an agreement to stabilise sectoral shares, upon which the subsidy scheme was contingent. Existing schools would have been dissuaded from increasing enrolments by such an agreement. Indeed, our discussions with officials in one prefecture are consistent with this view. This would also have been consistent with the Japanese consensus approach to decision-making. Finally, the government, whose permission would have been needed to start new schools and universities, substantially tightened its standards after 1970. All these explanations contributed to the outcome, but the last two are probably most important, suggesting that implicit and explicit government policies that accompany the subsidies can shape many of the effects; these are not immutable.

Table 11.3 Impact of the subsidies on private/public differentials in high schools

Per capita expenditures	1973		1980
(in thousand yen)			
Public	275.0		599.0
Private	196.9		546.0
Private/public	0.7		0.9
Student/faculty ratios	1970		1982
Public	19.1		17.2
Private	26.8		23.1
Private/public	1.4		1.3
Space per student	1974		1981
Public	10.0		11.5
Private	7.6		9.2
Private/public	0.8		0.8
Tuition and other fees per student	1973	1977	1982
Public	11 000	40 000	69 000
Private	93 000	302 000	402 000
Private/public	8.6	7.6	5.8
Tokyo: tuition and other fees per	1970		1982
1st year student			
Public	10 000		68 000
Private tuition			
and other fees	129 000		565 000
Private/public	12.9		8.3

Sources: Tables 6.2, 7.1, 7.5 and 7.7. Note that 1973 data on tuition and other fees is from a different source from data for 1977 or 1982. Hence the absolute numbers may not be completely comparable; in particular, the 1973 data probably omit some first-year fees in the private sector. Tokyo data is from: *Report on Issues of Political and Economic Questions in Public and Private Education*, p. 53.

While private enrolments did not increase, neither did they decline, despite the quotas that were built into the subsidy scheme. Most schools and universities continue to accept many more students than the allowed quota because the marginal costs are small and the additional tuition far exceeds the loss in subsidy. Thus, in 1981 the ratio of actual students to quota at universities was 150 per cent.[7] An incentive scheme that induces schools to reduce enrolments will not work unless it replaces the marginal profits they could otherwise earn,

Table 11.4   Effect of the subsidies on private–public differentials at universities

Per capital expenditures (in thousand yen)	1973		1980
Public	909.4		1982.0
Private	343.5		848.0
Private/public	0.38		0.43
Student/faculty ratios	*1970*		*1982*
Public	11.2		8.1
Private	37.3		25.6
Private/public	3.3		3.2
Space per student	*1974*		*1981*
Public	26.4		24.1
Private	8.7		9.2
Private/public	0.3		0.4
Tuition and after fees per student	*1973*	*1977*	*1982*
Public	31 000	146 000	316 000
Private	161 000	494 000	801 000
Private/public	5.2	3.4	2.5

Sources: Tables 6.2, 7.1, 7.5 and 7.7. Note that 1973 data on tuition and other fees are from a different source from data for 1977 or 1982. Hence the absolute numbers may not be completely comparable. In particular, the 1973 data probably omit some first-year fees in the private sector.

and this is too expensive for the government, when marginal costs are low and marginal revenue high. Moreover, the formula used for calculating the subsidy gives a declining marginal penalty as enrolments increase. Therefore, once a school has made the decision to exceed the quota, it will probably ignore the penalty and do so by a large amount.

The incentive scheme has had a clear impact, however, in other respects. Data on 'quality' indices such as expenditures per student and student/faculty ratios were presented earlier, but selective numbers are repeated here, in Tables 11.3 and 11.4, to demonstrate the effect of the subsidy.

The public–private differential in expenditure per student has clearly decreased, especially at the high school level. To a very small extent, this may be due to converging student/faculty ratios in the two sectors. However, for the most part the public–private ratios of real inputs have been unchanged. Instead, the most dramatic change has occurred with respect to teacher salaries, a factor which was not even mentioned in the initial scheme. As shown in Table 11.5, teachers in the private sector previously earned much less than those in the public sector – but by 1980 this relative position was reversed! In fact, the salary rise accounts for the largest part of the increase and convergence in expenditures per student, much more than the real gains noted above. (Interestingly, the private kindergartens did not get subsidies and the relative position of their teachers did not improve over this period.)

How do we explain this development? The more elastic the product

Table 11.5   Effect of the subsidies on teachers' monthly salaries (in yen)

High School				
Salaries for teachers,				
age 35–9	*1965*	*1971*	*1974*	*1977*
Public	48 100	76 000	133 000	178 800
Private	42 400	73 900	127 600	188 300
Private/public	0.88	0.97	0.97	1.05

University				
Salaries for teachers,				
age 50–4	*1965*	*1971*	*1974*	*1977*
Public	96 400	147 000	223 800	306 700
Private	82 500	139 400	218 400	321 700
Private/public	0.86	0.95	0.98	1.05

*Salaries for lecturers**		
	1975	*1981*
Public	197 200	273 500
Private	169 900	300 900
Private/public	0.86	1.1

Kindergarten				
Average salaries for				
kindergarten	*1965*	*1971*	*1975*	*1977*
Public	45 000	64 300	117 400	166 000
Private	28 600	46 200	76 900	120 700
Private/public	0.64	0.72	0.66	0.73

*Full professors and assistant professors experienced similar increases in relative salaries over this period.
Sources: 1971–7 data from: *National Educational Standards*, p. 94; 1965 data by age from *Educational Standards in Japan*, 1970, p. 226; data on lecturers' salaries provided by Shogo Ichikawa, National Institute of Educational Research.

demand and inelastic the supply of teachers, the more we would expect this outcome in a normal profit-maximising market situation. But here we are dealing with non-profit enterprises operating in what is probably a negotiated market between government and private schools. Given that non-profit enterprises cannot legally distribute the subsidies to owners in the form of higher profits, and given the fact that market shares (i.e. total enrolments) were probably predetermined, this meant that the subsidies could either be passed on to a given number of consumers in the form of lower tuition fees or to producer-workers in the form of higher wages and a larger quantity of inputs. The former might give schools the opportunity to be more selective among students, the latter the opportunity to be more selective among faculty and to provide better instruction, each improving its 'quality' and prestige in different ways. We conjecture that the school managers opted for some combination of these alternatives which maximised their utility, a combination which showed up in a dampened rate of increase in tuition fees, a modest decrease in student/faculty ratios, and a dramatic salary rise.

In the long run this may mean that higher quality teachers can be attracted, but in the short run it simply means that the same teachers get more money. This outcome is also consistent with observations in other countries: one of the main effects of government subsidies to education is a redistribution to teachers and, indeed, they are often the major group lobbying for such subsidies and benefitting from them.[8] Clearly, producer interests as well as and often even more than consumer interests are involved. But the teachers are political enemies of the ruling party, the LDP, in Japan. The Foundation is now considering adding another term to its incentive formula, designed to prevent private school salaries from rising faster than (and therefore pulling up) those in public schools.[9]

Note that the institution of subsidies did not bring with it extensive regulation in Japan, as it did in many other countries.[10] Perhaps this was because the academic content of the schools was already tightly controlled by the Ministry of Education, while the huge financial variations within the private sector would have defied uniform standards. Three important regulatory devices, however, were included. First, the Ministry of Education was instructed not to permit the establishment of new colleges or universities, a slowdown which has indeed occurred, as already noted. This was necessary to prevent the subsidies from being open-ended – a blank cheque – as has been the case in other countries. Second, the Ministry was given the right to withhold subsidies from, cut off faculty salaries in, and, indeed, close down, any institution where there were continued student revolts. The ultimate object of the reform was to end the revolts and, given the threat and the subsidy (the stick and the carrot), this right of closure has never had to be used.[9] Third, all private schools are now required to submit detailed financial statements to the Foundation, one object being to detect instances of disguised profit distribution. In most countries private schools are reluctant to provide such information, and it is therefore exceedingly difficult to obtain. In Chapter 5 we observed that disguised profits may constitute one rationale for the founding of private schools. Discussions with Foundation and Ministry officials indicate that instances of inflated salaries of founders, lucrative business contracts, etc., have indeed been noted – but may now be inhibited by the financial reporting requirement. In this sense, the subsidy scheme has made some school founders worse rather than better off (and some have voluntarily turned down the subsidies, as a result).[11]

THE TOKYO REFORM

Periodically, Japanese local governments have undertaken 'egalitarian' measures designed to equalise public schools, eliminating the rigid pecking order described above. The most important such reform was instituted in the Tokyo high school system in 1967. Whereas, in the past, students could apply to more than one public high school and attend the best one at which they were accepted – a system which leads to a ranked stratification of students and schools – after 1967 students were given much more limited choice. The city was divided into several small districts, each containing some 'good' and some 'bad' high schools. Students could apply to one such district but within each district they were randomly assigned by a computerised process designed to equalise student quality across schools. The intent was to mitigate the extreme differentiation in academic climates and reputations. What was the effect?

We would predict that random assignment of students would equalise the public schools, but those who cared most about the quality of education, the academic climate and reputation of their school (and could afford the price) would opt out to the private sector. And that is exactly what happened. Tokyo public schools were indeed 'equalised', dropping entirely from the national 'top ten' list which they had previously dominated. Whereas in most prefectures public high schools are clustered at the top (academic) or bottom (vocational), of the pecking order, in Tokyo they are now clustered in the middle. The total number of graduating seniors from Tokyo public schools admitted to national universities dropped precipitously.

The converse was happening in the private sector. Students who were dissatisfied with the public high schools to which they were assigned, shifted to private schools. These schools, facing an increased demand for their services, could respond by increasing their capacity (admitting more students) or becoming more selective; we know, with hindsight, that they chose the latter.

What objectives and constraints led to this decision? First of all, a model of prestige maximisation would produce similar results; American and British private schools would probably react to increased demand by becoming more selective, hence more prestigious. Second, the government was busy opening new public schools during this period, and probably would not readily have granted charters to new competing private high schools. As discussed earlier, we infer that a 'gentlemen's agreement' existed between the public and private sectors to maintain stable market shares, indeed, to permit the public share to grow slightly. Such an agreement could be reinforced by the locally-administered system of subsidies to private high schools, instituted in the early 1970s, which made it important for private schools to keep the goodwill of public officials. Most important, since the total number of places in the public sector remained unchanged, aggregate demand left over for the private sector may not have changed either, but the nature of the demand certainly did change: the better students now preferred the private schools.

As a consequence of all these factors, the Tokyo private schools became more selective with respect to student intake, which improved their examination scores and made them still more attractive to others. A long-standing equilibrium in prestige hierarchy was disturbed and an upward spiral set off for the private sector. Unlike most of the rest of Japan, and unlike the earlier situation in Tokyo, the high schools in Tokyo with the best record of college entrance are now private schools.

Whereas in 1960 fewer than 10 per cent of the students entering Tokyo University were from private high schools, this number had risen to 30 per cent in 1975 and 45 per cent in 1983.[12] In 1955 the top ten high schools supplying students to Tokyo University were mostly public, but by 1975 they were almost all private.[13] With 40 per cent of

Tokyo University students coming from Tokyo prefecture, the Tokyo reform bears much of the responsibility for this change. In 1983, 77 per cent of Tokyo residents entering Tokyo University came from private high schools.[14] Since these private schools have high tuition charges, they are more accessible to the rich. In particular, tuition and other fees are higher in the 'better' private schools with a higher acceptance rate at universities, according to a regression analysis we have conducted (see Chapter 6). Thus, a reform designed to be egalitarian has, in this sense, had the opposite effect.

The exit of students from the academic public schools created some openings there for low-ranked students from poor families who previously were forced to attend vocational public schools or private schools as a last resort. This group did indeed benefit from the reform – but the middle-ranked working-class student lost.[15] Whether this constitutes more or less equity is open to question.

A comparable situation prevails in Kyoto, which greatly restricted the students' choice of public school during the period following the Second World War. In 1975, the 'top twenty' high schools in sending students to Kyoto University did not include one public high school from Kyoto, although public schools from many other prefectures were included.[16] Similarly, when public school redistricting cut off the access of suburban families to Kobe's best public schools, they sent their children instead to a good private school, Nada, which consequently could be more selective and became the 'best' school in the country.[17]

The Tokyo reform, as well as the experience of Kyoto and Kobe, embodies an important lesson for the USA, the UK and other countries concerned with the quality of the public school system. When public schools are varied, competitive and selective, they are more likely to be the preferred schools. Those with higher incomes and taste for education will stay within a differentiated public system because they will probably be grouped with others who have similar characteristics in schools which, because of their high quality student input, achieve a high gross output (better examination results, university entrance rates, etc.). Such schools will therefore have a superior reputation even if they do not in fact have a higher value added for any given student. But their value added may also be higher, because of the peer group effect: students learn more when they are grouped together with other high-achieving students. A differentiated public system has the disadvantage of stratifying opportunities and quality within the public sector, and of putting pressure on students at an early age – for which the Japanese system has been much criticised;

but it has the advantage that the poor will not be excluded from the best schools by purely financial considerations.

A non-selective, non-competitive public school system, on the other hand, offers more uniform opportunity and quality to everyone within it, but also increases the dissatisfaction with the public sector and the outflow to the private sector. And the outflow will come from those willing and able to pay for superior education: those with higher income or taste for education. The private sector will thus become the élite sector and, since academic and price barriers now coincide, the best education (and corresponding jobs) will be less accessible to the poor. As we discussed in Chapter 9, the system which most redistributes public resources in the short run does not necessarily maximise access of the lower classes to élite opportunities, in the long run. In this instance, such a trade-off may have been made. We will return to this theme in the Conclusion, because it embodies one of the major lessons of the Japanese experiment.

The Tokyo reform may be compared with a similar reform which took place in England at about the same time. During the late 1960s and 1970s a massive shift occurred from a highly selective system of secondary education to a non-selective comprehensive system in the public sector. Moreover, in London a system of assignment was instituted which assured a roughly equal ability balance in all schools: families could indicate their preferred choice, but the final match of student to school was made centrally, with a limit placed on the number of high- and low-ability students that each school could have. As in Tokyo, this reform meant that some low-ranking students who previously could not have gained entrance to the academic state (grammar) schools now had the opportunity to pursue a pre-university course in a state (comprehensive) school. Did this also mean that some high-ranking students were now induced to opt out to the private sector, which remained selective?

From the available data, it is difficult to tell. Private schools in England were on top of the hierarchy before the state changeover to comprehensive schools and they remain on top today. Anecdotal evidence suggests that private schools place more weight on academic criteria for admission than they did previously and have become more oriented towards success on the O-level, A-level and university entrance exams. They have even grown slightly in size, despite large increases in fees; however, there has been no large-scale opting out.[18] At the same time, there is much talk of the unhappiness of middle-class parents with the state schools.

The top-rated state grammar schools, whose records were on par

with the private sector, have almost totally disappeared; in this sense
there is an increasing gap between the two sectors. But other state
schools have now improved. Along similar lines, if students learn
more when they are put together with other bright students from high
socioeconomic backgrounds (the 'peer group' effect), it may well be
that lower-ability students from poor backgrounds have gained while
high-ability working-class students have lost as a result of this reform,
raising the same ambiguity regarding equity that we found in the case
of the Tokyo reform.[19]

Unfortunately, we do not have concrete data on the admissions
standards of private schools; secondary exit examinations and university entrance criteria have been modified; and 'value added' by the
schools is difficult to compare when both student intake and output
measures are changing.[20] Thus it is difficult to make rigorous statements about the private reaction to the public reform in England.
However, it does appear that there are winners and losers and the
losers may contemplate cutting their losses by opting out. We will
discuss in the Conclusion some of the forces that limit this effect.

WHAT NEXT?

In 1980 Japan instituted yet another reform, this time at the university
level. Whereas previously each national university held its entrance
examination on a different date, so that students could apply to
several, from 1980 all examinations were to be held on the same date,
so each student can now apply to only one per year. In making this
choice, a student must now assess a university's quality as well as his
chance of passing its entrance exam, with a trade-off between the two.
In the future, some superior students will not apply to the best
university to which they might be admitted, because of the possibility
of failure; instead, their places will be taken by less able, less risk-
averse students. This will downgrade the selectivity of the top
universities and raise that of the lower-ranked national universities.
Some good students, aiming too high, will fail the national examination they choose and will, instead, enter a private university (which
still hold their entrance examinations on different days); this option,
of course, is mainly open to wealthier families. One would predict that
this reform, also intended to make the public sector more 'egalitarian', will have the effect, as well, of upgrading and enlarging the
private sector, and increasing the advantage accruing to families with
high incomes – but it is still too early to test this hypothesis.

Summary and Conclusions

In this final section we summarise our findings, place them in international perspective, and draw out implications for public policy in the USA and the UK.

Perhaps the most striking observation is that, under certain circumstances, it is possible to have widespread educational consumption without public production or large direct public expenditures. The rate of high school graduation in Japan is greater than that in the USA and the rate of higher education attendance is second only to the USA. Much of this expansion has taken place within the past three decades, and within the private sector.

In many economic models of education, it is presumed that government financing is necessary in order to achieve a socially optimal amount, i.e. individuals would underspend privately because of the existence of externalities and the inability to use human capital as collateral for loans. In Japan the private benefit has apparently been great enough to induce large numbers of people to seek high school and university education, and much of this has been financed through personal savings (in effect, parents make 'loans' to their children, in return for an implicit promise that children will help to care for their parents later on).

The private sector developed in Japan, not because of cultural heterogeneity, as in other countries (e.g. Holland and Belgium) but as a response to excess demand, which the public sector was not satisfying. Stimuli from the labour market led to a strong effective demand, with many people willing to finance their own education, convinced that it was a good investment as well as an important status symbol. Supporting this effective demand were two unusual conditions: a sustained *GNP* growth rate of 10 per cent per year during much of this period and a household plus business savings propensity of over 30 per cent, possibly the highest in the world, with 'education of children' given as one of the major reasons for saving.[1] It is not clear that the same private demand for education would develop under more normal growth and savings conditions.

We have discussed the variety of pecuniary and non-pecuniary motives which led to a large private supply, with many people willing to start private schools and universities, despite their non-profit status. The role of religious entrepreneurs deserves special note in Japan, as in most other countries. Much of this role was historical:

179

Christian missionaries trying to use education to mould tastes and values prior to the Second World War. Nevertheless, their legacy remains, their example spread to secular entrepreneurs, and in prefectures where their presence was strongest the private sector is now largest, receiving substantial public subsidies. While religious organisations were closely tied to the state (the public non-profit sector) in other countries and in earlier periods, where separation exists they often constitute an alternative service provider to the state, in the private non-profit sector, and this is also true of Japan.

Underlying the elastic supply of private schools in Japan have been three major facilitating factors: they could be small-scale with low capital requirements, hence few natural entry barriers; cheap labour was readily available to run them; and bank credit was extended on a privileged basis, to cover the cost of buildings and equipment. The first of these resulted from the nature of the educational system: high schools are typically small-scale, while Japanese universities often specialise in a narrow group of subjects rather than 'covering the waterfront' and private universities usually chose the inexpensive labour-intensive fields. A society wishing to develop its pure science, basic research, or comprehensive universities may not be able to do so through a privately financed educational system.

The second factor arose from basic labour-market institutions: early retirement for men and limited opportunities for women provided a rich source of underemployed educated labour upon which the private schools drew heavily. While the details vary from country to country, low-wage labour is a common characteristic of private schools, particularly those with no government subsidies. In a labour market without these artificial barriers, the private schools would have had a difficult time competing for teachers and covering their costs. On the other hand, given the existence of these pockets of underemployment, the private sector was more able than the public to utilise the resources and keep its costs low.

The third factor – access to bank credit – resulted from a conscious decision by the ruling group to foster private sector growth, as a preferable alternative to public production and spending. We shall discuss later other facilitating actions by the government, without which the dramatic expansion of private education could not have taken place.

The presence of these three factors meant that individual entrepreneurs could easily start and operate a private school or university, benefiting in the form of wages, prestige and, possibly disguised profit distribution. The risk was small, donations of labour and capital were not needed, opportunity costs were covered. The absence of one or more of these facilitating factors in other sectors, such as social service, health and culture (which could not be small-scale or did not have access to liberal bank loans), meant that the private non-profit sector grew more slowly, despite limited government production, in these areas.

Probably the key force explaining the growth of the private educational sector in Japan, as elsewhere, was conscious government policy. Government set the stage for excess demand by creating a mass high quality public elementary school system but a limited supply of public secondary schools and universities. Government then permitted private high schools and universities to start, greatly relaxing the standards it had previously set, and encouraging banks to make liberal loans available during a period of credit rationing. Finally, when many schools were in danger of bankruptcy, unable to repay their debts, government followed through on what may be viewed as implicit insurance of bank loans, by agreeing to subsidise the schools.

This observation, too, is common across many modern countries; rarely do we find a large private sector in education without some direct or indirect support. This positive correlation occurs both as cause and effect: such support seems necessary for the private sector to grow large and, once large, it is politically powerful enough to obtain further support.

Ultimately, then, the role of the private sector depends on public policy and this, in turn, depends on who controls the government. In Japan, a policy of limited public spending, hence substantial private production and financing of secondary and higher education, was shown to be in the best interest of the supporters of the Liberal Democratic Party which governed the country during most of the post-war period: big business and its managerial classes (who did not want to subsidise the education of the working class beyond compulsory levels) and rural areas (where demand for education was low). We may contrast Japan with Sweden, another culturally homogeneous country with rapid post-war educational growth, where a governing party with a very different support base (the Social Democratic Party, affiliated with the unions) reached the opposite decision about how this expansion should be funded and produced – there, the private sector hardly exists.

What difference does it make that much of secondary and higher education is privately provided in Japan? The public and private schools differ in selectivity and prestige, public ranking over private in most but not all cases. This is contrary to what we expect in the USA and the UK but is a common pattern in many countries, particularly in developing countries where the private sector is driven by excess demand. In content and technique, however, public and private schools are very much alike: high schools following the same curriculum and training their students to pass the university entrance examinations, and universities seeking to make their students attractive to the most prestigious employers. In the basic sense of what is taught, how, and towards what end, the public *versus* private division of responsibility may not matter.

One of the major differences between the public and private sectors has been the lower cost per student, particularly lower teacher costs, and the greater variability in these costs, in the private schools. This cost advantage, which may be alternatively interpreted as evidence of lesser quality or greater efficiency, was an important factor leading to the development of a large private sector. Had all the enrolment expansion been confined to the public sector, it would probably have involved more uniform and higher expenditures per student (possibly better quality), hence a greater opportunity cost of education. The trade-off between cost or quality on the one hand and quantity on the other probably would have meant that fewer students could have been accommodated. The private sector, then, enabled more rapid growth in the face of limited resources. This may be an important lesson for other countries wishing to educate large numbers with scarce resources.

However, the very growth of the private sector ultimately set up political pressure for subsidies and, as we have seen, the main effect of the subsidies was to reduce the cost advantage. This impact is paradoxical because it also reduces the higher efficiency and social rate of return which private schools have hitherto offered. Thus, the private sector is tending to look even more like the public, a convergence which is also true of large private sectors in other modern countries.

Possibly the major consequence of privatised education concerns its distributional consequences. It is important to note that the disparate distributional consequences stem, not from the private production of education, but from the private funding that was used in Japan. In modern countries where private production is a response to cultural heterogeneity, as in Holland and Belgium, private schools tend to be

publicly funded and the class breakdown and distributional consequences of the public and private systems are very similar.

Tuition-fee barriers to private high schools in Japan have led them
to serve the rich, disproportionately. At the university level tuition-fee
barriers have kept the poor out of private institutions while cultural
barriers and foregone earnings have kept them out of public institutions, so the two sectors are equally skewed (albeit not so much as in
many other countries). Nevertheless, tax shares exceed enrolment
shares for the upper classes in both sectors, so that government
funding would be redistributional in either sector. Under these
circumstances, heavy reliance on a private system, which is largely
privately funded, implies that opportunities for such redistributions-
in-kind through education have been by-passed, as a matter of
deliberate public choice.

The recently instituted subsidies represent a partial reversal of this
policy, designed to enlarge the support base of the LDP. Subsidies
increase the amount of redistribution for the given group of students
and, if they result in reduced tuition fees, hence larger enrolment
shares for the lower classes, they spread the redistribution still further.
While the first of these effects has already happened in Japan, the
second, as we have seen, is more problematic. To the extent that the
subsidies simply raise teacher salaries rather than increasing real
inputs or lowering tuition fees, they may constitute a redistribution to
the producers and not only the consumers of education.

*   *   *

What are the implications of the Japanese experience for public policy
in the USA and the UK, the question with which we started? If we
shift to a policy of tuition tax-credits or vouchers, i.e. more government support of private schools, can we learn something from Japan
about how the public and private sectors would respond?

An important caveat is in order here, before we begin, concerning
the interconnectedness between the various levels of the educational
system and between the educational system and the rest of society. In
order to understand the Japanese high schools, we must understand
how the universities choose their students, and in order to understand
the universities, we must understand employers' recruitment patterns.
Conversely, if we want to change the educational system, perhaps we
must start by changing the labour market, since education is often
viewed as a means to an economic end by its consumers. In all cases,

our ability to make such changes will be limited by historical legacies, e.g. entrenched interests and reputational factors which change only with a lag. The public and private schools operate within this broader societal and historical framework, which differs from country to country, and one must be particularly careful, therefore, in drawing cross-national inferences. With this caveat firmly in mind, let us see what lessons we in the West can learn from the Japanese experience.

If public policies favouring the private sector (such as tuition tax-credits or vouchers) were implemented here, what effect would this have on prices and enrolments in the private sector? Note that in Japan, the benefits from subsidies were not passed on to consumers in the form of lower prices;[2] we did not observe a higher quantity demanded, an enlarged capacity of old schools or an influx of new ones. We did, however, observe higher expenditures per student, and particularly higher teacher salaries, developing in the private sector. In effect, much of the subsidy was transferred to the teachers. While the higher salaries may improve new teacher quality in the long run, they also constitute a large infra-marginal rent to the existing stock of teachers in the short run. Would this be the effect in the USA and the UK too?

In the USA and the UK, any public support for the private sector is unlikely to be accompanied by an agreement on fixed market shares, as may have been the case in Japan. The outcome is therefore more likely to depend on competitive market forces, such as the elasticity of product demand and factor supply in the private sector, the availability of new non-profit entrepreneurship, and the trade-off in the older schools between quantity and selectivity, as well as the teachers' non-market response. It is difficult, therefore, to draw a direct inference on this question from the Japanese case.

Suppose, for example, that a voucher or subsidy scheme were instituted in the USA. As one possibility, the higher revenue per student (from public plus private sources) might induce schools to take in more students (assuming they faced an excess demand or waiting list to begin with). As another possibility, the existing schools might lower their price to compensate for the voucher, using (student) quality rationing in place of price rationing. This would increase their prestige but it would not increase private school places in the short run. In both cases, the increased profitability and/or prestige of private education might attract new entrants to the market, lower the price and increase places supplied in the long run – provided that individuals perceived incentives for starting schools and accreditation barriers did not deter them. As still another possibility, the teachers might organise and try to capture the subsidy in the form of higher wages, in which case the lower price and higher enrolments might never occur. This was roughly the situation in Japan. Most likely, the final outcome in the US or UK would be some combination of these three scenarios.

Probably the larger the subsidy the more likely that some of it would initially be passed along to students in the form of a lower effective price; hence also, the more likely it would be to attract lower-income students and alter the socioeconomic class breakdown of private enrolments. In other words, the consequences of a large subsidy scheme, as in Holland, might be qualitatively different from that of a small subsidy scheme. In general, however, empirical evidence from other countries as well as Japan suggests that not all the subsidies would be passed forward, that costs rise and producers as well as consumers in the private sector gain when subsidies are instituted.

If enrolments increased in the private sector would this lead to diminished support for US public schools? The answer to this question is unclear on *a priori* grounds. Suppose that school budgets are responsive to the preferences of the voting population, in a democracy. Then, if many people have opted out to the private sector, the average or median voter may prefer lower expenditures per pupil in the public schools. This effect will be particularly strong if the people who opt out are those who care most about quality of education.

On the other hand, the tax-cost per unit of quality in the public schools is now less, because there are fewer public school places; hence this is a counteracting force which may lead to higher expenditures per student, particularly if people outside the system derive some external benefit from having a well-educated citizenry. In the short run, additionally, institutional constraints (e.g. job security arrangements) would limit the feasible decline – but probably in ways that would be detrimental to quality for the system as a whole. (For example, more secondary school teachers might be needed but these could not be hired because the system is declining and has more than the optimal number of tenured primary school teachers.) The net outcome regarding expenditure per student and quality in the public schools is therefore uncertain on *a priori* grounds and this outcome might be quite different in the short and long run.

In Japan, when subsidies were instituted, political support for the public sector, which remains costly and prestigious, did not erode. As fiscal problems have hit Japan, public universities have been expected to cover slightly more of their expenses out of higher fees, but this was a cost they could readily absorb given their hugh excess demand. Thus empirical experience of other countries suggests that a large subsidised private sector need not imply declining expenditures and quality in the public schools. This is especially the case if the private subsidies depend positively on public school budgets (as in Holland) or if public schools are allowed to compete for students (as in Japan). More will be said on the latter point later.

One of our fears is that a more privatised system is likely to segregate along religious or linguistic lines, an outcome some (but not all) would like to avoid. Such segregation, of course, did not happen in Japan – largely because Japan is such a homogeneous country, culturally and ethnically. However, it has occurred in other countries, such as Holland, Belgium and India. Japan's homogeneity gave it more latitude *vis-à-vis* its educational system than other countries have, because it did not have to pay a price in terms of religious or ethnic segregation for its heavy reliance on private education. The probability of cultural segmentation in other countries is underlined when we realise that much of the entrepreneurship in the private educational sector comes from religious organisations or from groups with particular linguistic, caste, or national affiliations. Thus, this fear cannot be ignored, even though it did not materialise in Japan. Many private schools would probably be ideologically motivated and affiliated in the USA and the UK, particularly if they are expected to operate as non-profit organisations.

Another fear is that a more privatised system will lead to greater segregation by socioeconomic class, with the rich having access to higher quality education than the poor. Together with class segregation might go racial segregation, in many American and English cities. This, again, is a problem that Japan does not face, given its racial homogeneity.

Unfortunately, we do not have data broken down by institution in Japan, which would be most useful for analysing this question, since we are really interested in socioeconomic segregation on an institution-by-institution basis.[3] We do know that in the USA and the UK the non-religious part of the private sector tends to be more biased towards the rich than is the public sector, but this is not true of higher education in Japan nor is it true in other countries (such as Holland) where private sectors play an important role. In Japan, as we have seen, public universities are the preferred élite institutions and the socioeconomic background of students is roughly the same in the two sectors. Government regulation of tuition and admissions criteria may strongly influence the outcome here; for example, subsidised private schools in Holland are not permitted to charge tuition fees, which means that they are not limited to the upper classes by price rationing. However, such controls are not found in Japan. What, then, determines the class structure of the two sectors?

We suspect that a key to the answer is found in the degree of variety and selectivity within the public sector: public schools and universities are more likely to remain on top of the hierarchy if they are differentiated, competitive, selective. Those public schools which select the best students will also have the best 'perceived quality' according to two indices which students and their families frequently use: first they have the highest gross output (exit examination results, university entrance rates, job success), and this enhances their reputation even if it is due to their superior student input rather than to the value added by the school. And second, they may indeed have a superior value added, because of the peer-group effect which we discussed in the preceding chapter. In this scenario, families with greater incomes and taste for education will have better access to the top-rated public schools and many will satisfy their preferences within the public sector as their first choice on academic grounds, even apart from any price advantage they receive. The public sector will serve the middle and upper classes as well as the poor under these circumstances, so its socioeconomic composition may not be very different from that of the private sector. (Of course, great differences will exist within the public sector regarding student input, gross output and reputation, with the lowest-ranked schools such as vocational schools in Japan and the old secondary moderns in England serving a predominantly lower-class constituency.)

When public schools cannot differentiate their product and select their students, because this is proscribed as a matter of policy, private schools will leap into the vacuum. They will offer programmes designed to attract the best students and they consequently offer the highest 'perceived quality' for the reasons already given. This quality advantage then offsets the price advantage of the public sector, for those who can afford to pay. Both because of the price rationing, and because the 'best' students academically are likely to come from families with high incomes, such families will now be overrepresented in the private sector relative to the public. The public schools are now more homogeneous in terms of student input, gross output and reputation, but they serve a very different socioeconomic clientele from the private schools. This is the 'creaming and segregation' outcome which is feared by the opponents of privatisation.

Underlying this situation, where public schools cannot compete and select, is the educational redistribution which they bring about because of the peer-group effect upon student learning. Suppose the amount learned by each student depends positively on the ability and prior achievement (sometimes proxied by the socioeconomic background) of other students in the classroom. Then each student will prefer to be in an environment where the average level of ability is high and, in a school or classroom with mixed ability, education or human capital can be said to be 'redistributed' from the more to the less bright. In a public school monopoly, bright students have no recourse against this redistribution. However, once private schools are permitted (as they are in all democratic countries), high ability students may opt into them, thereby preventing educational redistribution, and those who do so will come disproportionately from families with high incomes.

Viewed in this light, devices such as neighbourhood schools combined with residential segregation and internal tracking or setting in the USA and the UK may be viewed as attempts by the middle and upper classes to institute quasi-selection when explicit selection along academic or income lines is proscribed, in order to prevent the redistribution of human capital and enable them to use the state schools. However, these mechanisms are effective only to a limited extent. Together with the price advantage of public schools they serve to keep most of the middle classes in the public sector – but more dissatisfied than in the Japanese schools, which are openly and strongly selective.

Some policy-makers would favour more proscriptions against private schools, to minimise still further opting-out and enable greater homogeneity and redistribution of human capital through the public schools. Private schools can be denied tax advantages and can be socially frowned upon, as in Sweden, but to prohibit them entirely runs counter to libertarian values in most modern democracies. Others would favour the opposite approach, facilitating parental satisfaction via exit to the private sector by policies such as tuition tax-credits or voucher schemes. If these are implemented, the above analysis suggests that they must be accompanied by policies permitting more differentiation and competition within the public sector in order to maintain the status hierarchy. (Higher spending within the public sector is another possible compensatory policy, although its marginal productivity is far from clear.) Otherwise, public schools will lose more of their good students (i.e. those of high ability and upper socioeconomic background) and their perceived quality will consequently decline still further.

The notion of differentiation, competition and selection within the public sector runs counter to the American ideal of open-access public schools and the more recent English concept of comprehensive education, at the primary and secondary levels. However, it is not inconsistent with practices such as school choice based on residential proximity and internal tracking, which, as already noted, achieve some of the same ends. Moreover, it is consistent with magnet schools that are developing in some American cities, with specialised schools (such as the Bronx High School of Science or the High School of Music and Art in New York City) which have long had excellent reputations, with the possibly emerging British colleges of technology, and with highly competitive and selective, hence prestigious, public universities such as the University of California, Oxford and Cambridge.

In other words, if the middle and upper classes in a society will strive to avoid a redistribution of human capital through the peer-group effect, we may face an unhappy choice between differentiation versus homogeneity, perceived quality and parental satisfaction on the one hand *versus* equality on the other, within the public sector. The Tokyo reform led to a system which is more equal but has less perceived quality. Similarly, we may face a trade-off between equality within the public system and equality overall, as when the Tokyo reform led to more equality in the public sector but perhaps less for society overall, because of a larger gap between the public and private sectors.

When differentiation and selectivity are permitted, those with greater incomes and taste for education remain within the public system, which helps to maintain its status and political support. In this situation the rich can benefit disproportionately from the 'élite' schools without paying privately (a non-egalitarian outcome), but at the same time those students from poor backgrounds who qualify are not kept out of these schools by high tuition-fee barriers. When the student bodies in the public schools are homogenised, roughly the same mixture in one school as another, those with greater incomes and taste for education are more likely to flee to the private sector, which then becomes élite. The public system is more equal, but is also perceived as being lower quality, a source of parental discontent. And since the poor are now excluded from the élite schools by economic as well as social barriers, it is not clear that equality for society as a whole has gone up. These are important trade-offs and social choices for the USA and the UK to consider, particularly if we move towards policies favouring greater privatisation of education.

Notes and References

Introduction

1. For fuller accounts of the private sector in other countries, see Estelle James, 'Benefits and Costs of Privatized Public Services: Lessons from the Dutch Educational System'; 'The Private Provision of Public Services: A Comparison of Sweden and Holland'; 'The Public/Private Division of Responsibility for Education: An International Comparison; and 'Differences in the Role of the Private Education Sector in Modern and Developing Countries'.
2. See Andrea Boltho, *Japan: An Economic Survey, 1953–63*, pp. 166–8.
3. Data supplied by Japan Foundation for the Promotion of Private Schools.
4. See, for example, William Cummings, *Education and Equality in Japan*; Thomas P. Rohlen, *Japan's High Schools*, and W. Cummings, I. Amano and K. Kitamura, *Changes in the Japanese University*.

1 Historical Background of Education in Japan

1. For fuller accounts of the history of Japanese education, see: *Japan's Modern Educational System: A History of the First Hundred Years*; Ronald Anderson, *Education in Japan: A Century of Modern Development*; Herbert Passin, *Society and Education in Japan*. R. P. Dore, *Education in Tokugawa Japan*, is the basic source for information presented on Tokugawa education.
2. Dore, *Education in Tokugawa Japan*, p. 81.
3. Koya Azumi, *Higher Education and Business Recruitment in Japan*, p. 83.
4. Dore, *Education in Tokugawa Japan*, p. 181.
5. Ibid, pp. 317–22.
6. Marjorie Cruickshank, *Church and State in English Education,* pp. 11, (17); Brian Simon, *Studies in the History of Education 1780–1870*, p. 347; and E. G. West, *Education and the State*, pp. 126–173.
7. Dore, *Education in Tokugawa Japan*, pp. 271–90.
8. Anderson, *Education in Japan*, p. 15.
9. *Japan's Modern Educational System: A History of the First Hundred Years*, p. 464.
10. Illustrative enrolment figures for 1931 are: elementary schools, 10 381 290; middle schools, 336 186; girls' high schools, 362 625; vocational schools, 292 015; youth schools (part-time schools for employed youth), 1 271 970; higher schools, 20 844; universities, 69 985; all normal schools, 41 617. (Ministry of Education, Science and Culture, *Japan's Modern Educational System*, pp. 458–9).
11. Illustrative enrolment figures for 1981 are: elementary schools, 11 924 653; junior high schools, 5 299 282; high schools, 4 682 827; junior

colleges, 372 406; universities, 1 822 117 (Ministry of Education, *Mombu Tokei Yoran, 1982*, p. 16).

2 The School Environment

1. William Cummings, *Education and Equality in Japan*. This is the most complete description of elementary schools in Japan. Many of these points have also been confirmed in our own observations and discussions.
2. Ibid, p. 39.
3. John Singleton, *Nichu: A Japanese School* pp. 68–9. This is a classic source on junior high schools.
4. Thomas P. Rohlen, *Japan's High Schools* pp. 128–33. This is the best source of observations of high schools, extensively utilised in the following paragraphs.
5. The following discussion is based on interviews with faculty members and students at national and private universities.
6. Cummings, *Education and Equality*, pp. 159–71; Rohlen, *Japan's High Schools*, pp. 3–5; and our own observations.
7. Rohlen, *Japan's High Schools*, pp. 128–33.
8. *Educational standards in Japan*, pp. 258–9.
9. Rohlen, *Japan's High Schools*, especially chap. 1 and Part II.
10. See *High School Survey Report: The Basis of Private High School Study*.
11. *Educational Standards in Japan*, 1975, p. 35.
12. Cummings, *Education and Equality*, p. 88.

3 Current Issues and non-issues in Japanese Education

1. Also see Benjamin Duke, *Japan's Militant Teachers: A History of the Left Wing Teachers' Movement*; and Donald Thurston, *Teachers and Politics in Japan*. These two books are the standard source on the history of educational politics in post-war Japan.
2. Robert J. Smith, *Ancestor Worship in Contemporary Japan*.

4 Overview of the Private Sector

1. Moreover, the ratio of standard deviation to mean was lower in Japan than in most other countries, indicating a relatively small variability in achievement. See Torsten Husen (ed.), *International Study of Achievement in Mathematics*, vol. II, pp. 2–3.
2. See L. C. Comber and J. P. Reeves (eds), *Science Education in Nineteen Countries*, pp. 119, 120, 122, 150. In contrast, England ranked below average in both the science and mathematics tests for the population as a whole, but above average when only the small population of students in their final year of pre-university education was considered.

3. See Shogo Ichikawa, 'Finance of Higher Education', in W. K. Cummings, I. Amano and K. Kitamura (eds), *Changes in the Japanese University* p. 44. Also see OECD, *Reviews of National Policies for Education: Japan*, p. 77.
4. *Mombusho*, p. 36; *Digest of Educational Statistics*, 1982, pp. 65, 92; and Department of Education and Science, *Statistics of School Leavers*, Table CD. Also see Table 1.4 of this book.
5. Ibid. Also see Table 1.3 of this book. For comparison, 43 per cent of the relevant age group entered higher education in the USA and 19 per cent entered higher and further education in England and Wales during this period. See *Educational Standards in Japan*, 1975, pp. 266–7. The relative size of the private sector in Japan varies from 76 per cent to 84 per cent depending on whether we are talking about undergraduates or undergraduates plus graduates, universities or universities plus junior colleges, entering students or all students enrolled.The reader should be aware that in different parts of this book we will be referring to somewhat different concepts and therefore the corresponding numbers given will vary slightly.
6. *Educational Standards in Japan*, 1975, p. 213, gives average years as 11.1 in Japan, 12.0 in the USA, 11.0 in the UK, for age group 25–34, in 1970. By 1980 the Japanese average had become even higher because of the expansion of higher education in the 1960s and 1970s. Data on public–private enrolments in the US is from *Digest of Educational Statistics*, 1982.
7. *Educational Standards in Japan*, 1975, pp. 186, 191, 349, 350.
8. Thus we observe the private percentage peaking in 1964–5, together with the number of high school entrants, both in Tokyo and nationwide. (See Table 1.4 and Ken Ogata, *Introduction to Educational Economics*, p. 136.)
9. For an enlightening description of each of these school-types see Thomas P. Rohlen, *Japan's High Schools*.
10. See *High School Survey Report: The Basis of Private High School Study*.
11. For a breakdown of success rates and *ronin* applicants by field, see *Educational Standards in Japan*, 1975, p. 269. For a clear depiction of changes in proportion of *ronin* entrants, see p. 39.
12. For a fuller discussion of *juku* see Rohlen, *Japan's High Schools*, pp. 87, 101, 104, 107.
13. See T. J. Pempel, 'The Politics of Enrollment Expansion in Japanese Universities', pp. 67–86.
14. Ibid.

5 The Founding Decision: Who Starts Private Schools and Why?

1. Most private schools in the USA are run by the Catholic Church and most non-Catholic schools were started by other religious groups (e.g. Quakers, Congregationalists) even if they have now lost their denomina-

tional connotations. This is true of most private primary and secondary schools as well as illustrious universities such as Harvard and Yale.

In the case of England, the religious affiliation of private schools is much clearer in a historical context: many nineteenth-century schools were non-governmental, started by voluntary religious organisations – the Church of England, the Catholics and the Dissenters. Most of these voluntary schools began to receive modest government subsidies, which increased through the mid-nineteenth and early twentieth centuries. These subsidies now cover all current costs and 85 per cent of capital costs for 'aided' schools, which are therefore considered part of the state-maintained sector. Only the small non-subsidised sector is now considered private (or independent) in England. However, by definitions used in other countries, subsidised schools run by religious organisations are also considered private and these, in fact constitute the largest part of the 'private' sector in the UK.

2. *Religion in Japan.*

3. As one example of this segmentation: among high schools sending more than half their students to private universities, 60 per cent are private (and often affiliated to a particular university). Among schools sending more than half their students to national universities, 90 per cent are public. See Hata, *Journal of Education Department, Nagoya University*, vol. I, 1975, p. 141.

4. For a general discussion of sales or output maximisation, see William Baumol, *Business Behavior, Value and Growth* (New York: Harcourt, Brace, revised edition, 1967). For a discussion of its importance in Japan, where earnings are typically reinvested and time-horizons long, see Peter Drucker, 'Economic Realities and Enterprise Strategy', in Ezra Vogel, *Modern Japanese Organization and Decision-Making*, pp. 228–244. Sales maximisation may then be a proxy for long-run profit maximisation.

5. *Japan Times*, 2 August, 1983, p. 2.

6. See Ken Ogata, *Private University*.

7. Ken Ogata, *Introduction to Educational Economics: Finance in Private Universities*.

8. See Roger Geiger, *Private Sectors in Higher Education: Structure, Function and Change*.

9. *Educational Standards in Japan*, 1975, p. 356. Some of these 'donations' are required for admission, etc.

10. Ogata, *Introduction to Educational Economics*, pp. 76 and 105.

11. This contrasts with typical 30 per cent debt-financing of enterprises in the USA. See OECD, *Reviews of National Policies for Education: Japan*, p. 159; and Drucker in Vogel, *Modern Japanese Organisation*, pp. 228–44.

12. *Educational Standards in Japan*, 1970, pp. 247–9.

13. See Akira Ninomiya, *Private Universities in Japan*, p. 25; and Shogo Ichikawa in Cummings *et al.* (eds), *Changes in the Japanese University*, p.59.

6 Private Benefits, Costs and Pecking Order among Schools

1. See Ninomiya, *Private Universities*, p. 25, and Ichikawa in Cummings *et al.* (eds) *Changes in the Japanese University*, p. 59. Note that, despite the rise in private/public tuition rates during the 1960s, private tuition per student as a percentage of consumption expenditures per capita in Japan fell over the same period, from 0.62 in 1950 to 0.41 in 1965 and 0.35 in 1968. Indeed, the rapid increase in income in post-war Japan was a major factor facilitating the rapid increase in private universities and private tuition. For purposes of comparison, in 1965 average private university tuition constituted 0.65 of consumption of per capita in the USA and average public university tuition was 0.15 of consumption of per capita in the UK. See *Educational Standards in Japan*, 1970, p. 250.
2. Ibid. Of course, much of the current expenditures at American universities are for research rather than instruction while at Japanese private universities there is little research. See James, 'Product Mix and Cost Disaggregation', and Chapter 7.
3. Masakazu Yano, 'Rates of Return from Education and Resource Allocation', in Shogo Ichikawa, *Allocation of Educational Resources in Japan*.
4. Much of the following discussion is about the relationship between university education and the labour market in Japan. The relationship between high-school education and the labour market, during a somewhat earlier period, was explored in Mary Jean Bowman, *Educational Choice and Labor Markets in Japan*.
5. Cummings, *Education and Equality*, p. 209.
6. OECD, *Reviews of National Policies*, pp. 81–2.
7. Rohlen, *Japan's High Schols*, pp. 90–1; and *Sandei Mainichi*, 29 May 1977.
8. Ikuhiko Hata, *A Study of Bureaucracy: Unperishable Power, 1868–1983*.
9. Ibid.
10. *Shukan Yomiuri*, 24 June 1975, and *Sandei Mainichi*, 16 March 1976, as quoted in Rohlen, *Japan's High Schools*, p. 89.
11. See *Social Framework of Private Universities*, pp. 125–90.
12. Cummings, *Education and Equality*, p. 27.
13. *Social Framework of Private Universities*, p. 151.
14. For the relationship between wages and size of enterprise in international perspective, see A. Boltho, *Japan: An Economic Survey*, p. 28.
15. *Educational Standards in Japan*, 1975, p. 268.
16. Ibid, p. 300.
17. Ibid, p. 325.
18. Ibid, p. 109.
19. See Geiger, *Private Sectors*, p. 54.
20. See *High School Survey Report*, part of the *Study on Autonomy and Public Role of Private Schools*.
21. See Masaharu Hata, *Journal of Education Department*, Nagoya University, vol. I, 1975 and vol. II, 1976.
22. Data sources were: *Private School Founders and Their Academic Philosophy; List of Private Junior High and High Schools; Guide to Tokyo Private Junior High and High Schools.*

7   Quality, Efficiency and Social Returns

1. See Ichikawa in Cummings, *et al.*, *Changes in the Japanese University*, pp. 43 and 53. Thus, in Japan the proportion of enrolments in the private sector exceeds the proportion of total educational expenditure in that sector, whereas the opposite is true in the USA.
2. *Educational Standards in Japan*, 1975, pp. 175, 343, and data supplied to us by the National Institute for Educational Research.
3. Our calculations from data supplied by the National Institute for Educational Research.
4. A. Ninomiya, *Private Universities in Japan*, p. 18.
5. *Educational Standards in Japan*, 1975, p. 54.
6. Also see *Educational Standards in Japan*, 1975, pp. 330–1, for similar 1974 data.
7. *Japan Statistical Yearbook*, 1982, p. 630, data for 1980.
8. Calculations made by authors from data supplied by Shogo Ichikawa, National Institute for Educational Research. The last figure relates to forty-two public and fifty-three private universities that grant Ph.D.s in two or more faculties.
9. *Educational Standards in Japan*, 1975, p. 52.
10. OECD, *Reviews of National Policies for Education*, p. 77.
11. Rohlen, *Japan's High Schools*, p. 23.
12. *Educational Standards in Japan*, 1975, pp. 318–20.
13. See Ichikawa in Cummings, *et al.*, *Changes in the Japanese University*, p. 57.
14. See Pempel, 'The Politics of Enrolment Expansion'.
15. *Educational Standards in Japan*, 1975, pp. 318–20.
16. Shogo Ichikawa, 'Educational Expenditure in Real Terms and the Factors for Its Increase', in Ichikawa, *Allocation of Educational Resources*, pp. 39, 244.
17. Data supplied to us by the Foundation for the Promotion of Private Schools.
18. Our own calculations from data supplied by the National Institute of Economic Research.
19. See Rohlen, *Japan's High Schools*, p. 19. Also see *Educational Standards in Japan*, 1975, p. 122, for international comparisons.
20. Moreover, higher education in Japan may be valued for its screening function rather than its function of creating human capital, and class size may be particularly irrelevant to screening. It is also possible that Japanese consumers favour a high-cost public sector and a low-cost private sector, on grounds that expenditures in the former generate externalities (e.g. national prestige) while the latter do not. If cost and quality differentials in these two sectors are desired by society, efficiency comparisons are even more difficult to make.
21. See Husen, *International Study of Achievement*; and Comber and Reeves, *Science Education in Nineteen Countries*.
22. *Educational Standards in Japan*, 1975, p. 323.
23. Ibid, pp. 322, 128–9.
24. See A. Boltho, p. 37, for evidence that age–earnings profiles rise more

steeply in Japan than in most other countries. Teachers' peak salaries in Japan are treble beginning salaries while in the USA they are double beginning salaries.

25. *Educational Standards in Japan*, 1975, p. 323. Converted at 1985 exchange rates.
26. Ibid, pp. 330–1.
27. See Ichikawa in Cummings *et al.*, *Changes in the Japanese University*, p. 44.
28. For a discussion of the lax atmosphere at Japanese universities, based on observations by an American professor who lectured at several, see John F. Zeugner, 'The Puzzle of Higher Education in Japan', *Change*, January 1984, pp. 24–31.

8 Socioeconomic Distribution and Redistributional Effects of Education: Japan

1. A. Boltho, *Japan: An Economic Survey*, pp. 36–7; Masanori Hashimoto and John Raisian, 'Employment Tenure and Earnings Profiles in Japan and the United States', pp. 721–35; and Haruo Shimada, *Earnings Structure and Human Investment: A Comparison Between the US and Japan*.
2. Kikuchi, 'Access to Education and the Income Distribution Effects', in Ichikawa, *Allocation of Educational Resources in Japan*, pp. 152–7.
3. Derived from marriage and fertility data in UN *Demographic Yearbook* for 1958, 1968, 1982.
4. Pursuing the above line of argument further, the first child is in high school when the father is aged 41–8, the second child when the father is aged 45–52. Thus, within the 'relevant' age category 35–54, men who are younger than 45 or older than 48 will have either none or one child in secondary school, while those between the ages of 45 and 48 are almost certain to have one and possibly two. That is, those who are most likely to have a child in high school are middle-seniority within this age group, which would lead the middle quintiles to appear overrepresented, even if access were, in fact, equal for everyone.

   Similar reasoning at the university level (parental ages 40–59) leads us to the expectation that men aged 48–52 are most likely to have a child at university. This is close to but not at the peak earning period. Hence, it may lead to a modest overstatement of the advantage the rich have, at the university level.

   Thus, the relative share of the top income quintiles is most overstated for the primary and junior high levels, where both the public and private sectors are less income-biased than they appear. This distortion is largely absent, however, at the high school and university levels, where differences between the top and bottom quintiles are more likely to be a true reflection of income bias.
5. See Rohlen, *Japan's High Schools*, p. 130.
6. See Cummings, *Education and Equality in Japan*, pp. 225–7.
7. This section draws heavily on data presented in Jyoji Kikuchi, 'Access to

Education and the Income Redistributive Effects', in Shogo Ichikawa (ed.) *Allocation of Educational Resources*. However, in calculating cohort tax and enrolment shares we use a different method from that of Kikuchi.

8. The importance of adjusting for lifetime cohort quintiles is seen if we compare these figures with those presented by Kikuchi in Ichikawa, *Allocation of Educational Resources*, pp. 205–10, where tax and enrolment shares are based on current income for the relevant age group and national income quintiles are used. Kikuchi's results are very sensitive to the age of the family in question, since this determines its tax share, whereas our results, which are based on estimated lifetime tax share within a cohort, are independent of age. For young families, Kikuchi shows a smaller redistrbutive effect than we do at the compulsory and high school levels (because there are few young families in the top quintile, and their apparent tax share declines more than their apparent enrolment share). The opposite is true for older families. We believe it is more valid conceptually to define redistributive effects in a way which depends on lifetime income and standing within a cohort, not on the income and age which a family happens to have in the year their child attended school.

9. Until now we have been measuring redistribution according to students' family background. If, instead, we ask what are the redistributive effects based on students' future income, a stronger difference appears between the two sectors. Given employer recruitment patterns in Japan, public university graduates are likely to end up with the most remunerative and prestigious jobs in civil service and private enterprise. Thus, viewed from the vantage point of family background or future income and status, one could easily argue for subsidising private universities on equity grounds. Also see *Educational Standards in Japan*, 1975, p. 265, and Table 7.9 in this book.

10. In 1973, the government in Japan spent only 5.5 per cent of its national income on education, compared with 7.1 per cent in the USA and 7.7 per cent in the UK. Of this total, 14 per cent went to higher education in Japan, while the comparable figures for the USA and the UK were 23 and 20 per cent respectively. Thus government spending on higher education was only 0.7 per cent of the national income in Japan, 1.1 per cent in the USA, and 1.5 per cent in the UK. See *Educational Standards in Japan*, 1975, pp. 186, 191, 349 and 350.

11. See Table 4.1 and *Educational Standards in Japan*, 1975, pp. 261–9.

12. For example, Cummings, *Education and Equality*, and Pempel, 'Politics of Enrolment Expansion' have not mentioned the Prime Minister's data, relying solely on *Mombusho* data, thereby giving what we believe to be a distorted view of the public–private enrolment bias and changes in enrolment distribution through time.

13. The *Mombusho* data is based on a random sample of 30 000 students who are asked to complete an extensive survey on various aspects of student life, including family income. One stated objective of this survey is to obtain data relevant to the government's loan programme, which is based partially on need. The Prime Minister's data are based on a stratified sample of 8000 households; the households are requested to keep daily

income and expenditure records for six months. This is considered a more reliable data source. This point of view was confirmed to us in conversations with Shogo Ichikawa and in correspondence with Jyoji Kikuchi, who wrote the chapter on income distributional effects in Ichikawa, *Allocation of Educational Resources*, in which much of the data discussed here is presented.

14. Calculated from figures in Thomas Rohlen. 'Is Japanese Education Becoming Less Egalitarian?' p. 43.

9 The Distribution of Education, Income and Political Power: International Comparisons

1. Relative expenditures for each socioeconomic group would have to be adjusted to reflect the higher support grant received by lower-class students on a means-tested basis. However, this does not change the picture very much: relative expenditures per person in the relevant age category are still 5:1 for the top and bottom socioeconomic groups, after this adjustment. See Julian Le Grand, 'The Distribution of Public Expenditures in Education', pp. 63–8. An offsetting adjustment would be necessary to take account of the fact that the upper classes are more likely to attend universities, such as Oxford and Cambridge, with higher expenditures per student.

2. See A. H. Halsey, A. F. Heath and J. M. Ridge, *Origins and Destinations: Family, Class and Education in Modern Britain*, p. 141. Note that 'class' is defined in this study somewhat differently from 'class' in Table 9.1, since Halsey, Heath and Ridge group together skilled and unskilled manual labour in their bottom class, but their overall point continues to apply.

3. Ibid, p. 152.

4. Ibid, pp. 53, 179.

5. 'The Effects of Taxes and Benefits on Household Income, 1977', pp. 97–130.

6. See, for example, W. Lee Hansen and Burton Weisbrod, 'The Distribution of Cost and Direct Benefits of Public Higher Education: The Case of California'; W. Lee Hansen and Burton Weisbrod, *Benefits, Costs and Finance of Public Education*; Joseph Peckman, 'The Distributional Effects of Public Higher Education in California'; Robert J. Hartman, 'A Comment on the Peckman–Weisbrod Controversy'; John F. Crean, 'The Income Redistributive Effects of Public Spending on Higher Education'; Joseph McGuire, 'The Distribution of Subsidy to Students in California Public Higher Education'; Joseph Hight and Richard Pollock, 'Income Distribution Effects of Higher Education Expenditures in California, Florida and Hawaii'; Douglas Windham, *Education, Equality and Income Distribution*; Estelle James, 'Cost, Benefit and Envy: Alternative Measures of the Redistributive Effects of Higher Education'; and Estelle James, 'Product Mix and Cost Disaggregation: A Reinterpretation of the Economies of Higher Education', pp. 157, 186.

7. Hight and Pollock, 'Income Distribution Effects'.

8. Census of the Population, Vol. I, Characteristics of the Population, Chapter D, "Detailed Characteristics," Table 198 for Florida and California (Washington, D.C.: Bureau of the Census, 1970).
9. It is difficult, of course, to separate out the family background and pure school effects in determining whether the school itself enhances life chances. Evidence of school effects at the secondary level for the UK is presented in A. H. Halsey, A. F. Heath and J. M. Ridge, *Origins and Destinations*; for Scotland in Andrew McPherson and J. Douglas Willms, 'Certification, Class Conflict, Religion and Community'; for the US in James Coleman, Thomas Hoffer and Sally Kilgore, *High School Achievement*; and at the university level in Weisbrod and Karpoff, 'Monetary Returns to College Education, Student Ability and College Quality.'
10. *1975–Nen SSM Chosa: Kiso Tokeihyo* (Report of Basis Statistics from the 1975 SSM Survey), as quoted in Cummings, *Education and Equality*, p. 47. For a discussion of the close ties between the large employers' association, the LDP and the Ministry of Education, see Yung H. Park, 'Big Business and Education Policy in Japan', pp. 315–35.
11. *Educational Standards in Japan*, 1975, pp. 214–17.
12. *Japan Statistical Yearbook*, 1972, pp. 65, 104, 642.

10 Analysis of Prefectural Differences

1. Symbols and data sources appear in Appendix at end of Chapter 10.
2. *PUB* was interpreted here as an indication of public supply, since the full time public high schools are filled to capacity, in contrast to the situation in open access systems, where *PUB* would indicate the demand for public education rather than the supply. Thus in Japan the negative effect of *PUB* is interpreted as evidence of excess demand whereas in open access systems it indicates differentiated demand. In either case, in a situation where most age-eligible students attend high school a smaller attendance in public schools necessarily implies larger private enrolments, so the significance of *PUB* and the high R^2 in equations with *PUB* is not as interesting as the significance of other variables and high R^2 of other equations.
3. See E. James, 'The Public–Private Division of Responsibility for Education: An International Comparison'.
4. It is important to note that we have treated *PSS* as a positive indicator of quality, not a negative indicator of efficiency. It would have been useful to include in our regression an indicator of the relative costs of providing equal-quality public and private education. As shown above, expenditures per student in private schools have been 70–90 per cent those in public schools. This might lead people to choose a smaller public system, if they believe that quality is the same in the two sectors and private efficiency is greater. On the other hand, a lower ratio of private to public *PSS* may indicate that private quality is less, not that efficiency is greater. In any event, data on spending per student in private schools was not available by prefecture, so we could not use this ratio in our analysis.
5. E. James, 'The Public-Private Division of Responsibility for Education', and 'Differences in the Role of the Private Education Sector in Modern and Developing Countries'.

6. The wealthy prefectures do end up getting more education than the poor ones. The larger private sector allowed a higher proportion of junior high school pupils to advance to high school in high income prefectures, despite the lower number of public school places there. We estimated this relationship and found:

$$AR = 71.9 + 0.01\ PCI \qquad R^2 = 0.33$$
$$(4.7)*$$

where AR = advancement rate of males from junior high to high school, 1975. According to the above analysis, this is an equilibrium condition resulting from a higher demand for secondary education in high income prefectures, met by a supply from the private sector. Running the same regression based on 1963 data we obtained a larger coefficient of PCI and a higher R^2 – suggesting that disparities in demand for education induced by income differentials have narrowed during the 1960s and 1970s.

$$AR = 44.9 + 0.15\ PCI \qquad R^2 = 0.47 \qquad \text{(data for 1963)}$$
$$(6.1)*$$

11   Recent Government Reforms: Two Case Studies

1. For a discussion of the forces that led to more social service expenditures, see John C. Campbell, 'The Old People Boom and Japanese Policy-making', pp. 321–57.
2. See A. Ninomiya, *Private Universities in Japan*. By 1973 the debt:asset ratio of private universities and junior colleges was over 40 per cent. At least sixty-nine universities were reporting deficits. Also see Ichikawa in Cummings, *et al*, *Changes in the Japanese University*, p. 59.
3. See Ogata, *Introduction to Educational Economics*, p. 189; and Ichikawa in Cummings *et al.*, *Changes in the Japanese University*, p. 61.
4. See Ichikawa in Cummings, *et al.*, *Changes in the Japanese University*, p. 61.
5. Based on A. Ninomiya, *Private Universities*, p. 32, and discussions with officials of the Foundation for the Promotion of Private Schools.
6. Ogata, *Introduction to Educational Economics*, p. 194.
7. Our calculations based on data provided by the National Institute for Economic Research. Ichikawa gives a similar ratio for 1976 in Cummings *et al*, *Changes in the Japanese University*, p. 61.
8. For further discussion of this point, see E. James, 'The Private Provision of Public Services: A Comparison of Sweden and Holland'; E. James, 'Public Policies Toward Private Education'; and E. James, '*The Non-profit Sector: A Research Handbook*.
9. Based on our discussions with Foundation officials.
10. See E. James, 'Public Subsidies in the Private Non-profit Sector'.
11. Approximately seven or eight universities and junior colleges turn down the subsidies each year. The Foundation has also withheld subsidies from

a small number (fifteen to twenty) of institutions each year, because they are delinquent in repaying their loans or have other inadequate procedures. See Ogata, *Introduction to Educational Economics*, p. 194; and Masui Shizeo, *The Social Framework of Private Universities*, p. 177.

12. Rohlen, *Japan's High Schools* p. 21 and article in *Shukan Yomiuri*, April 3, 1983.
13. Rohlen, *Japan's High Schools*, p. 21.
14. Article in *Shukan Yomiuri*, 3 April 1983.
15. See Thomas Rohlen, 'Is Japanese Education Becoming Less Egalitarian?' pp. 37–70.
16. *Sandei Mainichi*, 6 April 1975, p. 172, as quoted in Rohlen, *Japan's High Schools*, p. 89.
17. See Roheln, *Japan's High Schools*.
18. Some supporting evidence on the increasing academic orientation of private schools is given in Irene Fox, *Private Schools and Public Issues*; John Rae, *The Public Schools Revolution*; R. Salter and T. Tapper, *Power and Policy in Education: The Case of Independent Schooling*. Small increases in private–sector size appear in annual publications of the Department of Education and Science and the Independent Sector Information Service (ISIS). The annual ISIS Census also shows private-school fees to be increasing faster than the cost-of-living index or average teacher salaries, over the past decade.
19. For convincing statistical evidence of this peer-group effect (or 'contextual effect') in the Scottish context see J. Douglas Willms, 'The Balance Thesis: Contextual Effects of Ability on Pupils' O-Grade Examination Results', pp. 33–41; J. Douglas Willms, 'Social Class Segregation and its Relationship to Pupils' Examination Results in Scotland', pp. 224–41; and Andrew McPherson and J. Douglas Willms, 'Certification, Class Conflict, Religion and Community: A Socio-historical explanation of the Effectiveness of Contemporary Schools'.
20. One of the main attempts to measure academic value added in public selective versus comprehensive schools, after controlling for student intake, indicates that comprehensives do not do as well as the high-ranking grammar schools, but do better than secondary moderns, which admitted those students who did not get into the selective grammar schools. On average, comprehensives do about as well as the grammar-plus-secondary-modern combination. This evidence is consistent with the importance of the 'peer-group effect' although it does not isolate that effect. See Jane Steedman, *Examination Results in Selective and Non-selective Schools*; and Jane Steedman, *Progress in Secondary Schools*.

Summary and Conclusions

1. A. Boltho, *Japan: An Economic Survey, 1953–64*, pp. 9, 84, 91.
2. It is possible that private tuition fees would have risen much faster without the subsidies; however declines in nominal or real tuition fees were not observed.

3. However, on socioeconomic segregation by school in Scotland, see Willms, 'Social Class Segregation'; McPherson and Willms, 'Certification, Class Conflict, Religion and Community'.

Bibliography

ANDERSON, RONALD, *Education in Japan: A Century of Modern Development* (Washington, DC: HEW, US Government Printing Office, 1975).

AZUMI, KOYA, *Higher Education and Business Recruitment in Japan* (New York: Teachers' College Press, 1969).

BAUMOL, WILLIAM, *Business Behavior, Value and Growth* (New York: Harcourt, Brace, revised edition, 1967).

BOLTHO, ANDREA, *Japan: An Economic Survey, 1953–64* (Oxford: Oxford University Press, 1975).

BOWMAN, MARY JEAN, *Educational Choice and Labor Markets in Japan* (Chicago: University of Chicago Press, 1981).

CAMPBELL, JOHN C., 'The People Boom and Japanese Policy Making', *Journal of Japanese Studies*, vol. 5, no. 2, Summer 1979.

Census of the Population, vol. I., Characteristics of the Population, Chapter D, 'Detailed Characteristics', Table 198 for Florida and California (Washington, DC: Bureau of the Census, 1970).

Christian Education In Japan, Report of a Commission, International Missionary Council, New York, 1932.

COLEMAN, JAMES, HOFFER, THOMAS and KILGORE, SALLY, *High School Achievement: Public, Catholic and Private Schools Compared* (New York: Basic Books, 1982).

COMBER, L. C. and REEVES J. P., (eds) *Science Education in Nineteen Countries* (New York: John Wiley, 1973).

CREAN, JOHN F., 'The Income Redistributive Effects of Public Spending on Higher Education', *Journal of Human Resources*, 10, Winter 1975, pp. 116–23. CRUICKSHANK, MARJORIE, *Church and State in English Education* (London, Macmillan, 1964).

CUMMINGS, WILLIAM, *Education and Equality in Japan* (Princeton, New Jersey: Princeton University Press, 1980).

CUMMINGS, W., AMANO, I. and KITAMURA, K., *Changes in the Japanese University* (New York: Praeger, 1979).

DEPARTMENT OF EDUCATION AND SCIENCE, *Statistics of School Leavers* (London: DES, 1980).

Digest of Educational Statistics, (HEW, US, 1982).

DORE, R.P., *Education In Tokugawa Japan* (Berkeley: University of California Press, 1965).

DUKE, BENJAMIN, *Japan's Militant Teachers: A History of the Left Wing Teachers Movement* (Honolulu: University of Hawaii Press, 1973).

Education in 1960 (Tokyo: Ministry of Education, 1960).

Education in 1968–70 (Tokyo: Ministry of Education, 1970).

Educational Standards in Japan (Tokyo: Ministry of Education, 1964).

Educational Standards in Japan (Tokyo: Ministry of Education, 1970).

Educational Standards in Japan (Tokyo: Ministry of Education, 1975).

'The Effects of Taxes and Benefits on Household Income, 1977', *Economic Trends*, 303 (London: Central Statistical Office, 1979).

FOX, IRENE, *Private Schools and Public Issues* (London: MacMillan, 1985).

GEIGER, ROGER, *Private Sectors in Higher Education: Structure, Function and Change* (Ann Arbor: University of Michigan Press, 1986).

GOLDBERGER, A. S., *Econometric Theory* (New York: Wiley, 1964).

Guide to Tokyo Private Junior High and High Schools (Tokyo to Shiritsu Chugakko Kotogakko Kyokai) (Tokyo: Tokyo Association of Private Junior High and High Schools, 1983).

HALSEY, A. H., HEATH, A. F. and RIDGE, J. M., *Origins and Destinations* (Oxford: Clarendon Press, 1980).

HANSEN, W. LEE and WEISBROD, BURTON, 'The Distribution of Cost and Direct Benefits of Public Higher Education: The Case of California', *Journal of Human Resources*, 4, Spring 1969.

HANSEN, W. LEE and WEISBROD, BURTON, *Benefits, Costs and Finance of Public Education* (L: Markham 1969).

HARTMAN, ROBERT J., 'A Comment on the Peckman–Weisbrod Controversy', *Journal of Human Resources*, 5, Fall 1970.

HASHIMOTO, MASANORI and RAISIAN, JOHN, 'Employment Tenure and Earnings Profiles in Japan and the US', *American Economic Review*, 75, September 1985.

HATA, IKUHIKO, *A Study of Bureaucracy: Unperishable Power, 1968–1983*, Kodansha, 1983 (Kanryo no Kenkyu: Fumetsu no Power, 1968–1983).

HATA, MASAHARU, *Journal of Education Department, Nagoya University*, vol. I, 1975.

HATA, MASAHARU, *Journal of Education Department, Nagoya University*, vol. II, 1976.

High School Survey Report: The Basis of Private High School Study (Tokyo: National Institute for Educational Research, 1977).

High School Survey Report: Study of Autonomy and Public Role of Private Schools (Tokyo: National Institute for Educational Research, 1977).

HIGHT, JOSEPH and POLLOCK, RICHARD, 'Income Distribution Effects of Higher Education Expenditures in California, Florida and Hawaii', *Journal of Human Resources*, 8, Summer, 1973.

HUSEN, TORSTEN (ed.) *International Study of Achievement in Mathematics*, vol. II (New York: John Wiley, 1967).

ICHIKAWA, SHOGO, *Allocation of Educational Resources in Japan* (Tokyo: National Institute for Educational Research, 1978).

JAMES, ESTELLE, 'Cost, Benefit and Envy: Alternative Measures of the Redistributive Effects of Higher Education', in H. Tuckman and E. Whalen (eds) *Subsidies to Higher Education*, (New York: Praeger, 1980).

JAMES, ESTELLE, 'Product Mix and Cost Disaggregation: A Reinterpretation of the Economics of Higher Education', *Journal of Human Resources*, Spring, 1978.

JAMES, ESTELLE, 'Benefits and Costs of Privatized Services: Lessons from the Dutch Educational System', *Comparative Education Review*, December 1984.

JAMES, ESTELLE, 'Differences in the Role of the Private Education Sector in Modern and Developing Countries', International Conference on the Economics of Education, Dijon, 1986.

JAMES, ESTELLE, 'The Private Provision of Public Services: A Comparison of Sweden and Holland', in E. James (ed.), *The Nonprofit sector in International Perspective: studies in Comparative Culture and Policy* (New York: Oxford University Press, 1988).

JAMES, ESTELLE, 'Public Policies Toward Private Education', World Bank Discussion Paper, 1987.

JAMES, ESTELLE, 'The Private Nonprofit Provision of Education: A Theoretical Model and Application to Japan', *Journal of Comparative Economics*, 10, 1986.

JAMES, ESTELLE, 'The Public/Private Division of Responsibility for Education: an International Comparison', *Economics of Education Review*, 1986.

JAMES, ESTELLE, 'Public Subsidies in the Private Non-profit Sector', paper presented at Independent Sector Research Forum, 1985.

JAMES, ESTELLE, 'The Nonprofit Sector in Comparative Perspective' in W. Powell (ed.) *The Nonprofit Sector: A Research Handbook* (New Haven: Yale University Press, 1987).

JAMES, ESTELLE and BENJAMIN, GAIL, 'Educational Distribution and Income Redistribution Through Education', *Journal of Human Resources*, 22, 1987.

Japan Times, 2 August 1983.

Japan's Modern Educational System: A History of the First Hundred Years (Tokyo: Ministry of Education, 1980, translation of 1972 Japanese edition).

Japan Statistical Yearbook, 1982, 1983, 1972.

LE GRAND, JULIEN, 'The Distribution of Public Expenditure on Education', *Economica*, 49, 1982.

List of Private Junior High and High Schools (Zenkoku Shiritsu Chugakko Kotogakko Meibo) (Tokyo: Japan Private Junior High and High School Federation, 1983).

MADDALA, G. S., 'Limited–Dependent Variables and Qualitative Variables in Econometrics', (Cambridge: Cambridge University Press, 1983).

MCGUIRE, JOSEPH, 'The Distribution of Subsidy to Students in California Public Higher Education', *Journal of Human Resources*, 11, Summer, 1976.

MCPHERSON, ANDREW and WILLMS, J. DOUGLAS, 'Certification, Class Conflict, Religion and Community: A Socio-historical explanation of the Effectiveness of Contemporary Schools', in A. C. Kerckhoff (ed.) *Research in Sociology of Education and Socialization*, vol. 6, (Greenwich, Connecticut: JAI Press, 1986).

Mombusho (Tokyo: Ministry of Education, 1981).

Ministry of Education, *Report on University and College Student Life* (Tokyo, 1961).

National Educational Standards (Waga Kuni no Kyuiku Suijen), (Tokyo: Ministry of Education, 1981).

NINOMIYA, AKIRA, *Private Universities in Japan* (Tokyo: Private Universities Union of Japan, 1977).

Obunsha, August, 1983.

OECD, *Reviews of National Policies for Education: Japan* (Paris, OECD, 1971).

Office of Prime Minister, *Annual Report on the Family Income and Expenditure Survey*, (Tokyo, 1976).

OGATA, KEN, *Private University* (Shiritsu Saigaki) (Tokyo: Nihon Keizai Shinbun-sha, 1977).

OGATA, KEN, *Introduction to Educational Economics: Finance in Private Universities* (Kyoiku Keizairon Zyosetsu: Shiritsu Daigaku no Zaisei) (Tokyo: Toyo Keizai Shinposha, 1978).

PARK, YUNG H., 'Big Business and Education Policy in Japan' *Asian Survey*, vol. XXII, no. 3, March 1982, pp. 315–35.

PASSIN, HERBERT, *Society and Education in Japan* (New York: Teachers College Press, Columbia University, 1965).

PECKMAN, JOSEPH, 'The Distributional Effects of Public Higher Education in California', *Journal of Human Resources*, 5, Summer, 1970.

PEMPEL, T. J., 'The Politics of Enrollment Expansion in Japanese Universities', *Journal of Asian Studies*, vol. XXXIII, no. 1, November 1973.

Private School Founders and Their Academic Philosophy (Nihon Chugakko Kotagakko Rengokai) (Tokyo: Japan Private Junior High and High School Federation, 1981).

RAE, JOHN, *The Public Schools Revolution* (London: Faber & Faber, 1981).

Religion in Japan (Foreign Press Center, 1980).

Report of Basic Statistics from the 1975 SSM Survey (*1975–Nen SSM Chosa*: Kiso Tokeihyo) as cited in William Cummings, *Education and Equality in Japan* (Princeton, New Jersey: Princeton University Press, 1980).

Report on Issues of Political and Economic Questions in Public and Private Education, School Affairs Division, Tokyo Government, 1983 (*Koshi Kyotsu Kyoiku Gyozaisei Mondai Chosa Hokokusho*, by Tokyoto Somukyoku Gakujibu).

Report on Survey of School Standards (Gakko Kihon Chosa Mokoku sho) (Tokyo: Ministry of Education, 1982).

ROHLEN, THOMAS P., *Japan's High Schools* (Berkeley, University of California Press, 1983).

ROHLEN, THOMAS, 'Is Japanese Education Becoming Less Egalitarian?' *Journal of Japanese Studies*, vol. 3, 1977.

SALTER, B. and TAPPER, T, *Power and Policy in Education: The Case of Independent Schooling* (London: Falmer Press, 1985).

Sandei Mainichi, 6 April 1975.

Sandei Mainichi, 29 May 1977.

SHIMADA, HARUO, *Earnings Structure and Human Investment: A Comparison Between the US and Japan* (Tokyo: Keio Economic Observatory, 1981).

SHIZEO, MASUI, *The Social Framework of Private Universities* (Shiritsu Daigaku no Shakaiteki Kozo) (Tokyo: National Institute of Educational Research, 1978).

SIMON, BRIAN, *Studies in the History of Education, 1780–1870* (London: Lawrence & Wishart, 1960).

SINGLETON, JOHN, *Nichu: A Japanese School* (New York: Holt, Rinehart & Winston, 1967).

SMITH, ROBERT J., *Ancestor Worship in Contemporary Japan* (Stanford, California: Stanford University Press, 1974).

Social Framework of Private Universities (Shiritsu Daigaku no Shakaiteki Kozo) (Tokyo: National Institute for Educational Research, 1978).

Shukan Yomiuri, 3 April 1983.

STEEDMAN, JANE, *Examination Results in Selective and Non-selective Schools* (London: National Children's Bureau, 1983).

STEEDMAN, JANE, *Progress in Secondary Schools* (London: National Children's Bureau, 1980).

Summary of Educational Statistics (Mombu tōkei yōran) (Tokyo: Ministry of Education, 1982).

THURSTON, DONALD, *Teachers and Politics in Japan* (Princeton: Princeton University Press, 1973).

UN, *Demographic Yearbook*, 1958, 1968, 1982.

VOGEL, EZRA, *Modern Japanese Organization and Decision Making* (Berkeley: University of California Press, 1975).

WEISBROD, BURTON and KARPOFF, P. 'Monetary Return to College Education, Student Ability and College Quality', *Review of Economics and Statistics*, 50, November 1968.

WEST, E. G., *Education and the State* (London: Institute of Economic Affairs, 1970).

WILLMS, J. DOUGLAS, 'The Balance Thesis: Contextual Effects of Ability on Pupils' O-Grade Examination Results', *Oxford Review of Education*, 11, 1985.

WILLMS, J. DOUGLAS, 'Social Class Segregation and its Relationship to Pupils' Exmaination Results in Scotland', *American Sociological Review*, 51, 1986.

WINDHAM, DOUGLAS, *Education, Equality and Income Redistribution* (Lexington, Massachusetts: Heath, 1970).

ZEUGNER, JOHN F., 'The Puzzle of Higher Education in Japan', *Change*, January, 1984.

ZELLNER, A., and LEE, T. H., 'Joint Estimation of Relationships Involving Discrete Random Variables', *Econometrica*, vol. 33, 1965.

Index

Junior high schools – *cont.*
  guidance regarding high school
    entrance exams, 30–1
  income bias in enrolments, *see*
    Socioeconomic distribution of
    enrolments
  juvenile delinquency in, 45
  number of schools and students, 20
  redistributional effects of public
    spending on, 126, 127, 128–9
Juvenile delinquency, 45

Karpoff, P., 200
Keio University, 78, 79, 84, 169
Kikuchi, Jyoji, 113, 121, 122, 126,
    134, 197, 198, 199
Kilgore, Sally, 200
Kindergarten
  as choice point, 34–5
  free play in, 27
  government subsidies for private
    schools, 172
  group activities, 26–7
  independent behaviour encouraged
    in, 27–8
  transition from home to school,
    focus on, 25–6
Kitamura, K., 191, 193
Kohlen, Thomas, 199
Kokugaku (national learning), 14–15
Kyoto University, 54, 77, 78, 79, 84,
    106, 142, 176

Labour-market channelling through
    educational system, xiv, 77–83
Latin American higher-education sys-
    tems, 144
LDP, *see* Liberal Democratic Party
Lee, T. H., 200
Le Grand, Julian, 138, 199
Lessons of the Japanese experience
  caveat regarding, 183–4
  cultural segregation due to privati-
    sation, 186
  educational redistribution due to
    privatisation, 188
  government subsidies to private
    education, 184–6
  public education reforms to accom-

pany government subsidies for
    private education, 188–90
  socioeconomic segregation due to
    privatisation, 186–8
Liberal Democratic Party (LDP), xv,
    58, 146, 148, 163, 166, 173, 181
Lifetime employment, 80–1
Local control of education, 41, 47–8

McGuire, Joseph, 199
McPherson, Andrew, 200, 202, 203
Magnet schools, 189
Marriage and child-bearing cycle of
    typical Japanese family, 114–15
Mathematical achievement rates, 53
Meiji Restoration era, 3, 11–15, 16, 17
Ministry of Education (*Mombusho*),
    18, 19
  American Occupation, impact of,
    41, 42
  censorship of textbooks, 44–5
  control of textbooks and curricu-
    lum, 32, 42–3, 44–5
  exam-oriented curriculum, deve-
    lopment of, 45–7
  government subsidies to private
    education, role in, 168, 173
  local controls, attitude toward, 47–
    8
  moral education, plans for, 44
  popular support for, 43
Mombusho, see Ministry of Education
Moral education
  in *Bakufu* schools, 7–8
  elimination of, 18, 19
  meaning for the Japanese, 13–15
  reintroduction of, 43–4
Mothers' club meetings, 27

National and regional examinations,
    43
Nationalism, 45
Ninomiya, Akira, 66, 194, 195, 196,
    201
Non-issues in Japanese education,
    48–50

Obunsha publishing firm, 84

218   *Index*

LC94.J3 J36 1988   010101 000
James, Estelle.
Public policy and private educ

0 2002 0009562 4
YORK COLLEGE OF PENNSYLVANIA 17403

LC 94 .J3 J36 1988
James, Estelle.
Public policy and private
  education in Japan

DISCARDED

LIBRARY